AXES CHOPS & HOT LICKS

RITCHIE YORKE

Contents

INTRODUCTION

There was a different vibe abroad when I had the pleasure of originally launching the first edition of Axes Chops & Hot Licks (The Canadian Rock Music Scene) back in 1971.

There was a lot of hope rising out there on the northern hit-making highway. Murmurs from the fringe, whispers from the galleries. Like the north country in May, there was a new form emerging from the remnants of last year's life.

There was a growing sense that local talent wasn't all that bad, after all. Perhaps it might stand up against the big-timers on the world stages. Lots of maybes.

You couldn't deny the existence of a vision that Maple music talent might rise up. Some optimists saw it capable of conquering all... a little further on down the line.

There was a spreading conviction that Canadians were about to lurch forward into a whole new era of commercial music endeavor. And it would all prove to be – in one way or another – quite literally true.

Undoubtedly Canadian artists and composers have flourished in the Canadian content era. Having been given a chance to provide musical entertainment to fellow Canadians, these talents have flowered in a wondrous way.

Would that opportunity have come their way had there not been legislated Canadian content is a moot point and one which will be debated ad infinitum in future Canadian culture wars? There are many variations on tap to answer this question. But I'd have to say that in my humble opinion, most Canadian artists to emerge since 1971 would have struggled for exposure without the multiple benefits of Cancon. Life in left field is particularly tough on foreigners trying to crack America with an unorthodox track which falls outside of the conventional boxes.

Australians talk about the ``tyranny of distance'' – the difficulties of being geographically so far removed from the American heartland - as being the biggest stumbling block for Aussie artists trying to crack the US charts. Canadians I believe are confronted by an equally troublesome obstacle – what I've termed the ``quandary of closeness'' - in trying to establish a beach head on American soil. Neither route to the top of the American charts is a simple exercise in toil and tribulation.

The Canadian content era has opened the doors to a multitude of domestic artists – some utterly commercial, a significant number not so much so – which has been a boon to the local talent register. No longer do young artists with obvious potential have to march off to the nearest airport or U.S.-connecting highway to find a place to showcase their talents.

Now they can make that crucial shuffle on local soil with all of the benefits which that entails. The equation adds up to a fresh splash of hope for the homegrown artist. It's hard to construct anything negative around that concept.

I wish I could come right out and make the claim that I always knew this was going to happen. Because I did and I didn't. All in the same breath. I never for one moment doubted the potential of Canadian artists in being able to bring home the bacon and curate the hits.

I instinctively knew the Maple music makers would be able to cut it with the best in the business – as they have done many times over – once they were given a chance.

Getting the chance is what had been missing before, and it's what has changed the scenario into its present operational form.

It's naturally nice to see and hear that my faith in Canadian music makers has been completely confirmed.

I still feel that it was eminently predictable. The talented home-grown writers, composers and performers would inevitably win through in the end. By sheer force and grace.

I would like to believe that the job has been done.

Zoom forward to August 2015 where your ink-stained wretch finds himself installed back in Toronto and attending the opening night's performance of a fascinating new musical production, Oh Canada What a Feeling!

More than a year and a half in the making, Oh Canada was produced by a stellar team headed up by Jeff Parry featuring writer Martin Melhuish, who is himself something of a legend in Maple musicland.

The production's first meeting took place in March 2014 in Winnipeg during the Juno Awards and I was honored to be invited to the initial gathering. I always felt that the concept of this show would be a winner. It could hardly be anything less. If ever a country had a reason to celebrate its musical beginnings, it is Canada.

For so long lost in the wilderness upstream from Niagara Falls, the sound of Maple music has leapt out at the world with astonishing veracity.

The story of its rise is captured in colorful fashion within the confines of Oh Canada. Many of its stars are appropriately celebrated – from early winners such as Paul Anka, the Guess Who (so named to overcome the ``death wish'' familiarity factor which daunts so many would-be participants), Neil Young, Joni Mitchell, The Band, Steppenwolf's John Kay and Gordon Lightfoot, through to newer bright lights like Crowbar, kd Lang, Rush, Bryan Adams, Tom Cochrane, Gino Vanelli, Trooper and Loverboy.

Not surprisingly, Oh Canada What a Feeling! catches the updraft of Canadian music on the rise and into the mainstream. It lights up the feeling which accompanied the breakthrough of Canadian content into the main North American current.

I found it particularly intriguing to peruse the opening night appraisal by eminent music journalist David Farrell, the head of the fyi music Canada online outlet. ``Judging from pre-show banter, the audience attending last night was skeptical whether a musical parading a collection of Canadian songs on stage could win them over, but the thoughtfully selected repertoire clearly resonated with those attending, and the ensemble cast took turns stirring inner emotions with performances that more than did justice to songs that are part of our national psyche,'' Mr Farrell wrote.

``It is a show that needs more production values and perhaps needed to be put through its paces in smaller venues before landing in such a conspicuous setting. That said, the audience was on its feet demanding an encore and Trooper's "We're Here For A Good Time" was the perfect choice as it melted any inhibitions this button-down collared crowd had. The troupe then launched into the show's title song (with Crowbar in the audience), and by the time they reprised with Neil Young's "Rockin' In the Free World" the house was on its feet letting its appreciation be known. They were, after all, there for a good time — and what they wished for was delivered with oh, such unreserved feeling!''

Given that it was very early days on what is hoped to be long and absolutely national circuit, The Feeling show has started off well. The big question from now on is - of course - does it have the legs?

Judging, as one must, from the stride of its ``bouquet bearers'', the key tunes which anchor this production have already stood the test of time.

Diana, Snowbird, American Woman, Helpless, Four Strong Winds, The Weight, Shakin' All Over and I've Been Everywhere don't really need to make any extra statement. They've delivered the news that neon-signs their presence.

Oh Canada, what a special maple-flavored feeling you've brought to the music world. Almost as delicious as maple syrup!!! How good is that?

You could only hope for more axes, chops and hot licks out of Canada!!

RITCHIE YORKE,

High Park, Toronto

August 19 2015

1. IN THE BEGINNING

Where does one look for contemporary Canadian culture? In the richly decorated concert halls with their steady stream of international celebrities from other countries? In the art galleries with their cliquish exhibitions of favoritism? In the cinemas where Hollywood has tight hold on the reins? On the television set, where mediocrity dominates mass entertainment?

A good deal of originality in the Canadian arts of the seventies is to be found among a relatively new breed - the rock musician. You will often hear more about Canada on tiny pieces of black plastic and in rock clubs and folk houses than in any ballet performance, symphony concert or theatrical production.

Canada lives under the cultural umbrella of the United States media. Artistic development in this country has been overwhelmingly influenced by our neighbour to the south. Until a few years ago in the entertainment world, it was only those Canadians who had left Canada to pursue their careers elsewhere who were accepted at home. It was impossible to become a star in Canada without a well-stamped passport. Nowhere was this more evident in the sixties than the pop music field. If the average Canadian rock radio station was anything to go by, there was no such animal as Canadian music. It simply did not exist.

The average Top Forty station was programmed by an American broadcasting consultant, who told the station what to play, how to play it, and who to hire and fire. The station played either English or American records or both; it employed primarily American dee jays; and it modelled itself after the best (or worst, whichever way you personally hear it) U.S. stations in Boston, Chicago and New York. The yardstick of success was just how close you could come to sounding exactly like these American stations.

Few people took the trouble to speculate on the booming music industry of other countries, only a handful wondered why Canada was the only English-speaking country in the world without a domestic music and record scene. Music business people in other countries had no idea that Canada had any fine rock musicians. They heard next to nothing coming from Canada. But they did realize the obvious - Canada was the largest record-buying market for American rock music in the world outside of the U.S. itself.

Because of this, almost all record companies in Canada were foreign owned. They were mere branch offices of huge operations in New York, Los Angeles and London. As primarily distributors they had little or no interest in costly domestic talent development. After all, why bother to search out a talented group and spend thousands of dollars recording them, when it was possible to simply hop down to the Customs office, and pick up the master tapes of already established U.S. and English hits. What's the use of growing your own tomatoes if you can buy them inexpensively at the nearest supermarket? The sort of people who like to grow their own did not become visible in Canada until the end of the sixties.

Canada blindly followed whatever the Americans were doing. *Billboard*, the U.S. music business weekly, was the bible. If a particular record was doing well in the States—be it about universal love, race riots in Alabama or California girls—it immediately gained access to Canadian airwaves, television, newspapers and magazines.

This situation probably would have continued for the next three decades if something drastic hadn't been done about it. The man who did more than anyone else seems an unlikely saviour. An ex-cop and beer company public relations man, Walt Grealis pioneered the acceptance of Canadian music in its country of origin. During the eight years he has been running *RPM*, a weekly Canadian music business magazine, he has taken more than his share of abuse for his stand.

Grealis' views were highly influential in the Canadian Radio-Television Commission's decision to force Canadian radio broadcasters to play thirty percent domestic content. He has long been a thorn in the side of Canadian apathy. And he has profited very little from his crusade to bring other Canadians fame and fortune. *RPM* had lost money every year up to 1970.

Grealis, who's now forty-three, looks back over those long years with little nostalgia; but somehow he leaves the impression that if he had his time over, he'd have done exactly the same things.

"My introduction to the music business came about in a rather strange manner. I'd been working with the Toronto City Police when I decided to take a break and spend the summer as the social host of a hotel in Bermuda. The natives taught me all sorts of Calypso dances and even talked me into singing with one of the local bands.

When I returned to Toronto, I went into public relations with a brewery. The beer business was a completely different game, but working in their PR department brought me into contact with entertainment and sporting personalities.

"A couple of years later, I took a job with Apex Records. Shortly after that, London Records asked me to set up a promotion department for their Ontario distributor. That was when I realized the imbalance in the Canadian music scene. Canada simply had no recording industry.

"I decided to try and do something about it. I liquidated everything I had and put it into a small newspaper. It was going to be a shit-disturbing sheet ... Canadian artists had really been suffering. Advanced recording techniques were unknown and the records that were made in Canada were bad. Because there was no exposure of them, there was no way they could get better. It was a vicious circle."

The debut issue of Canada's first and only music trade magazine came out in February of 1964. Its arrival was greeted with a less than enthusiastic reception. "The majority of people told me to get lost," Grealis recalls with a grin. "My biggest enemies were the record companies."

Grealis quickly went out on a limb by editorially plugging Canadian records. "I didn't really know why I did that. The records were poor, there was no quality control, no technique. Production was a fly-by-the-seat-of-your-pants sort of thing. The reason was that no one cared. America came in clear and strong with a switch of a television channel. Why should Canada try and be different?"

The cities most affected by U.S. TV saturation were those close to the border. "In Edmonton and Calgary you find the real Canada. Toronto was just a second class American city. There were no independent thinkers. "Canada has a ridiculous collection of hand-me-down people."

At first Grealis wasn't sure whether it was the foreign-owned record companies or the U.S.-emulating broadcasters who were most at fault for the lack of a domestic music scene in Canada. "Gradually I began to see clearly the apathy of broadcasters. A promotion man would take in a Canadian record and they'd throw it into the garbage in front of him. Those things actually happened."

Don Troiano, the veteran lead guitarist of Bush, tells the story of a record which had been cut by a Toronto group of the early sixties,

Richie Knight and the Mid-Knights: "They'd just finished making a record with their own money. It was after midnight and they took a soft cut into the all-night disc jockey at CHUM. They assured him that they weren't asking the station to promote or regularly play their record, but that they would just like to hear it once over the radio to see how it sounded. The disc jockey took the record, smashed it, and told the group to piss off."

"Nobody," says Grealis, "seemed to realize the power of the broadcasters. If they had decided to push Canadian talent, we could have a domestic music industry almost overnight."

One of Grealis' few supporters was Stan Klees, a then struggling record producer who had some success later in the sixties. Klees became a close friend, and according to Grealis, was "the catalyst I needed. Klees is the one who really started it all. He gave me a shot in the arm to get me going."

Says Klees in return: "Canada has been very fortunate to have someone with a sense of responsibility like Walt Grealis. He's been a big daddy to the industry."

A year after he'd started *RPM*, Grealis still hadn't seen a nickel of profit. But he had become even more dedicated to his cause. "Our culture was suffering, I felt. We were imitators and followers. How can you be proud of a country like that?"

The reaction to *RPM* was growing with each new issue, but Grealis was still not getting support in Toronto. "Vancouver and Toronto people thought it was a joke, but that made me even more determined.

"I had a fairly low impression of Canadian broadcasters at that time; they all looked to CHUM for leadership. Toronto was the largest English city in the country. The other stations thought CHUM had the sweet smell of success."

Because of its national influence, CHUM could have single-handedly created a music scene in Canada. Yet in my opinion the station traditionally did the least for Canadian talent. CHUM's music director in the mid-sixties was Bob McAdorey. One of his most revealing lines appeared in a Toronto newspaper in July of 1967: "Ninety percent of Canadian radio stations refuse to play an unproven record whether it's from Czechoslovakia or Tilsonburg. They don't feel any obligations to prove themselves heroes."

By allowing themselves to become the disciples of American hit charts, most Canadian stations locked out almost any possibility of success for domestically produced records. The U.S. chart list was their sole programming guide; they based program decisions on what they read in *Cashbox* and *Billboard*; they were not capable of judging the commercial potential of new music.

But they were aware of the power they possessed. CHUM's Bob McAdorey again, July 1966: "If CHUM was playing the record a group could sing *God Save the Queen* and the kids would buy it." The CHUM chart was distributed to record stores throughout southern Ontario and to radio stations across the country. Most store buyers used it as the guideline on what to order, in much the same manner as CHUM used the U.S. hit lists for programming decisions. Thus, the Canadian consumer was being fed directly from the heart of the U.S. music industry. It passed from American magazine to Canadian radio station to the Toronto disc dealer to the local record buyer. The Americans could not have secured more thorough domination of the Canadian record market if they had deliberately planned it.

In 1966, there were several developments in the Toronto music scene which indicated that Canada might be about to take its place in the global music picture. Local groups gained massive popularity at Toronto dances and concerts, many of which were emceed by city disc jockeys. Some dee jays ran their own dances and made a lot of money doing it.

Booking agencies sprang up, several promoters were able to accumulate large profits, and CHUM was right in there pushing the so-called "Toronto sound".

"In 1966, I made more money than I thought I'd make in a lifetime," said Ron Scribner, one of the principals in the Bigland booking agency.

Grealis recalls that CHUM was surprisingly "part of the overall excitement. One Canadian producer had five or six records on the CHUM chart at one time. The station became very nationalistic. There was a live show once a week featuring Canadian groups. It really looked like they were sincere about it.

"Then a few little things entered the picture. It came out that one booking agent had his thumb on a Toronto dee jay. A bandwagon was starting up and everyone wanted to get on it. Lots of people were in there viciously fighting for a few bucks. There were young girls, evenings on the town, all sorts of payola. The management of the station in question got wind of what was going on, and they quickly put a stop to it. They felt that the only way to prevent local interests from coercing the disc jockeys was to simply cut back on Canadian records." Grealis concludes that "CHUM developed a policy of anti-Canadianism to protect itself from the leeches who would do anything to get the station to play their records. We were right back where we started."

Grealis believes that Canadian print media had also contributed to this false start of the domestic music scene. "An American group would come to Toronto to play at Massey Hall and one of the big Canadian acts would open the show. But the Canadians were always ripped to shreds by the critics. The press has been one of the big disabilities in this country."

A few months after this setback, an idea came to him. The Ontario government was conducting a "Buy Canadian" campaign, and Grealis contemplated the role of the federal government (which after all, policed the broadcasting industry) in the development of Canadian music. He came up with the possibility of government legislation making it mandatory for this country's broadcasters to play a fixed percentage of Canadian records. It was not a new idea; indeed, only a few years earlier the concept had been examined and then somewhat rapidly shelved by the Board of Broadcast Governors, the predecessor to the CRTC as governmental controlling body of radio and television in Canada.

In a public announcement dated November 9, 1961, the BBG stated: "The Board gave the closest consideration to various methods of determining and enforcing a minimum Canadian content in the broadcasting of radio stations, but was unable to conclude that any of the possible alternatives was administratively feasible."

To some, the conclusion seemed too short-sighted, especially in retrospect. Enforced domestic content of radio and TV had been introduced in other countries and had been highly successful. The BBG has subsequently received much criticism for that conclusion. Nevertheless, the fact remained that the BBG had definitely demonstrated a lack of desire to stand up to the radio station license holders. There were some occasions when the BBG rather more appeared to reflect the opinions and interests of the broadcasters, than of the general populace.

The BBG finally reached the end of its reign in March 1968. For some observers, such as Walt Grealis, the future could only be an improvement in breaking down the long preserved status quo of Canadian broadcasters. When the creation of the Canadian Radio-Television Commission was announced (its full-time commissioners were Pierre Juneau, chairman; Harry J. Boyle, Pat Pearce, Hal Dornan and Rheal Therrien), Grealis decided the time to act had come.

"At first we were a little put off by the appointment of a French Canadian from the National Film Board as chairman. Then it dawned on us that being a French Canadian, Pierre Juneau would realize the value of cultural development."

French Canada has had a prosperous local recording industry for many years. A complete star system had evolved and it was possible to sell more records in Quebec than the rest of the country combined. In the early sixties, many of the French Canadian discs were of poor quality, but French language radio station support spurred them on to greater achievement. By the start of the seventies, several Quebec hits had gained chart success in France.

Juneau's determination was obvious from the outset. Says Grealis: "We made sure that all the members of the CRTC received copies of *RPM*. They needed advice and help. They were not entirely familiar with the broadcasting-record business in Canada. But they were open-minded."

Grealis launched a ten-part in-depth study of legislated radio. Among other things it pointed out: "Between thirty million and eighty million dollars of the music industry's annual gross is leaving the country in the form of various royalties; there are few countries in the world which do not legislate to control their culture, their acts and their music; Canada can offer a midget of art to the world, a little bit of literature, very little theatre, very little dance and next to no music ... we have failed to provide ourselves with a cultural background distinct to our people."

The eloquence and compassion of the series had deep effect on the CRTC. But meanwhile the radio stations laughed off legislation as just another crazy idea from the oddballs at *RPM*. There was isolated discussion of the idea in the popular press, yet the small support accorded Grealis was of enormous help. In August of 1968, the *Globe and Mail* scooped the country with a full page feature headlined "Can a Law Put Canada on the Hit Parade?" Despite the triteness of the title, the story revealed a very real problem. The comments on legislation by leading Toronto disc jockeys of the time are well worth repetition. CKFH's John Donabie: "I don't want to play third class records. Canada lacks technicians"; CHUM's Jay

Nelson: "The legislation strikes me as something you just say 'no comment' to"; CHUM-FM's Hugh Currie: "The legislation would mean simply spoonfeeding Canadian talent"; CKFH's Don Daynard: "Forced Canadian content hasn't done much for Canadian television. Few Canadian records are up to the American standards. Besides, the good ones get played."

Garry Ferrier, program director of CHUM-FM, stated that "you can't shove Canadianism down people's throats." CKFH general manager Barry Nesbitt said: "I don't need anyone to tell me how to program this station. We play as much Canadian product as we can."

Sam the Record Man's Mel Mostov offered a different viewpoint: "No Canadian records can succeed here unless you have an in with a disc jockey. I'd welcome legislation, although it's insane the Commission should have to go that far." A survey by Walt Grealis, prominently mentioned in the *Globe and Mail* story, showed that in nine major Canadian cities, stations were playing less than one half of one percent of totally Canadian records.

Early in 1969, the Guess Who - the phenomenally successful rock group from Winnipeg - added further fuel to the fire when its single of *These Eyes* became a U.S. million seller after it had been ignored by many of Canada's foremost rock stations.

Sensing what could be a trend, *Billboard* magazine published a special forty-four page *Spotlight on Canada* issue on May 24, 1969, which brought the problems of the Canadian market into international focus. It, too, was carefully examined by the studious members of the CRTC. It, too, made a contribution to the steadily growing clamor for CRTC intervention.

Anticipating that something might be in the wind, a group of the largest rock stations in Canada formed the Maple Leaf System in June 1969 with the announced intention of "developing and encouraging Canadian talent on an organized national basis." One might well wonder why it had taken so long for radio stations to discover that there was indeed such a thing as Canadian talent. The real reason for the formation of the MLS was to try to throw the CRTC off the track, to demonstrate a sincere effort among broadcasters to expose Canadian artists on domestic airwaves, to dismiss the need for legislation. It was a shrewd move, well-timed and very convincing.

Even Walt Grealis was to some extent taken for a ride on the MLS. "At first I was suspicious, but I decided to help wherever I could. They appointed me MLS coordinator. They thought they had silenced one of their noisiest critics."

The first chairman of the MLS was J. Robert Wood of CHUM, the station which seemed to be directly responsible for the formation of the MLS. Later when criticism and industry disappointment in the MLS reached high levels, Wood abdicated and Roy Hennessy of CKLG Vancouver took over. Nevin Grant of CROC Hamilton (long a recognized Canadian talent supporter) became the third chairman late in 1970.

The full membership of the MLS included CKLG Vancouver, CHED Edmonton, (which left in April 1970 after a policy disagreement), CKXL Calgary, CKOM Saskatoon, CKCK Regina, CFRW Winnipeg, CHLO St. Thomas, CKPT Peterborough (a CHUM-owned station), CKOC Hamilton, CFRA Ottawa (another CHUM station), CFOX Montreal, CJCH Halifax (another CHUM station) and CHUM Toronto.

Although the MLS did aid in the national success of several Canadian discs, it never realized its full expectations. Grealis resigned early in 1970.

Eventually the bombshell fell. On February 12, 1970, the CRTC announced its proposed Canadian content legislation. It was a tremendous shock to broadcasters, but many still doubted that the proposal would become law.

The CRTC held its Canadian content hearings in Ottawa, April 14-22, and the broadcasting industry assembled a massive lobby to defeat the legislation proposal. The supporters present spoke only as individuals but were numerous - members of various music groups, Pierre Berton, Bruno Gerussi, a representative of CAPAC, and others. There were no representatives of either the Canadian recording industry (which stood to benefit more than anyone from the proposed legislation) or BMI, the U.S. owned performance rights association. Both were apparently afraid of antagonizing the broadcasters. They declined to stand up.

It looked to be a tough battle as the hearings proceeded. The hearts of the Commissioners appeared equally unmoved by the pleas of Canadian talent supporters, and the ridiculous rhetoric of the radio stations.

The broadcasters' trade association tried to protest the proposed legislation as being unconstitutional, a foolish stand which resulted in some stations breaking away from its membership. Hundreds of excuses were presented to prove that the programming of Canadian records would cause enormous hardship, financial and otherwise for the stations and their listeners. It was a pitiful performance.

The absence of any real evidence that the Canadian recording industry would be able to supply enough discs for stations to program thirty percent domestic content was disheartening for supporters watching from the sidelines. And the majority of broadcasters were still convinced that they would win.

Then on May 22, 1970, a CRTC press release announced that Canadian content legislation would take effect from January 18, 1971. For the first twelve months after January 18, 1971, all radio broadcasters would be required to program at least thirty percent Canadian compositions daily between 6:00 A.M. and 12:00 P.M. A composition was considered Canadian if it fulfilled one of four conditions: (a) the instrumentation or lyrics were principally performed by a Canadian; (b) the music was composed by a Canadian; (c) the lyrics were written by a Canadian; (d) the live performance was wholly recorded in Canada.

In the second year of legislation, two of the four conditions would be required in at least thirty percent of all musical compositions programmed by each station; and then in the third year (i.e. after January 18, 1973) at least five percent of all music played must have either music or lyrics composed by a Canadian in addition to the thirty percent with at least two of the four qualifying conditions mentioned above.

For the purposes of the legislation, the Commission deems a person Canadian if (a) he is a Canadian citizen; (b) he is a landed immigrant as defined in the Immigration Act, or (c) his ordinary place of residence was in Canada during the six months immediately preceding his contribution to the musical composition in question.

Comments from radio license holders were as expected. Allan Waters, president of CHUM, stated: "There isn't enough Canadian music available, by which we mean available and playable." Waters said it was unreasonable to ask a station like CHUM to more than double its Canadian content in such a short period.

It was difficult to feel any sympathy for the wailing broadcasters; they'd had their chance and blown it. They had had enough warning that legislation was being considered - if they had any foresight, they would have jumped into Canadian talent with their clothes on and perhaps would have eliminated the need for legislation. But they didn't. And they found themselves at the mercy of a gallant little band of Canadians intent on giving Canadian pop culture a chance.

At last Canadian music would be heard on the country's airwaves. Finally Canadian musicians would be given a chance to compete fairly with Americans and others in their own land. It was a triumph of immeasurable proportions; a new era was dawning.

2. THE GIANT'S AWAKENING

Before 1970 rolled around, Canada's representation on the world music charts had been almost non-existent. There had been a couple of freak singles like the Guess Who's *Shakin' All Over* and *My Girl Sloopy* by Little Caesar and the Consuls in the mid-sixties, but it wasn't until March 1969 that the Guess Who totally blasted through the border barrier and sold a million copies of *These Eyes*.

Later in the year, the Winnipeg foursome scored again with a double-sided hit *Laughing/Undun*. In December, the Guess Who's third single *No Time* was released in the U.S. At the same time, the Original Caste unexpectedly scored an American hit with *One Tin Soldier*.

But that was the extent of the long-overdue Canadian invasion. Then came 1970, and the twelve months that followed constituted the most exciting and energetic period ever in the history of Canadian music. In the midst of the unprecedented interest in Canadian talent, sparked by the Canadian Radio-Television Commission recommendations, some record companies decided to risk further investment in local recording.

The result of this thawing of the traditional apathy towards Canadian talent was quite literally world-shattering. More Canadian hits made the world charts in 1970 than in any ten-year period previous. More and more U.S. record executives started to talk about the so-called "Canadian Sound" and almost overnight, Canada became a force to be reckoned with in the global music market.

A total of sixteen Canadian singles and six albums reached the *Billboard* U.S. sales charts during 1970. But the most incredible aspect of Canada's arrival in the international scene was that it had been accomplished in only a few months. In 1968, Canada didn't even rank among the first forty international record producers. In 1970, we were third!

It is interesting to look back over the 1970 charts and examine Canada's growing monthly influence in the American scene.

In March, the Guess Who's fourth single, *American Woman*, bombed into the Billboard Hot One Hundred at number forty-six, and went on to reach number one - the first ever Canadian single to do so. Nimbus 9, the company which produces the Guess Who, was so excited at this unprecedented success that they placed a hastily drawn sign above their doorway on Toronto's Hazelton Avenue. One doubts if many passers-by realized the enormous significance of a piece of cardboard reading *"American Woman* - Number One." At the same time, the Guess Who had two albums on the U.S. charts - *American Woman* and *Canned Wheat*.

A month later, the Poppy Family's first hit single, *Which Way You Goin' Billy?*, had reached the American Top Forty.

On May 16, *American Woman* was in its second week at number one, the Poppy Family had climbed to number seventeen and Edward Bear's ultra-commercial single, *You, Me and Mexico*, was bubbling under the Hot One Hundred. The *American Woman* album had soared to number nine, the first Canadian rock album to hit the U.S. top ten.

A month later, *Which Way You Goin' Billy?* had reached number two and become a million-seller. *American Woman* was still entrenched in the U.S. top ten, and the Poppy Family's album bounded into Billboard's Two Hundred Top LPs listing at number one hundred.

On July 18, two new Canadian singles registered their first week on the Hot One Hundred - number eighty-six was Anne Murray's *Snowbird*, and eighty-nine was *Hand Me Down World* by the Guess Who.

The *American Woman* LP, which had been certified as a gold disc, having passed the million dollar sales figure, was hanging on at number twenty and the Poppy Family album had climbed to seventy-nine.

The August 22 issue of *Billboard* was especially important in that it marked the first time that four Canadian discs were on the charts - *Hand Me Down World, Snowbird*, the second Poppy Family single, *That's Where I Went Wrong*, and Mashmakhan's *As the Years Go By*.

The Mashmakhan single was the first Canadian hit for Columbia, and represented that company's awakening interest in the music scene in Canada. Long content to prosper on its numerous successes with established U.S. product, Columbia suddenly started to think Canadian and the results spoke for themselves.

Other discs which had made brief U.S. chart appearances during 1970 included the Gordon Lightfoot album, *Sit Down Young Stranger*, and the singles by Terry Jacks (of the Poppy Family) with *I'm*

Gonna Capture You, Canada Goose with *Higher and Higher*, Steel River's *Ten Pound Note*, and King Biscuit Boy's first album, *Official Music*.

In the December 26 issue of *Billboard*, the annual awards to best selling artists were given; Canada, for the first time in its history, made a strong showing. In the Top Singles Artists category, the Guess Who were fourth (led only by the Jackson 5, Neil Diamond and Simon and Garfunkel), while the Poppy Family came in at thirty-fourth and Anne Murray at eighty-third. In the Top Album Artists area, the Guess Who were number thirty-three.

In the Top Groups section, the Guess Who were third, and the Poppy Family twentieth. In New Artists, the Poppy Family were seventh and Anne Murray twenty-fourth.

The Guess Who's producer. Jack Richardson, came in at twenty-third, above such well known international record makers as Bones Howe, Phil Spector, Lou Adler, Tony Macauley, Gamble-Huff and Felix Pappalardi.

Canada had four titles in the World's Top One Hundred Singles of 1970 - *American Woman* at number three, *Which Way You Goin' Billy?* at twenty-seven, *Snowbird* at forty-second and the Guess Who's *No Time* at seventy.

In addition, *Cashbox* magazine, the second largest world music trade publication, named the Guess Who as the number one singles artists of 1970, above any other recording group anywhere.

It had been an incredible year for international acceptance of Canadian talent. Some of the Canadian-made hits went on to achieve similar success in Europe, including *American Woman, Which Way You Goin' Billy?* and *Snowbird*.

This compilation of Canada's representation on the world charts obviously does not include the performances of Canadian artists then living outside their homeland. If one were to take into account hits by Steppenwolf, The Band, Andy Kim, Neil Young and Joni Mitchell, Canada's percentage approaches the English total.

Not surprisingly, all of this sudden and unexpected hit action from Canada caused quite a flurry in the U.S. record industry. Several major American companies dispatched talent scouts into Canada. In the latter part of 1970, U.S. consumer papers and radio stations gave more prominence to the invasion of the so-called "Canadian Sound" than the country of its origin.

The attention of the U.S. thus gained, Canada became a focal point for enterprising Americans looking for a guide to tomorrow's pop world. Hype plays a very large part in the record industry's thought processes, and the abundance of Canadian copy in U.S. magazines and papers soon had the Americans convinced that Canada might be the next big production market for world hits. England had been saturated with recording; in fact, on several occasions U.S. record companies signed English groups (for example Led Zeppelin) before they were even formed. The name value of top rock musicians is awesome.

So why not Canada? American programmers - familiar with those Canadians who had moved south plus such groups as the Guess Who - looked to Canadian records for something a little out of the ordinary.

For the first time in their careers, Canadian record makers were able to tell their U.S. record companies of startling domestic chart action on their efforts. In the past, when trying to make U.S. distribution deals, Canadians were invariably faced with the question: "I like the record, but what's it doing in Canada? How many charts have you got? Where are you getting play?" Their only reply had traditionally been a stony silence and the result was no deal.

Several U.S. record companies were able to climb on the Canadian Sound bandwagon in 1970. RCA, which had signed the Guess Who due to the belief in the group by one executive (Don Burkhimer, who is now artists and repertoire director at Paramount Records in New York), picked up several other Canadian acts from their subsidiary company in Canada, including Simon Caine, Noah, and the Marshmallow Soup Group. Shelby Singleton, who owns Sun Records in Memphis, visited Toronto and signed up several acts, among them Madrigal. Polydor acquired the talents of the Bells; Bell picked up the Stampeders and Dr. Music.

But probably the most ardent interest came from Paramount Records. The company's key executives, president Bill Gallagher and A & R vice- president Jack Wiedemann, had been responsible for Columbia's entry into the U.S. rock scene in the late sixties. At Paramount, they teamed up with Neil Reshen (a young business consultant who had handled Frank Zappa) and saw in Canada what could be the world's next big music phenomenon.

Paramount made a deal with Love Productions in Toronto, buying world distribution rights to Crowbar and King Biscuit Boy. Their intuition quickly paid off with King Biscuit Boy's album, *Official Music*, entering the U.S. charts in December 1970. Paramount also signed

Everyday People, a group from the Maritimes, which enjoyed considerable success with its first single, *You Make Me Wonder*. Paramount's new president, Tony Martell, continued that company's interest in Canadian talent.

Although Canadian media in general may have treated the rapidly expanding local music scene with less than the respect and attention due it, the growth did not go unnoticed within the music industry itself. 1970 witnessed a spectacular growth in Canadian independent record production companies and labels. Jack Richardson, producer of the Guess Who, had led the way in 1969 by forming Nimbus 9, a production company. In the year prior to Canadian content legislation, almost a dozen independent record companies were established. The most noteworthy of these were Happy Sack Productions, Love Productions, True North Industries Limited, Tuesday Music Productions and Music World Creations.

Happy Sack, run by Brian Ahern, produces Anne Murray for Capitol Records. Love Productions, which is owned by Frank Davies, has its own label, Daffodil, on which it released King Biscuit Boy, Christmas and Crowbar prior to the start of legislation. Daffodil was the first of the independent labels to release a record from outside Canada (an album titled *Sinfonias*, featuring Waldo de Los Rios and his orchestra, which Daffodil leased from Hispavox Records in Spain) and the first record company of any kind in Canada to have its own label in another country. The first overseas Daffodil product was released in Australia and New Zealand, just after Canadian content legislation began. Capitol distributes Daffodil and its new subsidiary, Strawberry, in Canada.

True North Industries, owned by Bernard Finkelstein, has its True North label (which releases Bruce Cockburn, Syrinx and Luke Gibson) distributed by Columbia.

Greg Hambleton's Tuesday Music Productions owns the Tuesday label, distributed by Quality, which had notable success with singles by Steel River and Madrigal, prior to January 18, 1970.

Music World Creations, owned by veteran Canadian music plugger, Mel Shaw, releases the Stampeders through Quality Records.

The strong growth of these independent labels and the increasing interest in Canadian talent by the major foreign-owned record companies probably prevented a wholesale takeover of the infant Canadian scene by Americans.

When U.S. company talent scouts arrived in Canada looking for new artists, they found that the cream of the crop had already been signed by local producers. Obtaining international releasing rights to many of these Canadian artists often cost U.S. companies a small fortune. A good example is Crowbar and King Biscuit Boy. It was widely reported in the music trade press that Paramount would pay more than $250,000 over three years for world rights outside Canada for these two Daffodil acts. This is money which comes back into Canada in the form of royalties and will obviously be a boon to domestic record production.

The flow of money and Canada's increase in global music stature also brought about a boom in studio construction. In November, 1969, Terry Brown opened Toronto Sound Studios, the first sixteen-track operation in Canada. Since then, three other sixteen-track and one twenty-four track studio have opened in Toronto, and sixteen-track studios were planned for Montreal, Edmonton and Vancouver.

The absence of multi-track studios had been a major obstacle to Canadian musical development. But without radio exposure, there hadn't been much point in utilizing modern and expensive equipment and a world-standard studio was a hopeless financial risk. Almost all international hits are recorded on either eight-track or sixteen-track equipment, and to compete in the global marketplace, Canada had to have the necessary facilities. With the increasing acceptance of Canadian talent in 1969 by local broadcasters (due, in no small part, to growing content legislation rumors from Ottawa), hit-making facilities blossomed.

In one year, rock music had become Canada's fastest growing industry. From virtually nothing in the preceding year, 1970 brought an estimated ten million dollars into Canada from other record markets. The boom that so many had fervently hoped for was finally becoming a reality. Canada had seen the arrival of a music industry, economically stable and creatively rewarding.

Canada had taken her place among the world's leading producers of pop music; the country which had been silent for so long was making noises that would make 1970 an historic year for Canadian culture.

The Guess Who

The Guess Who expect to earn more than five million dollars during 1971. That estimate is made up of record, writing and publishing royalties (almost certain to be in excess of one million dollars), concert and television appearances (the group commanded $12,500 per show at the beginning of 1971) and return on investments made in the previous two years.

The Guess Who are big business. They own shopping plazas, hotels, U.S. chicken franchises and huge tracts of prime Canadian land. They represent close to fifty percent of all music income which began to flow into Canada early in 1970.

The Guess Who are one of the most popular rock groups in the world. According to *Cashbox* music magazine, the Guess Who sold more singles (45 rpm) records in 1970 than any other group or single artist in the world, the Beatles and Creedence Clearwater Revival inclusive. They have sold more records than all other Canadian artists combined, Anne Murray and Gordon Lightfoot among them. One of their albums, *American Woman*, remained on the American best-selling LP list for the entire year of 1970, and the same year, the title song of that album soared to the number one spot in the U.S., becoming the first Canadian rock disc to accomplish the feat.

All told, the Guess Who have sold about twenty-five million LPs and singles in less than two years.

They are regarded as one of the finest groups, in an artistic sense, in the world. Respected critics from almost every corner of the globe have sung their praises in most enthusiastic terms. The group's writing ability has exhausted the superlatives of many of their rock contemporaries, such as Creedence's John Fogerty. Their disc producer, Jack Richardson of Toronto, has been described as one of the best producers on the continent.

Apart from the Canadian Radio-Television Commission itself, they have done more for Canadian music and musicians than anyone or anything in history. They made it possible for Mashmakhan, Edward Bear, Anne Murray, Crowbar, the Poppy Family and possibly even Gordon Lightfoot himself to attain international popularity through hit records in the United States.

It is no small comment on the sad state of Canadian media in the seventies that the Guess Who - winners in a fiercely competitive

24

business - are such unsung heroes in their own land. Despite the fact that the Guess Who have received seven gold records as compared with Anne Murray's one, the "girl-next-door" from Halifax is far better known from coast to coast than any member of the Guess Who. You'd be fortunate to find one Canadian out of a hundred who could name all five members of the Guess Who. That yardstick can even be applied in the group's hometown of Winnipeg.

 Despite their active role in the city's business and financial circles, the Guess Who have never graced the front page of Winnipeg newspapers. One can read about them in the entertainment section, but they're not considered hard news in the prairie city. If the Guess Who were an English group - and they had contributed as much to British rock as they have to Canadian - it is not unlikely that the band would have long since hit the front page of *The Times* in London.

The Guess Who came out of the prairies with their roots still clinging to them and they disintegrated all of the carefully propagated myths about Canadian musical inferiority with one catchy little song, *These Eyes*. They did it with the help of no more than a handful of Canadian radio stations. Mass U.S. success was the only criteria that most Canadian broadcasters used to form an opinion on the musical merits of the Guess Who. Similarly, it was not until the group had won international recognition that Canadian television and magazines acknowledged their success.

The roots of the Guess Who reach back to 1958, a full thirteen years before the legislation era began. Along the way they've had several different names—Al and the Silvertones, and Chad Allen and the Expressions among them. The present name dates from 1965, and its origin is revealing of the Canadian music scene of that time.

George Struth, a top executive at Quality Records Limited in Toronto, recalls with some relish how he came up with the name Guess Who. "We'd had Chad Allen and the Expressions signed to us for several years, and in 1965 the group cut a record called *Shakin' All Over*. We at Quality were highly impressed by the record, and we were sure it could be a national hit if radio – if stations did not know the group was Canadian.

"The bias against Canadian discs would have forced some programme directors to hear imaginary defects and mistakes in the sound of the record. In short, they wouldn't have played it.

"In 1965, a lot of English groups were popular in Canada, and some of them had pretty strange names. I thought that if we renamed the Winnipeg group the Guess Who, the radio stations might mistake them for an English group. The Who.

"We sent the record out with a white label reading simply '*Shakin' All Over* by the Guess Who.' We were only trying to get the program directors to listen to the record, and our gimmick worked."

Shakin' All Over became a tremendous Canadian hit, and went on to climb into the American Top Forty chart. In England and Australia, the public thought it was England's The Who. It was a premature rehearsal for the success of the Guess Who in the States four years later. Management problems and record company misunderstandings prevented the Guess Who from following up *Shakin' All Over* in the U.S., although they did have a number of singles in Canada which, ironically, were far superior in quality to the first international hit.

Not coincidentally, Canadian radio stations had by then discovered that the Guess Who were not English; their ardor for the Winnipeg group's records paled considerably. Quality Records, who had engineered the first Guess Who victory, made what now seems a classic blunder when they sold the group's contract to Jack Richardson's newly-formed Nimbus 9 label for a mere $1,000.

There have been four distinct phases in the development of the Guess Who as Canada's foremost creators of contemporary music. The first began in 1958, when drummer Gary Peterson and guitarist Randy Bachman first joined a high school rock group. In 1962, bass player Jim Kale and singer Chad Allen teamed up with Bachman and Peterson to form Chad Allen and the Expressions. Three years later, Chad Allen left, Burton Cummings joined, and the name was changed to the Guess Who. In 1970, Randy Bachman split the group and was replaced by two lead guitarists, Kurt Winter and Greg Leskiw.

Gary Peterson is married, a keen skier and a hard-hitting rock drummer. Jim Kale is divorced, a hard drinker and a tasteful bass guitarist. Burton Cummings is an outstanding songwriter, a classically trained pianist and as good a lead singer as any in the world rock scene. Kurt Winter is dedicated to his music, an aggressive Jimi Hendrix and Frank Zappa fan, and a dazzling lead guitarist. Greg Leskiw, sometimes introverted, often sensitive, is a country-influenced picker. All are in their late twenties.

Since Winter and Leskiw joined the group, it has taken a further climb into the upper echelons of rock. Initially a singles group, the

Guess Who has subsequently joined the ranks of top rock album acts. The *Share the Land* album, as an example, has sold more than a million copies internationally.

In 1970, I saw the Guess Who play in Toronto, in Montreal (before 40,000 ecstatic fans at Man and His World), in San Francisco (three nights at the prestigious Winterland Ballroom) and I watched them record *Hand Me Down World* at RCA's Chicago studios. With each occasion, I became more convinced of the Guess Who's unique and original talents, and more impressed by the group's willingness to promote Canada and Canadian music around the world.

Burton Cummings

Burton Cummings is what you might call an impulsive composer. He rarely writes regularly, and when he does he expects things to come together rapidly, or else. Or else what?

"If I can't sit down and play a new tune right through or if it doesn't sound half-decent, then I get up and leave," explains Cummings. "I don't like having to work at songs ... if I have to do that, then I'll probably stop writing."

Cummings, one of the youngest members of the Guess Who, is assumed by many people to be the leader of the band. He is self-confident, sometimes very loud, mischievous and completely unpredictable. He sleeps all day and sings all night. He's the closest thing to the traditional English rock idol within the Guess Who.

His songs have covered a lot of ground—from *Laughing* to *Undun* to *American Woman*. His melodies are catchy, leading one to suppose that he strives towards commerciality. "Not really ... I think I'm just a naturally commercial writer. I was brought up with nothing but AM Top Forty radio. Singles are really my syndrome. I think about seventy percent of my songs could be singles."

Cummings pens many of his songs for the guitar, even though his proficiency at piano is evident to anyone who's ever heard a Guess Who album. A child prodigy, he received his degree in piano in 1966, and has the qualifications to teach at the Royal Conservatory of Toronto.

"They've done just about all they can do on guitar; the piano is coming in a little stronger in rock music these days. I've been playing an electric piano with the group for the past couple of years but the sound is always muddy and it's hell trying to get it up to the same level as the guitars."

Cummings joined the Guess Who in 1965, when Chad Allen left. He'd only played with one other group prior to that.

"I had spent four and a half years with a group called the Dead Runs. We went to Minneapolis in 1965 and cut four tracks. The day we got back, I had a call from Bob Burns, who was the manager of the Guess Who at the time. It was just after *Shakin' All Over*, and Burns asked me to join the band. I said yes right there.

"We covered a lot of the country in the sixties. I hated Toronto - it was too flashy with the mohair suits and light shows. I didn't like Vancouver either - everyone was into a Moby Grape thing and the whole Los Angeles trip. The Maritimes were nothing, and Montreal was too big. No one had ever heard of the Guess Who there. There wasn't much of a Canadian scene then. We weren't influenced by anything except a rehash of North Dakota AM radio.

"Most of my ambitions have been fulfilled in the two years we've made it. It sounds corny I know but back in the old days, I just lived to be on top. I was obsessed with it. I should have gone back to school because I always wanted to be a doctor, but I had this rock obsession.

"You know, the Guess Who really should not have stayed together as long as we did without making it. We had nineteen singles and five albums of nothing, and that's a lot of disappointment."

Of all Guess Who members, Cummings is probably the most sensitive to musical developments outside the group. Every few months, he's into something new. Shortly after the million-selling success of *These Eyes*, he raved about the Jefferson Airplane, the Asylum Choir, the Mothers, Chicago, Lenny Breau, Gary Burton and Simon and Garfunkel. By the end of 1970, he was a confirmed Jelly Roll Morton addict. "I started listening to Mose Allison and Georgie Fame. One day I was messing around in the studio with a Mose Allison tune, and Jack Richardson yelled out 'OK, Jelly Roll.' I asked him 'Jelly Roll who?' and he said 'Jelly Roll Morton!'

"Then I found out that all Morton's albums are on the RCA Vintage series, and as we record for RCA too, it wasn't too hard to get hold of some copies. Jelly Roll Morton was the father of Dixieland jazz. If you can get past the fact that it sounds like rotten rag time, and start listening to the guy playing, it's really good stuff. Jelly Roll was a piano player, and I guess that's why I'm interested in it."

Several critics have compared the decline of The Beatles with the rise of the Guess Who, and found in the latter's music the same sort of broad appeal which inevitably marked the Beatles' work.

"It's crazy," says Cummings. "You can't compare anyone to The Beatles. But, of course, it's easy to compare another group with something you're only remembering, and not seeing anymore.

"I must admit I sometimes find myself striving for some of the same things as the Beatles did. I try not to consciously, but I listened to them - they're there in my blood. The influence lingers."

Being a Canadian is something which Cummings is often very long-winded about. "It means I'm just a little bit better off. I don't really know enough about the rest of the world to really appreciate being a Canadian. I can only compare it with the U.S."

Cummings claims there's one big difference between Canadian and American youth. "The U.S. has the draft and that really changes people's attitudes. Living in Canada, you're exposed to the whole of U.S. mass media, you can't help but write U.S. oriented songs. It's an unconscious thing. You begin to understand U.S. tastes, and you program your stuff to it.

"I don't think there's anything intrinsically Canadian in our music. I am just a member of a band which expresses the way it sees the world. Of course, the level of musicianship in each country can be different, and I honestly think Canada's is the highest.

"The Canadian music scene, as a whole, has improved a hundred-fold within the last six years. I'll never forget a record that David Clayton-Thomas cut. It was called *Brainwashed* and it was sensational. But it went nowhere.

"Now all sorts of Canadian groups are getting off. Steel River, Mainline, the Poppy Family. I don't like the Poppy Family style but they've had a lot of success."

In the first flush of Guess Who success, rumors of Cummings' imminent departure were rife. Cummings was predicted to be leaving the group every other month.

"A lot of this came from the fact that I've always planned to do a solo album. But the only thing that's been done so far is the cover.

"Most of the material is written. It won't be a Guess Who album, but I suppose it will sound like us in parts. I'm going to sing the same, all the compositions are mine, but I will be using a few sidemen. I even plan to get in a Dixieland band. It's all a matter of getting some time to cut the album." Time is a precious commodity to the Guess Who. Because of the desperate need for a well-earned rest in early 1971, the group had no time to cut a follow-up to *Share the Land*. It was necessary to pull another single from the much programmed *Share the Land* album, *Hang Onto Your Life*.

"It was basically an anti-drug song," Cummings admits. "The first two lyric lines lay out the rap - 'Thinkin' 'bout the people gone by. Screamin' that I don't wanna die.'"

A unique pop figure, in Cummings' opinion, is Don Hunter, the Guess Who's manager. Cummings is perhaps a little closer to Hunter than the other members of the group. When the Guess Who and Hunter broke up one night in December 1970, it was Cummings who came around first the next morning. The two share a camaraderie that is rare indeed in rock.

"Ten years ago," relates Cummings, "I used to deliver papers to Don. He was an entertainer then, and the weirdest cat on my route. When I'd bash on the door early in the morning, Hunter would come out and bellow - it used to frighten the hell out of me." It wasn't until eight years later, when Hunter became the group's agent, that Cummings remembered their earlier association. "Hunter is the most unique manager in the world," is the way Cummings describes him.

Predictably, Cummings is a young man with wide interests. "I write a bit - I'm trying to get a book published that I wrote seven years ago. It's a series of poems and short stories, all dated and titled.

"I also like to play pinball machines like crazy. I make tapes and collect records. But I don't really have any hobbies. I just have a good time. Everyday something's happening. I'm living in a fairy-tale. I just want it to keep getting better and better. It's all been pretty phenomenal so far.

"Now Winnipeg means more to me than ever before. I used to hate those freezing winters, but now that I've missed some of them, I really dig the winter. I like Winnipeg - I'll live there always."

Jim Kale

Precisely speaking, Jim Kale is the original member of the Guess Who. As a young teenager, he lived a few doors from piano player

Bob Ashley. Ashley and Kale got together in 1957, added a couple of other school friends and formed Al and the Silvertones. When Al left, Randy Bachman was his replacement. When the rhythm guitarist split, drummer Gary Peterson was introduced to the circle.

"There was myself, Bob Ashley, Randy Bachman and Gary Peterson, plus Chad Allen - alias Allen Mobell. We went through a series of name things at the start of the sixties. For a while, we were Chad Allen and the Reflections, but the *Romeo and Juliet* record from the Reflections in Detroit ruined that. We settled on Chad Allen and the Expressions, which lasted until George Struth of Quality Records came up with the Guess Who in 1965. We are eternally grateful to him.

"Actually I must admit that I could never get used to saying Guess Who. But the meaning's changed over the years and I don't mind it now."

After the success spree following *Shakin' All Over*, the Guess Who went through some lean times. "In 1966, we spent the entire summer in Vancouver and on a six week fiasco tour through Alberta and Saskatchewan. We were supposed to be making three hundred dollars a night, six nights a week. But after reading the contract a second time, we discovered that we received the first three hundred in paid admissions. If that much didn't come, we got what was there. Sometimes it wasn't very much.

"But we were always very lucky - we never starved, somehow we always got by. But you'd often run into the guys who'd like to put pressure on you. They'd say, 'You work here, and do my TV show or you don't work in this area at all'."

Kale is extremely honest about the personal relationships within the group, particularly about how they used to be when Bachman was still a member. "If our group ever had to live together, the old group especially, it would be all over in a few days. We're too different.

"It's hard to imagine getting any group of musicians to live and think together on planes other than music. A lot of The Beatles best work was done after they had separated.

"But we have our ups and downs. They're basically all fine guys. We can communicate much more effectively now that Randy Bachman has left us. As long as I've known Gary Peterson, some thirteen years, we've never got on, but in the last six months, it's been a new ball game. We like to give each other room to move. We don't all stay on the same floor in hotels; we often travel separately."

Musically of course, it's a different story. "Even though we're still individually independent, we can appreciate the others' viewpoints. Kurt is really into progressive things like Frank Zappa, Burton too, but he likes John Sebastian a lot as well."

"I'm closest to Greg, I guess. We often sit down together and play James Taylor and The Band. In the whole group, I would say that Burton has the widest tastes in music. He gets into all sorts of things."

Kale is openly loyal to the Guess Who, and their success has given him a fair amount of self-assurance. "We stuck out a lot in getting to the top. There was all the Canadian radio bullshit, learning the business, bad record contracts ... it never seemed to end."

The release of *These Eyes* in March 1969, did not really change things in Canada. CHUM, for example, refused to play the single for four successive weeks, offering various reasons, all related to the fact that the disc had not yet become a U.S. hit. "When it started to move in the U.S., CHUM went right on it, and even claimed they'd broken the record, made the first release. Like hell they did." Kale still thinks of *These Eyes* as one of the group's best recorded performances.

Kale's ambitions include "working like hell in 1971 to make a lot of money" and establishing the Guess Who into a "kind of Creedence category."

The accomplishment of the first (as inevitable as it seems) will mean the fulfilling of one of Kale's long-standing dreams. "I'd like to maintain two residences - one in Winnipeg and another in Horse-shoe Bay, outside of Vancouver. I'm never going to leave home, but I could take Vancouver in the wintertime."

Jim Kale doesn't like to talk a lot, especially about himself. But one evening in Winnipeg, he did confess to a feeling of fate fulfilled with the Guess Who.

"There was always that belief that one of those days ... if I said yes, that I knew we were going to make it, I'd be exaggerating, but we always hoped for it."

Greg Leskiw

The night I first got into a serious rap with the Guess Who's lead guitarist, Greg Leskiw, he insisted on first trying on a new outfit he'd bought in San Francisco that afternoon - a blue Mickey Mouse shirt and a pair of cord bell-bottom jeans. That may not strike one as revelatory, but they were the first set of new clothes Leskiw had bought in over a year. He had literally worn the same outfit for the entire year. It was a combination of poverty and eccentricity.

Home to Leskiw, as to all the members of the Guess Who, is Winnipeg. He had arrived in Winnipeg some six years before when he was eighteen. He took up guitar a year later and played in various bands prior to joining Wild Rice, the last group he was with before the big time hit.

"I got in on the Wild Rice scene late in 1969. I had been driving a cab before that to keep myself alive. But I wasn't too happy musically. In the early summer of 1970, I decided to split the group and go to New York." The offer to join the Guess Who came before he could make the trip.

Leskiw says he finds no difficulty in playing in a group with two lead guitarists - Kurt Winter joined the Guess Who at the same time, making the Guess Who one of the few leading Canadian groups utilizing this unusual combination (Crowbar is another).

"Kurt and I have different styles - unpremeditated styles. I have a country feel but I also have blues. I think it has worked out fairly well."

Leskiw admires a fairly large number of his contemporaries. "I really like Don Troiano of Bush - he's really fine, a progressive innovator, Jimi Hendrix, Elvis Bishop, Michael Bloomfield, George Harrison, Django Reinhardt, the gypsy guitarist who goes back to the thirties, and Lenny Breau. Lenny is fantastic."

He is fairly vague in his attempt to define what sort of guitar player he would like to be. "I'd just like to be musical," he claims simply.

"This whole scene is incredible, it really is. For Chrissake, 1 remember touring out in western Canada in mid-winter when we didn't even have enough money to buy a decent truck. The holes in the floor were so big you could see the road as you drove along. It was bloody cold - forty below sometimes, and no heating."

He has little familiarity with the current Canadian music scene. Jerked from that decrepit old truck into a superficially glamorous world where a two hundred dollar room-service meal means next to nothing, Leskiw finds it hard to gain hold of any perspective.

"I guess Canadian music is becoming more commercial. It'll help those groups who deserve to be heard and so far haven't had the chance. The music will get better, it will become more original as time goes by."

Leskiw listens to a wide variety of music from classics to be-bop to jazz to country and western to Jimi Hendrix. "I've always had certain types of music in my head - that's one thing that hasn't changed."

He pauses to reflect, to try to slow down the orbit which he has been thrust into. It is difficult and it shows in his face. He is uncertain and insecure in a sense. Ask him what he wants out of his life: "I want to be happy in my sadness," he answers, as if he has never thought of it before.

Gary Peterson

The Canadian music scene badly needs responsible business people according to the Guess Who's drummer, Gary Peterson.

"It was Brian Epstein who took The Beatles to the world, and we need the same sort of clever promoters in Canada."

Peterson doesn't think that international experience is absolutely necessary. He believes that the mere desire to reach the heights of the Epsteins, the Parkers, the Grossmans, is sufficient to get the job done.

"We've had six or seven managers, and we outgrew all but one very quickly. The only exception was Don Hunter, and I don't think we'll ever outgrow him. When Don first came with us in 1968, he didn't know any more than anyone else in the Winnipeg scene. He just did more - went out and taught himself. And now, he's one of the best managers in the business.

"The Guess Who has always been a very practical band. We're honest with ourselves, which makes it easy to be honest to the public. We're five individuals - there's a lot of things the other guys do that I wouldn't. There needs to be a lot of tolerance of each other's actions and feelings.

"We stayed together so long because we were continually improving. We put almost all the money we made back into equipment. We financed our own recording sessions, many times having to go into debt to do it. But we were never financially destitute. We made good money for a group of our stature in the Canadian music industry of the sixties.

"We didn't give up but there were some tough times. You tend to forget them over the years. In 1966, we were stuck in England. We had been promised a tour by a record company whose name I won't mention. We had no contract signed when we left, and when we arrived, we found they wanted the moon and wouldn't give us the tour unless we signed.

"We didn't sign. While we were there trying to straighten things out, we recorded *Flying on the Ground Is Wrong* which was a moderate hit in Canada. It was also the first time that a Canadian band had recorded in London.

"We came back to Canada about $25,000 in the hole. But we had learned a lot about the international music business. The hardest things to take were not so much the financial hard times but the frustration of it all. It took so long to get the right people around us.

"A dispute continually went on within the group as to whether we should move to the States. A few other bands had and they seemed to be getting by. It was tempting to pick up and go somewhere else and try and go the star route. But we stayed where we were, kept plugging at it and finally it happened. If we had gone to Los Angeles or San Francisco, I don't think we'd be where we are now. We're just not a west coast sort of group."

A significant breakthrough for the group was their association with Jack Richardson in Toronto, and the work done on jingles and a premium record for Coca-Cola. Richardson saw potential in the group and financially backed their recording sessions. His role in the development and success of the Guess Who is no small one.

Says Peterson, "Jack acts as arbitrator in the studio. He interprets what we want, and he acts between us and the sound engineer. He has a good technical knowledge and anything we want he will try, even though he has the final decision. We get along well personally and professionally. Even if we weren't associated with Nimbus 9, I'm sure we'd want Jack to work with us."

Peterson's favorite Guess Who tracks include *No Time, Undun,*

Moan for you Joe, and *Hang Onto Your Life*. *No Time* has a good vocal, and a fine music track. It was nice instrumentation, and it reminded me of the Buffalo Springfield, a group which I'd loved. *Undun* gets close to the jazz idiom but I think I like *Hang Onto Your Life* best because it was created completely in the studio. We had fun and it came out well."

Peterson readily admits that the arrival of The Beatles had much impact on the then five-year-old group. "They were a tremendous influence. Before we got into our own material, we used to do early Beatles tunes. That was before anybody knew who we were.

"We corresponded with people in London and received tapes and records of stuff by the Shadows, and then, of course, The Beatles arrived. We took all our stuff from English records and material. Our first record was a tribute to Buddy Holly, which had been done in England by Mike Berry and the Outlaws. We were really into the Shadows stuff when it didn't mean a damn thing here. We also like some of the stuff by Gerry and the Pacemakers.

"There were really a lot of good English rock groups. Canadian kids had never heard that stuff, and when we did it, it seemed so different. Actually, it was just English groups stealing stuff from old American rhythm and blues groups, and then we took it from them.

"I like to think now that we have diversification within the Guess Who. I believe every one of our cuts is totally different from the next. But I don't think we're deliberately trying to appeal to everybody. We only try to appeal to ourselves. We're definitely not in one bag."

Nor are their musical tastes. The pop press has found the Guess Who a difficult group on which to hang a label.

Peterson's own musical influences - jazz, big band and country - were a vital catalyst of progression within the group. "I always liked Buddy Rich, Gene Krupa, Cozy Cole and Joe Morello. Very few of the rock drummers impressed me at all. Ringo Starr was probably the best, but he's not really a great drummer. Still he was tremendously effective in what he did on records. As a matter of fact, I've always felt that drums were traditionally the lagging instrument in rock. Other instruments progressed but drums remained poor."

Peterson has some astute observations on the Canadian music industry. "I don't think there was a music scene in Canada up until very recently; at least, not one comparable to that of the U.S. The CRTC regulations are good - they will force radio stations to play and create work for Canadians.

"It shouldn't have been necessary to legislate it. Eventually, I think, there'll be no need for it. But something was needed to get the ball rolling, and I believe the CRTC regulations are the answer. It would have made our career a lot easier if they had started ten years earlier."

Peterson is not complaining, however. He is the least temperamental member of the Guess Who. He invariably maintains a positive attitude, and there aren't many problems which can bring him down.

"I've relatively simple tastes and ambitions," he says. "I like to ski, play music, and make money. Basically I'm lazy. I can't be bothered making long range plans. I've been a musician for twenty-three years, and I'm likely to be one for another thirty.

"I just want to be happy. I want people to accept me. I want people to say I played well ... that for me is very important."

Kurt Winter

Kurt Winter is a rotund, practical and straightahead guitar player who takes almost everything seriously, particularly his music.

He joined the Guess Who with Greg Leskiw in the summer of 1970, the end of an eight-year career in countless Winnipeg rock groups, only one of which even came close to satisfying Winter's musical appetite.

"I began writing songs while a member of Brother, a trio. When I was asked to join the Guess Who, it was just like a continuation of doing my own material."

Less than a month after Winter became one of the Guess Who, the band flew to Chicago to cut a new single, a follow-up to the million-selling smash, *American Woman*. The song they chose was Winter's *Hand Me Down World*.

The lyrics had a strange common sense, no nonsense to them. Winter had written the song for Brother, and had actually cut a demo of it which was rejected by RCA Records in New York. "They liked the sound of the group, but not the song," says Winter, a slight grin playing on his mustachioed lips. "The Guess Who's *Hand Me Down World* was one of those six-hour singles. We whipped into the studio and did it. There wasn't much thought behind it."

In short, Winter the writer didn't like what they'd done to his song.

"It could've been better, played better, recorded better - it was all too swift. It was a pity because the facilities were there. I did think the engineering and production were good though."

Winter didn't suddenly step up his writing activity when he joined the Guess Who. "Once you get into writing, you don't plan, you just write. If you get an idea, it's there.

"There are a lot of groups in Canada still writing in the same bag - the acid bag where they just want to make a racket. For the overall scene, you have to play music as well. You need well thought-out melody lines. If you like, it's contrived, but The Beatles did it and did it successfully. I don't know if Canada is up to it yet."

Melody is a subject very close to Kurt Winter's heart. "I really dig Frank Zappa. He's even more melodic than the Beatles. He can write the freaky stuff but he can also get off some really beautiful melody lines. He is not recognized as being a musician, a composer, a producer, an engineer - all of which he is good at - people just think of him as a freak."

Winter agrees that stepping into the Guess Who from obscurity presented a number of unusual difficulties. "It wasn't easy. I had a lot of apprehensions about playing the part. Joining them was something I hadn't expected. It was a quick step to the top, missing all the bullshit. I'd been out on the training grounds too - for eight years - but they had two years of international experience. I had some catching up to do.

"The thing is that I enjoy playing good music - and this is good music - so I like it."

Don Hunter

It took Don Hunter more than a little time to find the right calling. He was a bowling instructor, a racing car driver, a dispatcher for a cab company; he even did a stint in a turkey factory.

He was a singer, too. But all that was before he became a rock group manager - the most successful in Canada, and a man with a global reputation. Bob Gibson, who is based in Los Angeles and is one of the finest pop publicists on the scene, probably speaks for a wide section of the music business when he says of Hunter: "His tenacity and energy levels are unmatched within the industry. He devotes full time to his craft; obviously he has succeeded and will only do bigger and better things."

Hunter is the manager of the Guess Who. It's an eighteen hours a day, seven days a week job. When the group goes out on the road, the only sleep Hunter gets is in transit.

A great many factors were involved in the launching of the Guess Who internationally, but one thing is sure - without Hunter, it would not have happened. Hunter first became involved with the Guess Who early in 1967, quite a few months before *These Eyes* opened the world market to the Winnipeg group.

Hunter, naturally, is the group's greatest supporter and a promoter of Canadian music in general. He is also one of the fiercest critics of Canadian broadcasting apathy. Now that the Guess Who have achieved such massive international success, Hunter is one of the very few people in Canada able to candidly speak his mind without worrying about radio station reprisal. As he puts it, "I don't care if this station or that station won't play our records. They'll be hits without them. So I say what I think, which is the way it should be."

For a manager whose skills have been compared with Brian Epstein and Colonel Tom Parker, Hunter is surprisingly unorthodox in appearance and manner. He never wears ties; he drinks a lot; he undergoes tremendous pressure but he can laugh at the most crucial problem; and he has amazing intuition. Hunter instinctively seems to make the right decision at the right time. He has learned fast the ways and whims of the international music scene, and he has been accepted and welcomed at every level of the world rock business. He explains it simply. "I was working for a booking agency and going to university in Winnipeg at the same time. The relationship with the agency wasn't working out, so I decided to strike out on my own.

"At about the same time, I met the Guess Who, and they were a little dissatisfied with their agency. They called me and I began working for them as an agent. The busier things got, the more duties I took on for the group, and it gradually worked into a management thing. After I had worked for a short while with the Guess Who, I realized that the group had something really special. They weren't into the usual feedback things or the stuff that everyone was doing. They were original.

"But I was pretty green. I wasn't sure exactly what they had going for them. In any case I figured that whatever time or work that I put into them would be well worth the effort.

"If you're looking for the formula that transformed the Guess Who into a world act, it's difficult to pin down. There were so many different things involved. For three consecutive records - *These Eyes* and the two previous - we did a saturation tour, went back and forth across the country. No matter where you went in Canada during those few months, you'd see a poster for a Guess Who concert. In addition, the promoters who were buying radio time for the concerts were putting a lot of pressure on stations to play the current Guess Who singles. So we had airtime in many areas where normally there wouldn't have been a hope in hell.

"On every gig, we played as the only act. If you go on as an opening act to a major concert attraction, nobody's going to listen because nobody cares. When *These Eyes* came out in the U.S. we did some television work as well. We also had a lot of independent promotion men behind the record and after the press.

"I'm not saying that our record company wasn't capable - I just wasn't going to take the chance. As far as I was concerned, we had one shot. If nothing happened the first time around in the U.S., we were right back at the beginning.

"Everybody knows the problems we had getting *These Eyes* played in Canada. One station in Saskatoon said the record wasn't good enough, CHUM in Toronto just didn't like it and wouldn't play it for a month. Then it reached the U.S. charts and it was a different story. If we hadn't told them it was a Canadian record, they probably would have played it. I know a radio station that played three Andy Kim records right up to number one before they found out he was Canadian. When I started with the Guess Who, I was told I needed a psychiatrist. 'They're Canadian,' people said, 'forget it.' Forget it my ass!

"The group went out early in 1971 at $12,500 per night, against a percentage of the gate gross. I intend to have that up to $20,000 per night by the end of 1971. Then we'd simply do one ninety-day tour a year and spend the rest of the time recording and looking after our business interests.

"You may be surprised to learn just how many business interests the Guess Who are involved with. You will probably also be amazed at how meticulously we plan and operate our activities. We have an accountant in Winnipeg who is extremely sharp in investment. There is a long-range investment program operating for the group; they actually don't see very much of the money as it comes in.

"Each member of the Guess Who clears about $20,000 annually. They're on the road six months out of the year, so that's like having $40,000 per annum if you're sitting at home all the time.

"We only keep operating money - everything else is invested. The group grossed about two million dollars in 1970; I expect this to reach four to five million in 1971. I guess you could say that the guys in the group are close to being millionaires. Maybe they are already. In any case, they're becoming a large corporate entity.

"They own a shopping centre in Alberta, part of a hotel in Jamaica, lots of Canadian stock and land, and three Colonel Sanders' Kentucky Fried Chicken franchises. The chicken franchises are in the States, but they're owned by a Canadian company, which is something of a reversal.

"But we are careful about rip-offs. We have just made a $250,000 deal for twenty-five dates in the U.S. during 1971. Part of the deal is that there is a ceiling of five dollars on ticket prices. I'd rather make a little less and see a packed house. And if you want to look at it from an economic point of view, you will make the money back in record sales. You don't lose a thing. Anyway, what kid can go around paying seven dollars to see a concert? It's ridiculous.

"Eventually we plan to form our own record label in Winnipeg; perhaps call it Turkey Records [presumably a reminder of Hunter's days in the factory]. We've already signed two groups - Brother and Wild Rice. In the summer of 1970, I took a Brother master to New York and three major labels turned it down. The songs were *Hand Me Down World* and *Bus Rider*, both later million-sellers for the Guess Who. For the most part, I have very little respect for record company artists and repertoire men or for their opinions."

There are a lot of reasons why Don Hunter is the most successful rock manager Canada has so far produced, not the least being the way in which he has studied the moves of the masters. "The genius of them all, in my opinion, was Colonel Tom. He set a lot of precedents. Brian Epstein was another; he had a flair for showmanship. Reb Foster has done well with Steppenwolf and Three Dog Night and Bush, and Albert Grossman has been to the top.

"A manager's job is to co-ordinate. He must surround himself with the best people in every area, such as a road manager with brawn and brains. He also needs a good press agent. You cannot rely on a record company to look after the press. The company publicity department usually has four or five people to look after forty acts. I want someone working on the Guess Who twenty-four hours a day.

"I might add that the Guess Who have left me more than enough rope to hang myself, but fortunately I've been lucky and everything's worked out for the best."

And the state of Canadian music? "I think the CRTC deserves a standing ovation for legislating for Canadian content. I don't know whether it's a built-in inferiority complex of Canadians, or whether it's a matter of our radio stations relying too heavily on U.S. programming consultants. Our pop music stations are often being programmed by Americans who are totally unaware of what's going on in Canada. They don't know the local records or the groups, unless they're already well-known on their side of the border. So if the station is getting its programming advice from someone in California, how is the Canadian disc ever going to be heard? If the government had only said 'Play local records,' you'd have heard them between two and four in the morning.

"It's unfortunate that legislation was required but the radio stations had their chance, and they did absolutely nothing. The CRTC decision is going to create a music industry in this country. If producers know that they've got a chance of being heard, they'll put money into making records. "

Like many westerners, Hunter is sensitive about the role Toronto has played in the early development of Canadian rock.

"We've made one big mistake in Canada - letting U.S. record companies race in and sign all those Toronto groups. We're not seeing too much originality out of Toronto. The Toronto scene has become very sterile and over-exploited. It's time that other parts of Canada were given a fair chance."

Hunter thinks that the Maple Leaf System network of key Top Forty stations is "a joke and a hype, the less said about it the better." He does believe that several people should share in the credit for the ultimate emergence of Canadian music.

"Our producer, Jack Richardson, is terribly underrated. He's one of the finest producers in the world. Walt Grealis, the publisher of *RPM*, has been on the local content bandwagon for years, and he's done a lot for the scene; there's Brian Ahern, Greg Hambleton, Ralph Harding, Don Tarlton, Wes Dakus and a few of the smaller radio stations who were into Canadian records before they were made to be.

"I honestly believe that the Canadian music scene should have happened five years ago. If the Guess Who had cut *These Eyes* five years earlier, I think the industry could have been sparked from there. Once you can break one group in its own country and into the world market, it's off to a start. In the case of Canada, the Guess Who started it. And we're all very proud of that."

Jack Richardson

Jack Richardson doesn't look like the average rock record producer. His hair doesn't fall below his collar line. He wears turtlenecks and suits. He does not work like the average record producer. His sessions bear no resemblance to the Sodom and Gomorrah image, there is no dope, no groupies, no hangers on. When Jack is in the studio making records, it's serious business. And unlike so many of his younger contemporaries, Jack Richardson is also a businessman.

Jack is no youngster, although his creative talents continue to thrill millions of kids all over Canada and throughout the world. Despite the generation gap between youth and the business world, Jack understands kids. So he should - he has four of his own. He doesn't live the lifestyle of the young, yet somehow he is one of them.

Forty-one-year-old Richardson is the producer of the Guess Who. His company, Nimbus 9, has probably made close to half a million dollars from Jack's studio work with the group. He has done so well with the Guess Who that American record companies are asking him to produce records with big-name U.S. acts.

To reach the upper strata of the producing profession, Richardson had to travel a hard road. He had to take chance after chance, risk after risk, even to the point of mortgaging his family's house to finish the first recording session with the then unknown Guess Who. The battles he fought have left their scars. Richardson looks back on the bad old days with some bitterness.

"I started playing music professionally when I was sixteen. I had a stand up fiddle bass that was almost as tall as I was. I guess over the next few years I played with most of the big bands in Canada. 1 was a member of a jazz octet which played the Stratford Festival in its first year.

"But at that time, I'd only played to put myself through school. When I left school I took a job as a production supervisor at Massey Ferguson. It was a good job, and later on, I had some regrets about leaving it.

"In 1960, I cast an eye over the music business as a potential full-time career. What I saw didn't give me much hope of supporting a family." Jack had met his wife Shirley, a singer, while playing a gig in Rouyn, Quebec in 1950. They were married soon after. "Finally I found a job with the McCann Ericksen advertising agency. I enjoyed it because of the lack of regimentation."

Noting that Richardson had a good rapport with music and youth, the agency gave him the task of producing the *Hi-Fi Club*, a Coca-Cola sponsored radio show which was aired on two dozen stations. The show ran for two and a half years. Richardson became an account executive for Coca-Cola.

"Part of my job was listening to the commercials brought in by freelance producers. Most of them were awful. I kept complaining about the poor quality and lack of imagination and finally the agency responded. They invited me to do them myself."

Richardson quickly settled into the new field of commercial production. He did so well that he won nine broadcasting awards. Eventually he came up with the novel idea of having pop artists cutting commercials for Coke, a concept that was not only to revolutionize Coca-Cola's international advertising, but would also change his own life in a way he could never have imagined.

The first artist used was Bobby Curtola. Meantime, Coke's American parent company passed on the new concept of outside artists doing the jingles. Richardson went to Nashville and cut more Canadian Coke ads with the local musicians - Boots Randolph, Chet Atkins, and others. Eight months after the idea had first been presented, Coke in the U.S. decided to pick up this style of endorsement. Richardson recorded jingles with a number of international artists, including Petula Clark and David Clayton-Thomas, the ex-Toronto singer who now fronts Blood, Sweat & Tears.

Not content to rest on his laurels, Richardson approached Coke with the idea of cutting special pop records as premiums for bottle liners, a sort of added sales incentive. The Coca-Cola people agreed, and Richardson soon produced two special albums - one with Bobby Curtola, the other with Michel Louvin and Margot LeFebvre - which became two of the biggest-selling LPs of all time in Canada. The Curtola LP sold 117,000 copies, and the French album 135,000. Even then the French were far more aware of their domestic talent than English Canadians.

Two years later, in 1968, Coke decided to do another disc promotion. This time Richardson chose a barely known Winnipeg group, the Guess Who, and an even lesser recognized band from Ottawa, the Staccatos. This combination album represented a far greater risk to Coca-Cola than the Curtola venture. Bobby Curtola appealed to a much broader section of the market (in particular, the female audience), while the Guess Who and the Staccatos were rock bands.

Richardson approached both groups, suggesting that in their own interests they should try and record original material. They'd do better financially because they would receive automatic royalties. The Staccatos had Les Emmerson, who had already demonstrated considerable composing talent, while the Guess Who were just beginning to write. Neither act had done particularly well on record, so there was little difficulty in acquiring the permission of their respective record companies to make these special discs. Paul White, then artists and repertoire director at Capitol Records, which had the Staccatos under contract, recalls, "We'd tried many times to cut a hit record with the group, but we just couldn't get any airplay. We thought the Coke deal would be a good chance for them to put some long-overdue money into their pockets. We said good luck to them."

Radio stations took very little notice when they heard Coke was making a Canadian rock premium record. "Several program directors called up to tell us how bad Canadian talent and Canadian records were," Richardson notes acidly. Unperturbed, Coke went ahead with the album, putting the tracks down at Hallmark Studios in Toronto. "Coke were very generous to both groups. They gave them a fair royalty and didn't deduct the recording costs. I guess the two groups wound up making about $40,000 between them. And in those days, that was a small fortune."

The album, available to buyers for $1.25 plus eight bottle liners, sold some 83,000 copies, far and away the biggest rock music seller ever at that point in Canadian rock history.

In the meantime, Richardson flew to Nashville with Quebec's Michel Louvin and Michele Richard to cut another French album for Coke. It was the first time that a French Canadian artist had recorded in Nashville.

But Richardson was absorbed in something far more significant - the idea of recording the Guess Who for the mass market. He'd detected something unique, "something you just couldn't put your finger on," while working in the studio, and it fascinated him. Yet the group was still signed to Quality Records in Toronto, and the

Coke record had given their career a boost. It seemed unlikely that Quality would release the Guess Who from their contractual obligations at this point. Richardson had long discussions with the Guess Who. They had been impressed with his enthusiasm, his working knowledge of the finer points of music, and above all, his ability to get their name onto the airwaves.

"The Coke album, despite all the dire predictions, received some 'political' play on those radio stations which enjoyed an annual advertising commitment from the Coke company," Richardson recalls.

Richardson discussed his ideas with the management of Quality Records, who surprisingly agreed to give the Guess Who a release from their contract at a cost of $1,000. "It was a lot of money to us at the time," Richardson says, "but in the long run, it seems that it cost Quality much more." If Quality had somehow persuaded Richardson that he should produce the group for Quality Records (in return for a production royalty) that company might have made millions of dollars.

Richardson was still working at McCann Ericksen, but he and two friends - jingle writer-arranger Ben McPeek and fellow agency executive, Peter Clayton - had decided to start their own record company. Between them, they raised enough money to record some tracks with the Guess Who at Hallmark Studios in Toronto. "But the session just didn't make it. The sound wasn't right. We had to scrap the tapes."

At that point, Richardson mortgaged his home. The record company, Nimbus 9 Productions, was founded in March 1968, with all three actively involved, along with accountant Al Macmillan. Enough money was scraped together to fly the Guess Who to New York to cut an album at A & R Studios, where studio time costs an average $150 an hour. "If it hadn't been for the money Ben was getting for his jingles, we would never have cut the album," Richardson says.

The LP was lovingly titled *Wheatfield Soul*, a proud reference to the group's origins. The album work began on September 19, 1968, continued for three days, and cost $9,800. While in New York, Richardson played some of the tracks to various record companies, and one of them, RCA, expressed interest in acquiring world release rights.

"We signed a contract with RCA at a cost to them of $3,000 which sounds ridiculous now," Richardson laughs. "But we did renegotiate the contract later, and RCA has been very good to us."

Richardson flew back into Toronto, and handed in his resignation at McCann Ericksen on October 1. "We had a lot of confidence in the group and our own abilities to somehow expose them to the world. Ben and I had a strange kind of belief that it would turn out all right in the end. And we thought that if nothing came to Nimbus, we could always return to an advertising agency."

Looking back now, Richardson says in the light of hindsight, "We were lucky. We had a good group with a lot of talent, and we had the right record company." This is far from adequate testimony to the talents of the people who manoeuvred it all into place.

It was decided to release one of the cuts as a single. The song selected was. *These Eyes*, which again, through the peephole of hindsight, could be said to be the most important record ever released in Canada.

The battle flared up between Nimbus and radio stations who would do anything to avoid playing the record, while at the same time, Richardson had to concentrate on launching *These Eyes* in the U.S.

"We were deathly afraid of *These Eyes* not making it because of lack of effort. We decided to do everything we could to help RCA push the Guess Who. We took the totally unprecedented step of hiring our own promotion men in New York, Chicago, Washington and Los Angeles. It cost us nearly five hundred dollars a week and God knows we couldn't afford it, but we had to do it just to satisfy ourselves."

It was a hard fight to get the record into American stations. Richardson remembers calling Don Burkhimer at RCA Records in New York one night to say he was quitting the music business. "I had literally just put my head down on the desk and cried. But next morning I woke up with fresh enthusiasm and I called Burkhimer to tell him I was back in business."

The stubborn belief in *These Eyes* by both RCA and Nimbus 9 eventually paid off. It was picked up by a few small U.S. stations, spread to the bigger ones, and then busted wide open as a national hit. *These Eyes* reached the top three of the American best sellers list, and sold a million copies. Needless to say, there were many red-faced, embarrassed Canadian broadcasters, such as CHUM, who suddenly had to play a Canadian record because it was turning up in all their U.S. music programming guides.

It had finally happened. A Canadian group produced by a Canadian had broken through into the U.S. charts, thereby opening the doors for a potential invasion of Canadian talent. After this one single - which returned about $35,000 in production royalties to Nimbus - the Guess Who effectively became an American group in the eyes of Canadian radio stations. Their records came out first in the U.S., were reviewed enthusiastically by the American music papers, and the Canadians—as always with new records— played them like sheep.

Although Richardson has since greatly diversified his methods and used a variety of musicians at the studio, his first love is the Guess Who. "They're the most satisfying bunch of guys I could ever hope to work with," he says. One of the reasons for this is that the Guess Who like to get the job done when they go into the studio. Unlike many of their contemporaries (such as Simon and Garfunkel, who spent a reported $168,000 cutting their *Bridge Over Troubled Waters* album) the Guess Who get it on when recording. "None of their albums has ever gone over $13,000 in total studio costs," Richardson says proudly.

The most enjoyable record he has cut with the Guess Who was *American Woman,* which reached number one in the U.S. and quite a few other markets. "When we went into the studio to cut the song, we had absolutely nothing going for us. We built it right there in the studio. It came together from nothing but a scratch of an idea."

Although Richardson has yet to find another act to rival the popularity of the Guess Who, his reputation has brought offers from U.S. record companies to cut a number of American acts, including Alice Cooper and Mitch Ryder. The U.S. companies found Richardson's modus operandi somewhat different than that to which they had become accustomed. When Warner Brothers invited Richardson (and Nimbus' Bob Ezrin) to cut an album with Alice Cooper early in 1971, they set a budget of $35,000 on the LP. "We did the album for less than half that," claims Richardson.

Almost all Richardson sessions - be they with Canadian groups such as Homestead and Cat, or with U.S. acts like Alice Cooper - take place at RCA's comparatively new studios in downtown Chicago. The constant commuting between Chicago and Toronto accounts for most of Richardson's one hundred thousand air miles and hotel bills of $12,000 annually.

Richardson still plays bass on the occasional session. "I also sing from time to time ... I have a pretty good falsetto. And I played cello and viola on a Cat single."

Ask Richardson to describe what type of producer he is, and he's momentarily stumped. He tugs at his chin. "God, I don't really know," he replies at length. "I like to do as much preparation as possible. In the studio, I try to capture the essence of a group, rather than the producer. I think I'm a constructive producer."

I wondered if Richardson agreed with Delaney Bramlett (of Bonnie and Delaney) that a few bad notes are not too detrimental to a song if the right feel is there.

He shrugs. "I think successful records have a good feel and good notes. I'm primarily a jazz record listener myself. I'm not really into the heavier aspects of rock music. I like more sophisticated things than Led Zeppelin. But I listen to everything - I listen to it in analytical fashion as competitive rock product. Bob Ezrin is much more into the hard rock scene than I am."

Ezrin is a young Toronto producer whom Richardson is grooming. He is one of the nine employees at Nimbus 9. Three of the people devote most of their time to Ben McPeek's thriving jingle business. The other six are intimately involved with the running of Canada's first truly independent record company.

Virtually all Canadian record companies are in fact branches of U.S. and U.K. parent operations. Capitol, for example, is owned by EMI in England; Columbia is owned by CBS in New York; London, by Decca in England.

"Since there was no Canadian music industry to speak of, there were none of the professional people needed to sustain and aid a new independent record company not able to rely on imported hits," explains Jack. "Initially we weren't dealing from a position of strength. Our lawyer in Canada was very good but he had no knowledge of the international music scene. Few lawyers did. There had been no need for specialized knowledge in this field.

"The same applies to publishing, which is the most lucrative sector of the music business. We're only now beginning to understand the intricate ins and outs of international music publishing. And this sort of knowledge is vital. The Guess Who's *American Woman* was a huge hit in Germany because the publisher was a livewire promotion man. In many European countries, having the right publisher can mean the difference between a hit or a flop."

Obtaining Canadian financial backing for music-oriented ventures is another major problem. "After the broadcasters, the single most stubborn obstacle to development in the Canadian rock industry is the lack of understanding money men. Quite naturally, the Canadian music business does not have a reputation as a lucrative investment opportunity. Very few people are willing to take the risk. More and more people are needed to take a flyer. You don't always win but the stakes are so high that one hit record can make up for a lot of misses.

"The new independent companies need that sort of assistance. Anybody can be a successful record producer. The established producers don't have a corner on all the ideas. Far from it."

Richardson won a *Billboard* Trendsetter award in 1969 for his efforts in prying open the red, white and blue chart doors to Canadian musicians. He declines due credit, but he will admit that Canadians now have a much easier time getting their product heard by U.S. record companies.

"Everyone involved here has an unparalleled opportunity to get their thing together. In the long haul, I think we're going to have a very viable music industry in Canada. And with so much hype in the States about the Canadian sound, I actually think, as a record producer, that one is better off to come from Canada than to be an American.

"A Canadian producer nowadays has no trouble having his product heard in New York or Los Angeles. There's no difficulty in getting an appointment. In the U.S., there's a mystique to Canada. They think we have a special sound or favorable weather or something."

And what of that much-heralded "Canadian sound," the latest "big thing" in the U.S. record company crystal balls? How does Richardson, as the most successful Canadian record producer, ever view the Canadian sound? Is it something unique? Do we have something that the Americans don't? Are Canadians blessed with some special attribute which makes it easier for them to create pop music? Is there really a Canadian sound, or is it all in the minds of American record executives?

"No, there isn't a Canadian flavor or sound in music. That kind of musical identity usually comes through a factor of isolation from the mainstream. Canada just doesn't have that. We're simply too close to the American experience, the American media, and the American market."

3. CANADA'S ROCK INVASION

For all their obvious ability and success, the Guess Who was not the only Canadian act to realize global recognition. The Winnipeg band had won the U.S. scene with a string of hit singles and albums, but they were soon joined by an ever-increasing number of talented young Canadians.

Some twenty Canadian acts have achieved American chart success since the Guess Who's initial conquest. It hasn't been easy for any of them, but they all recall how much harder it used to be.

Still others are now knocking on the door. It is beyond the scope of the imagination to predict how many more Canadian bands and writers will rise from the north country in the coming years. That young man who strums guitar in an Edmonton coffee house, or that noisy group rehearsing loudly in the family basement, or that girl in Sudbury who puts poetry to music ... any or all of them could be international stars in the not so distant future.

The point is that what was once impossible is now quite feasible. In this chapter we rap with the leaders of the Canadian rock invasion about their evolution, hassles, successes and ambitions.

The Bells

About three years ago, writer Rick Neufeld awoke one summer morning to a typical Manitoba scene. But on this particular day, Neufeld took special notice of the sights and sounds around him. A few days later, he decided to write a song about a morning in Manitoba. He called the tune *Moody Manitoba Morning*, and his publisher sent a tape of the song to the Five Bells, a Montreal group who had achieved some prominence in Canadian and U.S. club circuits.

The Five Bells were highly impressed by the tune and recorded it. It came out late in 1968, to a less than warm welcome. Few stations could be talked into programming it, even though it was a first class production. It wasn't on the *Billboard* U.S. charts.

The potential of the song was realized by George Hamilton IV, the noted Nashville country singer. Only problem was George reportedly wanted to change the title to *Moody Mississippi Morning* for the U.S. market. To his lasting credit, Neufeld wouldn't have anything to do with such an artistic abortion. The Five Bells' version wound up selling around 3,000 copies in Canada ("a liberal estimate," says Cliff Edwards, leader of the Bells) and it naturally followed that no one in the States would release it because of its supposedly poor performance in this country.

A couple of years and two big hits later, the Bells were discussing *Moody Manitoba Morning* with their U.S. record company, Polydor. "Polydor said they would be perfectly happy to release *Moody Manitoba Morning* as our third single. They had been getting a lot of U.S. radio play on the track, which was included on the *Fly Little White Dove Fly* album," says Edwards.

There had been a complete shift in attitudes since the first release of Moody *Manitoba Morning* and the surprise arrival of *Fly Little White Dove Fly* in late fall of 1970.

"The sessions were almost a desperation move," Cliff Edwards recalls. "The Five Bells' contract with Polydor was almost up, and we were really mixed up in our music policy. Finally I decided to have one more try. We went in with four songs, two of which were *Fly Little White Dove Fly* and *Stay Awhile*.

"It all happened so naturally. It seemed as though there had been no stop in time between *Moody Manitoba Morning* and *Fly*; one just flowed into the other."

The group changed its name from the Five Bells to the Bells (Cliff's wife, Anne, had quit the group to become a mother), the record was released and became an instant hit. It sold close to 35,000 copies in Canada alone, and briefly entered the U.S. charts. It represented a new exposure experience for the Bells, who had hitherto been restricted to the nightclub circuit.

"We began to get out of the club scene after five years. The economic situation had cut into the crowds at the clubs. The only clubs doing well were located in hotels. It was becoming increasingly difficult for night clubs to attract people away from the TV sets. Fewer groups were being hired by clubs. More solo artists were making it. The trend was a return to basic music.

"Up until the summer of 1970, we'd been spending forty weeks a year on the road and in clubs. But now we've diversified our interests and found wider exposure in all markets. We still do some selected clubs; but we're also doing concerts. The colleges are interested - usually they don't care whether you're a Canadian or a Greek group."

Edwards believes the CRTC Canadian content ruling has played a key role in the development of local music. "When it was first announced, there were a lot of down vibes from radio stations. But my thought was that no matter how bad it ultimately came out, it could only be better than it was at that time.

"Look at CKLW in Windsor. Six months ago, they wouldn't even speak to you if you were a Canadian artist. Now they're actually playing our records.

"The stations originally claimed there would be bad product on the air. But that's bullshit! Canadians are now going out to buy Canadian records, whether they know they're Canadian or not. And if you, as an artist or record company, make money on one record, you're obviously going to spend more on the next one, and so on. This is a high risk, total investment business. You aim for the top. The Bells' ambition is to be the biggest group in North America - really. We think our possibilities are limitless. That's the way most people think in the music business.

"A couple of years ago, you had to make it somewhere else before they'd give you a chance in Canada. But there's only twenty million people and not enough clubs to provide a consistent booking schedule; an act had to go somewhere else. Speaking for ourselves, though, we haven't been to the U.S. in months. We used to be there all the time, but we haven't had to go lately. We've been busy enough right here.

"The CRTC ruling will make five or six major artists in Canada in its first few months. And that's great, because the artists deserve it. They've got the skill and the talent, and now they're also getting a chance."

The Bells presently consist of six musicians - Cliff Edwards and sister Jackie singing, with Doug Gravelle (an original member) on drums, piano player Frank Mills, plus two fellows from Halifax, Charlie Clark and Michael Waye.

Jackie is visibly overwhelmed by the group's success. "It's weird," she says, in that soft purr of hers. "It really hasn't hit home yet. It's rather nice to see a response at least, to have that confident feeling when you walk out on stage."

"We've paid our dues," Cliff adds, "and we're still paying them. But we're now making good money; we're receiving offers and exposure. We really couldn't ask for much more. It's all come out in the wash. Our music apparently wasn't relevant a couple of years ago - now it is. We must have finally been in the right place at the right time. But after six years, you figure it's due time."

Chilliwack

For all of the strenuous musical activity which has taken place in British Columbia over the past few years, only three acts have managed to make any sort of a national and/or international impact - the Poppy Family, Tom Northcott and Chilliwack.

Of the three, only Chilliwack is in any way representative of the Canadian west coast hard rock boom of the 1968-69 period. If there had been any unified radio exposure of this B.C. phenomenon, it is quite likely that Vancouver may have become an important music centre. The possibility remains, but there is no doubt that one chance has already slipped by.

"What we needed in Vancouver," says Bill Henderson, the friendly, folksy Chilliwack multi-instrumentalist, "was a really powerful radio station like CHUM in Toronto. We certainly didn't need CHUM's attitudes to Canadian music, but we needed a station with that much power in the local record stores and that much influence across the country at other stations.

"The Vancouver stations were traditionally as bad for local talent as they were everywhere in Canada. But even when they did give you a chance, it didn't make much difference. You'd maybe sell a few hundred records, but it didn't spread nationally."

Henderson speaks fondly of the "golden days" of Vancouver rock, the period three years before legislation began. "There was a club called the Retinal Circus, which became the focal point in Vancouver for the entire rock scene. Everyone got to play their music. The bands included Black Snake, Mother Tucker's Yellow Duck, Papa Bear's Medicine Show, and Hydro Electric Streetcar. They all had fantastic followings in Vancouver.

"The audiences were into the music. You could play whatever came into your head. You didn't need to hype the audiences. The entire thing lasted for about a year. But nothing happened record-wise. The evolution of a peculiarly Vancouver sound was prevented by the lack of studios and experienced people. I think of all the groups in Vancouver during that period, we were the only ones who recorded with any frequency. We were certainly the only band to record in the States."

Chilliwack, which was at last beginning to win acclaim in eastern Canada when the legislation period began, had been together four years. During the first three, the group was known as the Collectors. They had two albums released ("the first one still sells as much as it ever did, but the second one went nowhere") and a hit single, *Looking At A Baby*.

"We never really did dig that name, the Collectors," Henderson says. "But there hadn't been much choice. We had cut a single for a record company when we were in our infancy; we still hadn't come up with a name for the group. So the record company came to us and said we had to use either the Collectors or the Connection. With that selection, which would you have gone with?

"It had been in our minds to change the name for at least a year prior to actually doing it. We came up with Chilliwack in the winter of 1969. When we got around to doing the new album which had a new sound and approach, it gave us a chance to make the change."

There have been only two major personnel changes within the framework of the group during its four-year lifetime. The first was the departure of Howie Vickers, the other, when Glen Miller left.

"We tried two bass players after Glen left, but it just didn't work out. They both had their good points. But since we three [Henderson, Claire Lawrence and Ross Turney] had been together so long, it was very hard to break in someone new - musically and personally - in just a couple of months. So we decided to become a trio. All of us play bass at various times and songs."

Both Henderson and Lawrence make their home on Salt Spring Island, three hours by ferry from Vancouver. They found out about the place through a newspaper ad for three cabins for sixty dollars a month. The group took them all. Henderson moved into one with his wife, one is for Lawrence and the other is used for rehearsing.

Chilliwack has two long range plans. "First, we want a hit record because that's the best way to launch ourselves. That's why we're trying so hard to get a number happening in the east.

"The other plan is to play music we can get off on at the same time. There have been times in the past when we've compromised ourselves musically, doing things that we thought the audience wanted to hear. That's bullshit, and we regret it.

"We don't care too much about what we play when we go out on stage. I don't think it matters, if you've got a lot of chops and can play well. Live gigs are our most important method of communication at present. If we don't enjoy ourselves doing the gigs, we might as well forget it and go back to Salt Spring Island."

Bruce Cockburn

"I'm a Canadian, true, but in a sense it's more or less by default. Canada is the country I dislike the least at the moment. But I'm not really into nationalism - I prefer to think of myself as being a member of the world.

"The Canadian music business is not yet as rotten as the U.S. scene. But it's showing signs of catching up."

Words by Bruce Cockburn, rising young star; a bestselling album behind him; soundtrack of one of the most successful Canadian movies in history; former rock band organist; extremely sensitive lyricist; an artist in full creative control of his career; bound to succeed.

One imagines Bruce Cockburn to be many things, most of which he is not. Cockburn effectively defies description. He is too elusive to be labelled, possessing little or no image. He is Canada's latest addition to the big-time of folkdom. He has yet to achieve international recognition, though you feel it coming when he plays. Yet he seems disinterested in the fame aspect of music-making.

By late 1971, perhaps 1972, Cockburn will likely have a steady following in the U.S. or Europe. But he will have been an unwilling partner to it all. He is a sensitive young man in an awfully abrasive industry.

Cockburn has risen slowly and with cautious steps through the ranks of folk music. He has climbed to a position only ever held once before - by Gordon Lightfoot. Surprisingly Cockburn doesn't dig Lightfoot. "I've never really been a great fan of Gordon's. We don't do the same music." Everyone loves Lightfoot. Well, don't they? To not like him and worse still, to say so, seems to indicate an admirable if unwise, rebellious spirit.

Cockburn left his hometown of Ottawa in 1964 to attend a two-year music course in Boston. "My first introduction to the Canadian scene was in 1966. I came back to Canada and joined an Ottawa group called The Children. We did some original material; I played organ.

"I began writing songs because the group always needed material. We broke up after eighteen months and I drifted from band to band, played harp in a blues band, guitar in an R & B band. Even had a 'psychedelic' group, the Flying Circus, doing my material. Finally in 1969, I got out of it.

"I'd worked as a solo act in Boston, and also in Europe, when I was bumming around. Going solo again was so much less complicated, a lot easier on my head. It meant, too, that I didn't have anyone to cover my mistakes. It takes much less for one person to survive than four or five. I had no sound equipment. My expenses weren't high." A Canada Council grant was also of assistance.

One of Cockburn's most significant successes in 1970 was the music score he wrote for the highly-acclaimed Don Shebib movie, *Goin' Down the Road*.

"A mutual friend of the producer called me up and asked if I'd like to do it. Apparently it was between Ian Tyson and myself, but Ian wanted to use his band. They either couldn't afford it, or didn't want a whole band. So I took it on."

As well, there was the limited (though far-reaching) Top Forty radio play on Cockburn's single of *Musical Friends*, from his debut album, and the warm reception given his second album, *High Winds and White Sky*.

"Most of what I do is not immediately accessible to most people. But some radio stations have taken the trouble to find things among my material which could suit their audiences. Some of the Toronto stations have been especially helpful. Ottawa wasn't so good. It's mainly hardcore Top Forty up there, and one of the stations is owned by CHUM. We've also got the Maple Leaf System happening in Ottawa, which stands in the way a bit. CHUM-AM are right into the Ted Randal trip [Randal is a Californian program consultant whose clients include CHUM].

"I believe the CRTC has definitely helped me. It's at least drawing everybody's attention to what's happening with Canadian artists. That can only be good."

The Cockburns (Bruce and wife Kitty) have no fixed abode. "We have a truck that we live in or out of, depending on the weather. Both of our parents have farms just outside Ottawa, and we spend quite a bit of time with them. Usually when I'm working, we stay with friends."

He played the small coffee houses, such as the Onion in Toronto, but there were a lot of times when he was short of work. "I took jobs I wouldn't take now," he admits. "Two months at the Electric Circus in Toronto for example. First act on the bill Friday and Saturday nights. It was a hard place to play, doing a gig like I do."

Probably the incident which put Cockburn into a position of picking and choosing his appearances was the signing of a record contract with the newly formed True North Records, owned by Bernie Finkelstein.

"I'd been out on my own for about a year when I bumped into Gene Martynec, formerly of the Kensington Market in Toronto. We had a couple of coffees, and got to rapping on our idea of what an album should consist of - he from the production side, me from the musical side. We found our ideas were pretty much the same.

"Gene knew Bernie personally, and also knew he was the only person with enough money to make an album. Bernie also wanted to start True North, so it seemed a good opportunity to fulfill all aspirations."

Six months after the album was released, Cockburn still liked it, which indicated that it had been no minor artistic triumph. "Put it this way," he says, "I don't dislike it. I don't listen to it ... I'm familiar enough with the songs on it, but I was very happy with the way it was produced."

He gives little thought or respect to ambition. "I don't think in terms of becoming famous or rich. If it happens, great. Otherwise, O.K.

"I'm trying to preserve the smallness of my scene as much as possible. If an audience comes in thinking of you as a star, it destroys the relationship you can achieve otherwise. I've seen enough of that already to realize where it could lead."

Crowbar

The snow was still falling in fat flakes when we drove into Bad Manors. It had been pouring down for six hours on and off, but mainly on. Huge drifts had swept down the hill from the barn and settled against the sturdy brick walls of the century-old farmhouse.

Inside we joined the five members of Crowbar and a few friends. We'd been invited out for a special occasion - the inauguration of the first Crowbar album, which the group had named after this massive old farmhouse outside Hamilton. Pun and all, *Bad Manors* sounded like an original title for an album.

But why all this fuss over one album? I'd been impressed by Crowbar ever since I first saw them - playing back-up for Ronnie Hawkins, making it extremely difficult for Joe Cocker to follow them onto the Fillmore East stage in New York. Playing their first major gig, Crowbar simply trooped out onto the Fillmore stage and gave the capacity audience (which included Bob Dylan) a taste of music unlike anything it had heard before. Several of the usually blase New York rock critics waxed ecstatic in the weeks to come.

Dick Lupoff, writing in *Crawdaddy*, one of the most important U.S. rock journals, proclaimed: "These guys have everything ... material, technique, stage presence. Beautiful!"

They had done an album with King Biscuit Boy. Released in July of 1970, the LP, *Official Music*, drew international attention to both King Biscuit Boy and Crowbar. Again, the critics were unanimous in their approval. Jim Beebe, one-time rock critic for the *Toronto Daily Star*, wrote: "It's obvious that Crowbar could play circles around Canned Heat, Ten Years After, Led Zeppelin and other equivalents. Crowbar should take the world by storm."

I saw Crowbar play several times with King Biscuit Boy. Their most memorable performance was given at the Strawberry Fields rock festival near Toronto in the summer of 1970. It was the second day of the hastily arranged festival, and the audience of about 50,000 had suffered through an afternoon of musical mediocrity. Just as the sun was setting, Crowbar climbed up on the massive stage with King Biscuit Boy. By the time they'd reached their usual set closer, the Biscuit's *Boogie*, the crowd was on its feet, screaming for more.

Biscuit had dazzled the crowd with his authentic harp playing and blues singing, and Kelly Jay (Crowbar keyboards' player) had amused them with his stage antics. Nobody had seen a band that tight in years. Six hours later, when the mesmeric Sly and the Family Stone were doing their carefully compiled number on the stage, one could still hear the occasional voice yelling out for the return of Crowbar.

A few weeks after, King Biscuit Boy and Crowbar parted company - he to write material for his second album, *Gooduns*, they to prepare for their own debut album. I guessed on the way to the farm that the album had turned out fairly well, and that Crowbar wanted it to be heard in conducive surroundings. Yet, I was unprepared for what happened that evening.

As best I remember, we listened to the tape of *Bad Manors* seven times during the night. No Canadian album could be this good. I realized at that time that even the most ardent Canadian music supporter can sometimes fall victim to the off-heard myth that Canadian records can occasionally be as good as, but never better than American product!

As we drove back to Toronto around noon the next morning, I was fully convinced that Crowbar was going to be the most important Canadian talent export to the world since the Guess Who.

A few days later, I called Nevin Grant, the music director of CKOC in Hamilton and the chairman of the Maple Leaf System. I had heard through the grapevine that Nevin had also been exposed to *Bad Manors*. I wondered if his reaction had been similar to my own. At first I was cautious. I told Nevin I'd heard *Bad Manors*, and that I'd been told he'd heard it too. Gradually I unfolded the story. In the end, I simply said: "I think that *Bad Manors* is as good as *Sgt. Pepper*."

Nevin breathed an audible sigh of relief. "Thank goodness," he said. "I thought I'd gone crazy. This is just about the most incredible record I've ever heard in my life. I was so knocked out I was afraid to tell other people about it until I had confirmation from at least one other person."

We agreed the album would sell in excess of a million copies. We agreed there were about six definite hit singles on the album. And we agreed that not even the traditional Canadian apathy could slow down this powerful LP.

Upon the album's release, the music media reacted in a manner completely unheard of in Canadian music. Larry Green, one of the most listened to disc jockeys at CHUM-FM in Toronto, described *Bad Manors* as "the best new album I've heard from anywhere in the past six months." That included releases by Elton John, George Harrison and John Lennon.

Crowbar was the first Canadian group to be launched in the legislation era. They might well become one of the most popular Canadian acts of all time. Within three months of the international release of *Bad Manors*, Crowbar had become the first still-resident Canadian group to receive critical acclaim from the U.S. rock press. Despite their countless gold records, the Guess Who are still regarded by many American rock critics as a bubblegum band, appealing to the lowest musical instincts. Such an opinion is obviously debatable, yet the fact remains that while the Guess Who have broken down the chart barriers, Crowbar must get the credit for having torn down the critical walls. Reviews of the album in the American rock press were among the most enthusiastic accorded any new rock act (Canadian or otherwise) of 1971.

Rolling Stone magazine said: "This is a good one, friends ... this LP is one of the happiest, raunchiest, freshest emanations of a life energy to pin the grid in many moons."

Creem magazine: "Mama get your dancing shoes on ... then steady yourself for the jivingest, rock 'n' boogie band in the land, 'cuz Crowbar is about to smash your body to rock 'n' roll Valhalla. ... They might just have to rearrange the whole music awards format because of this one album."

And to top it all, *Fusion's* well-respected Lester Bangs came through even more enthusiastically: "I don't know anything about them [Crowbar] and I hardly ever like white blues bands, but I like these albums [*Bad Manors* and *Official Music*] as much as anything I've heard in the last year, and you will too, because they're fantastic."

But none of this is surprising when one looks at the facts. The six members of Crowbar - Kelly Jay, Sonnie Bernardi, Jozef Chirowski, the Ghetto, Roly Greenway and Rheal Lanthier - have one hundred years of combined musical experience. All came up the hardest possible way, through the bars and then with Ronnie Hawkins. Levon Helm and The Band had done the same gruelling route five years previously.

Kelly Jay, who has played with almost everyone worthy of mention in the history of North American rock music, first became a rock 'n' roller in 1954. He's been through more bars than most alcoholics. He's seen and done a lot; it shows.

"I remember one time working with Ronnie Hawkins and he had all of us living in a three-floor walk-up warehouse. We slept on the floor with no mattresses or coverings. But at least we had a roof over our heads if it snowed.

"The most sensational thing I ever saw take place in a bar was the night a cat was shot in the leg. With the bullet still in his leg he chased the guy who'd shot him outside, and beat the shit out of him.

"I've seen women getting beer bottles in the face. I've seen a lot of things, but I'm glad I did. You can't buy the experience and outlook you acquire on the bar circuit."

Kelly was playing a bar in Pembrooke, Ontario, six years ago when he first met the Ghetto, Crowbar slide and lead guitarist. "I'd never met him but he'd agreed on the phone to play with the band. I went down to pick him up at the station, and honest to God, I almost died when I walked onto the platform. There was this cat with ears like bicycle pedals and his hair shaved up over his ears. He wore a plaid shirt, his pants were up around his shins and he was sixteen years old. I just couldn't believe it.

"I thought to myself, 'how am I going to get this kid into the clubs?' Then he told me he was strung-out on Wake-ups, those caffeine pills you buy at any drugstore. But we had to open that night - I taught Ghetto the parts while we drove up to Pembrooke.

"I'd never heard Ghetto play, but I had heard he was good. He just didn't look good. Nevertheless, we were soon up on stage without any rehearsals, and we had to back up a stripper plus two go-go girls, twins. The stripper had music charts too. We opened for a week, and were held over for another seven. And Ghetto was sensational.

"He looked like he should be playing with a Meccano set, but he picked up that guitar like a laser beam and shot through everybody in the club. He was deadly. Even the morons who hang out at bars could tell that Ghetto was good.

"Few people who go to bars have any idea of what good music is. That's the trouble with being a bar musician. When you get acclaim, it's for the wrong reasons. It was a long struggle, and unbelievably depressing. There was never anything better to look forward to. There seemed no way out of the rut."

Though no one in Crowbar suspected it at the time, joining up with Ronnie Hawkins proved to be the escape route.

Later, after the triumph at the Fillmore East, Crowbar began to realize that they were much more than a back-up band. "We wondered if the time hadn't come for us to try it on our own," says bass guitarist Roly Greenway.

"Things weren't too cool with Ronnie," adds Kelly Jay. "In Boston, we played the Tea Party and jammed with Johnny Winter and then Ronnie wanted us all to sleep in a '48 Mercury to save money on hotel bills."

They split from Ronnie in May 1970, and cut the *Official Music* album with King Biscuit Boy later that month. There were many days when the group could not - individually or collectively - put together enough small change to buy a hotdog.

With the aid of a loan from their production company, Crowbar set up residence at Bad Manors in June. They paid $250 a month rent for the old farmhouse plus a hundred acres of prime land overlooking Hamilton from the escarpment. They used to jam late into the evenings and people would come by and be dumbfounded by the quality of the music. They quickly gained a reputation as the best new band in Ontario and made some highly impressive appearances, including a gig at Massey Hall with Van Morrison.

After release of the *Official Music* album Stateside, Crowbar were signed by Paramount Records. All of their discs for the next three years will be released world-wide by Paramount, and the group will be flown to England once every eighteen months for concert appearances.

When *Bad Manors* exploded onto the market place, it seemed that Canada had finally found another act able to regularly compete in the top ten of the world charts. The Guess Who had done it; Crowbar were about to.

Ronnie Hawkins

Burton Cummings, the outspoken lead singer of the Guess Who, commented that Ronnie Hawkins was responsible for the boom in Canadian music.

"He's the guy who made it possible for Canadians to happen in America," said Cummings, "The Hawk deserves the credit." Some will agree, many will not. The Hawk is the sort of man one either loves or hates - ardently.

In any case, most would admit that Ronnie Hawkins has left an indelible impression on the Canadian music scene. The ironic thing is that Hawkins isn't even a Canadian citizen. Born in Arkansas, Hawkins first set foot in Canada in 1958, well after he was established in the U.S. as a nationally known rockabilly idol with such hits as *Forty Days, Mary Lou, Bo Diddley* and Who Do You Love to his credit.

"We were starvin' to death on the Memphis circuit," Ronnie recalls.

"Conway Twitty, a good friend of mine, said that there were places to play in Canada where you could stay for the whole week. In and around Memphis, we could only get two or three nights a week."

What Hawkins found when he crossed the Peace Bridge at Niagara Falls obviously pleased him, because Ontario soon became a part of his regular tour. In 1961, Toronto became his base, he married Wanda, and began to think of himself as a Canadian. He brought to the Toronto music scene something it had not known prior to his arrival - professionalism, a sense of the big-time, a positive rather than negative attitude. Because he was from the U.S. and an established star, Torontonians listened to him. And he taught them a lot. Being an American, Hawkins was not an automatic subscriber to the myths of the Toronto music scene. He was a free thinker.

"I guarantee that a thousand different people - bookers, managers, radio station managers, disc jockeys - told me that I could not push a Canadian group in Canada. They told me I was crazy to even think about it."

At first, Ronnie didn't need to give it much thought. He'd brought his own band up from Memphis (Levon Helm of The Band was a member) and for the first year, he did not hire any Canadian musicians. Eventually, his band from the south, with the exception of Levon Helm, returned home and Hawkins put together a group which later made both him and the band world famous. He called them the Hawks.

At the same time Hawkins was endeavoring to become a music businessman. He formed his own record label, Hawk, and used his own sessions as the launching pad for the label. Shortly after, he began to record other Canadian talent.

At this point, Toronto rock musicians had virtually no chance of obtaining any regular (if demeaning) club work. "The agents told me that the local groups were not polished enough, and I asked them how they were going to get this polish without working in bars. After a while, I insisted that Canadian groups be used at the clubs I played at, and I think that started a whole bar thing for Canadian rock 'n' rollers. It also cut down on the competition for the first two or three years while I was establishing myself." For all the undoubted help he has given other musicians throughout the years, Hawkins remains a man constantly concerned with his own welfare.

Bobby Curtola played with Hawkins when he started out in London, Ontario. Other acts which got their break through the Hawk included the Four Fables, Ray Hutchinson, Buddy Carlton, Larry Lee, King Biscuit Boy and Toby Lark.

In 1961, Hawkins had gone to England on the strength of a couple of hit records. Although he was, in his own words, "screwed out of $15,000 by a promoter who also took Eddy Cochrane and Gene Vincent for much more," the trip did give Hawkins a first-hand look at a market in much the same dismal condition as Canada's music scene.

"There were a few local kids like Cliff Richard and Billy Fury who became idols just by covering American hits before the originals were released in England. That never happened in Canada. Some tried it but the radio stations wouldn't play them.

"That's what pissed me off about Canada at first—the way radio stations treated Canadian musicians like they were dirt. Nobody can tell whether you're good or bad if you're not heard."

But Hawkins didn't speak out too strongly against the radio stations. "I was afraid they'd stop playing my records if I said anything," Hawkins admits. "They always played my stuff because I was from the States. There was always a guy at each of the stations who'd give me a push." Hawkins wasn't above rewarding such services with the occasional case of whisky, and his rapport with radio stations increased with each new release.

The Hawk had also gained a reputation as being the first with the latest. He introduced the Twist, go-go girls, and other bar diversions to the Toronto scene. His popularity spread and by the mid-sixties, just before the Hawks left to join Dylan, he had become the most popular entertainer in Ontario.

His group had had tremendous influence on local musicians. John Kay, lead singer of the Sparrow (which later split to the U.S. to become Steppenwolf), remembers that he used to spend night after night hanging out where Hawkins was playing.

After the Hawks, Hawkins worked for a while with Robbie Lane (who came to some prominence as host of the national TV show, *It's Happening*) and in 1967, put together another band, which included King Biscuit Boy, Jay Smith and Toby Lark. Hawkins' friendship with Gordon Lightfoot produced in 1967 the hit single, *Home from the Forest*. But the Hawk was still tied contractually to Roulette Records in the U.S., which had lost interest in his career but wanted to keep him around, "just in case."

By this time, Hawkins was a legend in the Canadian music business.

His interests extended into local teen clubs, a night club in London, property in Mississauga and close relationships with several of Toronto's most prominent families.

When 1969 rolled in, Hawkins was bored with the Ontario bar circuit. He'd been ploughing across it every few months for almost a decade, and he was ready for a change. It came from an unexpected quarter.

The rock journal *Rolling Stone* had been discussing a Canadian music special (based on the success of Canadians in the U.S.) and had heard quite a lot about the colorful Ronnie Hawkins. They found his recollections of old days with The Band rather tantalizing, and a writer was commissioned to pen a lengthy feature article on the Hawk. The story appeared in August 1969, and almost overnight, the name of Ronnie Hawkins again meant something in the U.S. His Roulette contract had expired and he was wooed by several record companies (Hawkins claims Paramount offered him a total of $300,000 for a three year contract).

He decided to go with Atlantic, and was flown to Muscle Shoals to cut an album with producers Jerry Wexler and Tom Dowd (whose accomplishments include all Aretha Franklin's recent recordings). He took King Biscuit Boy and drummer Larry Atamaniuk with him. Before the album was released however, Hawkins was caught up in an entirely different venture.

In London, in December 1969, I found myself in the office of John Lennon and Yoko Ono discussing their forthcoming peace campaign in Canada. The Lennons needed somewhere to stay during their visit to Toronto, and I suggested the Hawkins estate. Lennon needed a quiet spot, well away from the never ending assaults of the press; he enjoyed the company of rock 'n' rollers; and it appeared that the visit might provide the attention needed to get Hawkins' career back into orbit internationally.

It worked well. The Lennons enjoyed their stay with the Hawkins, Lennon was afforded a little peace and quiet and time to complete the signing of his lithographs, and Hawkins' album was given a huge boost by John Lennon's public recommendation. The Beatle suggested that *Down in the Alley* should be released as a single, and he made tapes endorsing the tune. With such endorsement, *Down in the Alley* was a hit in Canada, making the U.S. and Australian charts as well.

On the strength its success, Hawkins went on a 52,000 mile, fifteen-country tour. He was in a self-confessed "state of shock." He hadn't believed the extent of the Lennon life-style - the private railroad cars, meetings with the prime minister, phone calls from all over the world, the autograph hunters flocking onto his property hoping for a glimpse of the Lennons tearing about on snowmobiles.

But Lennon is whimsical. Hawkins saw the Lennons for the last time at a small Italian restaurant in London's Soho district early in February 1970. Shortly after, they dropped out of the planned Toronto Peace Festival, severing most of the newly established ties with Canadians. Meantime Hawkins' first Atlantic album had been released, but it did not capture the public's imagination. It was a bitter blow for the Hawk.

Even sensational appearances at New York's Fillmore East, the Boston Tea Party and Detroit's East Town Theatre failed to create interest in the album. Just as Hawkins was setting up a U.S. promotional tour, he parted company with his group, which had been winning rave reviews.

"Those boys are so deadly they could fuck up a crowbar in about fifteen seconds," was Hawkins' comment when the break-up occurred in the spring of 1970. The group subsequently renamed itself Crowbar and went on to achieve spectacular success in the world music scene.

It was an immense setback for Hawkins, who was so close to the big time he could almost taste it. He spent the rest of the summer in Edmonton getting both his head and a new band together. He emerged a few weeks before the legislation era with the new group, the Fedville University Collegiate Klan. And after a decade of appearing at Le Coq D'Or on Toronto's Yonge Street, he signed a twelve-month contract with the Town Tavern, another downtown club. It was all part of a master plan.

"I intend to put together three bands to work regularly at the Town Tavern," he said. "After a few months, they should be fairly good, and I'll try to record them. Maybe it will happen for them; if not they'll still have regular work. I learned from Crowbar that you have to keep your musicians working every night or they start feelin' sorry for themselves. They'll have a steady gig in the small time, but they'll be able to make a crack at the big time."

Hawkins has had so many groups he's lost count. Most of the best known rock musicians on this continent have played with him at one time or another. One musician, with an international reputation, recalls a studio session at which Hawkins was angered by a scraping noise on his acoustic guitar. "I told Ronnie that even Segovia can't prevent that noise, and he replied that that was why Segovia wasn't on this session."

Hawkins was thirty-six years old as the legislation era began. Midway through 1971, Atlantic dropped him in the U.S. after two relatively unsuccessful albums. The tours have come to an end; the old days seem to have passed.

"We veterans often look at the Canadian music business now, and wonder where we'd be if it had been like this ten years ago," Hawkins says. "These days, if kids will get out and hustle and work, they've got a real chance of hitting the top. The trouble is that most of the young punkers nowadays think it's always been this easy. They don't realize the hard times some of us went through.

"Musicians are all the same - they have no gratitude. And I should know. God knows how many musicians I've employed through the years. I made them rehearse and learn, and they went on to make the big time. I'd have given most of them my last dime, and I often did. Give 'em your heart and they want your soul."

King Biscuit Boy

Despite the fact that most of the leading Toronto groups of the mid-sixties were heavily committed to American blues music, Canada has never been seriously regarded as a blues market. Every town has its blues bands playing English interpretations of Negro blues, a lot of radio stations play blues records, and you meet a lot of people who say they're "really into blues." But Canada isn't its natural habitat. Our most favored music is soft, lyrical and sometimes gentle, the ilk of Lightfoot, Mitchell, Cockburn and even Cohen.

If the Toronto scene, circa 1965, had broken through in Canada and the rest of the world, this country would have received wide recognition as a blues centre. Canadian blues of that time was the equal of anything the English later produced. Although it was heard in countless Toronto clubs in that period, it was never put on record. Little of it remains.

Richard Newell's work is one of the exceptions, and an outstanding one at that. In 1970, Newell, under his stage name King Biscuit Boy, was the fifth Canadian artist to make the Billboard album charts. He was the first Canadian blues artist to do so.

The Biscuit is indeed a true blues artist. His voice can be as searing as a blowtorch on bare flesh, his phrasing the equal of any man alive. His harp playing has added a new dimension to the instrument. Without doubt, Biscuit is the finest harp player in the world today. His slide guitar playing isn't bad either.

In his "official" music (from whence came the title of his first Daffodil album) he combines the authentic feel of black urban blues with the hard rock sound of Toronto in 1965. The combination is not far short of devastating.

Credit is due to the Canadian broadcasting fraternity that the unorthodox *Official Music* had received wide recognition prior to the ushering in of legislated content quotas.

Richard Newell lives in a house on the fringes of downtown Hamilton. He has a couple of small turtles, a bathroom full of Mickey Mouse memorabilia, a hamster, an incredible collection of blues records, and a very sweet old lady, name of Jackie. Newell was born in Hamilton, and started playing harp in 1961 after hearing Little Walter blowing hard over a Nashville radio station. "I went out and bought myself a harmonica and taught myself to play by listening to records."

Biscuit first played in a band called the Barons. "They were only doing instrumentals before I joined them. We cut a record in 1961 called *Bottleneck*, after I turned the group onto Elmore James. I'd been a blues enthusiast since 1956 when I first heard *Deep Feeling* on the flip side of Chuck Berry's *School Days*. I got into more by listening to southern radio at night. Even though I didn't take up harp until 1961, I'd had one around the place for a long while. It just sat around the house waiting for me to play it.

"After a time, we changed the name of the Barons to Son Richard and the Chessmen. We played nothing but blues and rock 'n' roll. All the other bands were into Roy Orbison and Ronnie Hawkins songs. We were doing Chuck Berry, Little Richard, Hank Ballard, and Huey Smith - what was often called 'R & B.' "We played around Hamilton until 1963, and the following year, we worked mainly in Michigan. In 1965, we went to Germany to play U.S. army bases as Son Richard and the Gooduns, and they went nuts about us there."

Richard returned to Toronto and played with the Midknights in 1966 and 1967. In 1968, he joined the Ronnie Hawkins band. "Ron always boasted that he was first with the newest. He was the first cat to use a PA in bar gigs, he was the first out with an electric organ, and he was the first to have a harp player."

It was Hawkins who gave Newell his stage name. "Ronnie could never remember the names of his musicians, so he would make up simple names. He called me King Biscuit Boy after a radio show at KFFA in Helena, Arkansas. A local flour company, the King Biscuit Flour Company, sponsored a weekly live music show which was titled *The King Biscuit Time*. Sonny Boy Williamson, the great Negro harp player, was one of the regular musicians on the show.

"Ronnie rehearsed his first rock band in the KFFA studios, and he used to listen to the show. It all came together in his head that I should be King Biscuit Boy. He could remember that better than Richard Newell." It was also Hawkins who created "the legendary" tag which often precedes the use of Newell's name in rock journals.

Biscuit played with Hawkins for two years during the period in which the Hawk assembled the nucleus of Crowbar. He speaks highly of his days with Hawkins. "Ron is a great entertainer and businessman too. He's also the funniest cat in the world. Ron is the only star from the early rock days who just kept on playing, getting better and better. He has a talent for bringing out the best in musicians who probably wouldn't do it on their own."

After a prestigious tour with Hawkins, Biscuit left with Crowbar. Back in Toronto, penniless and out of work, he arranged to cut his first album for Daffodil Records, a newly formed Canadian independent label. He chose as his backup musicians members of Crowbar, Sea Train and the late Janis Joplin's Full Tilt Boogie Band. It was a powerhouse unit.

"When I'd first been approached about the album, I was doing only about five or six different songs on stage with Ronnie. So we went into the studio with those songs, and recorded three or four of them. The remainder of the album was put together in about two days.

"All of the songs had been in my mind for years and I knew what I wanted to do with them. It didn't take much effort to get it together. Overall, there was very little over-dubbing or instruments on the album. I wanted to do everything together because that's how I'd been playing for years. There wasn't any point in messing around with over-dubs."

Official Music drew ecstatic reviews in Canada, sold more than 10,000 copies in a few months, and took off in the U.S. and international market. Biscuit played a few gigs with Crowbar in the fall of

1970, and the combination yielded countless standing ovations. It is doubtful if Biscuit has a more enthusiastic supporter than Crowbar's Kelly Jay.

"Biscuit has the capability of completely taking your breath away, he's so good. He has impeccable judgment and taste in blues. I don't think there's a white man in the world to match him in the blues scene. I've been playing harp four years longer than Biscuit, but in the one year I spent playing with him in the Hawkins band, I learned more about harp playing than during the ten years before. He gets tones and sounds that have never before been heard coming out of a harmonica."

Biscuit has little to say about the domestic music industry in general, but does express regret that the recording of Canadian groups was so long in coming.

He keeps a tape of a rehearsal made in 1964. The tone is distorted, but the authenticity of the blues played at the session is unmistakable. Possibly the CRTC suggestions have come too late to revive original Canadian blues; possibly King Biscuit Boy can do more for its development than any amount of legislation.

Gordon Lightfoot

The white phone was ringing loudly in the tastefully decorated offices of Early Morning Productions on Toronto's Davenport Road. The young secretary answered, spoke a few words as she wrote down a series of figures, then smiled.

She handed the figures to Alexander Mair, general manager of Early Morning Productions, and a demurely hip ex-record company promotion man who now holds one of the key posts in Canadian music. Al perused the piece of paper as he climbed the stairs to the second floor.

At the rear of the building, Gordon Lightfoot was sitting in his private office, preparing for that which he regards as an unnecessary ordeal - the press interview. His hair was longer than it had ever been. Its length was complemented by his clothes: a striped brown and black long-sleeved T-shirt, a sleeveless denim jacket with fancy satin appliques, blue jeans well worn, fawn suede cowboy boots coated with mud, and to top it off, blue tinted glasses.

Al Mair handed Lightfoot the paper with the figures on it, and they both seemed delighted, though they were trying to hide the fact. Mair explained that these were the latest U.S. chart and sales reports on *If You Could Read My Mind*, and the album from which the hit single had come, *Sit Down Young Stranger*. The single was over 750,000 copies; the album at about 350,000. They were by far the largest Lightfoot sales figures of his career. The long established Canadian singer-composer had finally broken through into the vast U.S. and international markets. Coincidentally or not (Lightfoot says not), it was just a few weeks after the start of the legislation era.

Almost exactly three years earlier, we had first discussed the prospect of what a hit single might do for Gordon's then steadily growing U.S. audience. At that time Lightfoot had protested a shade too briskly that he really wasn't keen about the idea of pop stardom, or the sort of situation which a hit single might force on him.

"I think that would create a scene where I'd have to come up with another single, and another and another, to stay on top of it. Today you need ten straight hits to establish yourself as a singles artist."

He'd been satisfied with his progress - the weekend college gigs, the occasional Stateside TV appearance, growing FM-radio airplay of his albums. A hit single just didn't seem the right thing then.

But early 1971 was another story. He possessed a different state of mind, changed attitudes, a lot more confidence.

"I don't feel worried anymore," Lightfoot said, and he wasn't kidding. "I've got nineteen tracks in the can; there are three or four dynamite cuts in there. And I'm still writing every week. As long as I keep producing songs, I won't worry. In the last little while, I've really been getting down to it. Forcing myself to write. What do you want to call it? Discipline. I've just been getting down and confronting the empty pages on a regular basis. And I've been coming up with results."

He sat back with an air of satisfaction and fiddled with a pencil. "The new album is *Summerside of Life*, after one of the tunes of the LP, which might be a single. I never know for sure. There's a couple of tracks ..." He paused. "You know, I can't describe them. I don't even like to talk about them. But I am a little excited by some of the things we've got.

"We cut the whole album at Woodland Studios in Nashville, used Red Shea and Ricks Haynes [his concert accompanists] plus ten or twelve other players. No strings - just strong tracks. The album is a little funkier than *Sit Down Young Stranger*.

"And I've written other new material I'd like to include on the album. It's a matter of having time to cut them. But I don't like the writing thing to be the driving force of my life, all that matters. It's just something that has to be done.

"My life was getting a bit rocky in the fall of last year. I just couldn't handle my home life and then business. So I moved downtown, away from the big house [a veritable mansion, located in one of Toronto's most elegant suburban areas]. It's not a total removal thing. I get up to see Breita [his wife] and the kids once or twice a week. I spend a lot of time with them ... Breita and I are still pretty close. It just became a bit too much to carry both things."

As Lightfoot declines to discuss individual tunes, one must presume that the songs on *Sit Down Young Stranger* were strongly influenced by that particular period in his life. Listen to *If You Could Read My Mind* and you know that this man is not singing about some imaginary love affair. It is far too piercing, too devastatingly simply, to be the product of a composer's fantasy. He as much as admitted that in a conversation we had in April of 1970, regarding the imminent release of *Sit Down Young Stranger*. "In the last year and a half, my songs have become very personal. They're introspective things. It's not a good space to be in, but I guess everybody has to go through it."

His comment on his relationship to the singles market later that night proved to be fascinating. "I'd personally like to stick to albums, unless I come up with a stone smash single. When you're essentially an album artist, you have to wait until it happens. If I were to have a single hit, I'd like it to be on my terms."

But it was one of his most personal songs which finally put Lightfoot at the top of the world charts. Initially, Reprise released *Me and Bobby McGhee* as a single from the album. It did fairly well in Canada, but virtually nothing south of the border. Then a radio station in Seattle, Washington, began playing *If You Could Read My Mind*. Audience reaction was so strong that the station asked Reprise to release it as a single. The response in Seattle soon spread, and within a month, virtually every rock and MOR station in the U.S. had either charted it, or were about to.

"We were lucky. Reprise knew what to do when it started to happen. If United Artists had been involved, the whole thing would probably have been botched up."

United Artists was the first U.S. label to sign Lightfoot. "UA released five of my albums over a period of three years [*Lightfoot, The Way I Feel, Did She Mention My Name?, Back Here on Earth* and *Sunday Concert*] and there were no hit singles. Still, the albums were popular. By the time we left UA, we were doing as many as 70,000 copies of an album. But we still hadn't been in the charts. Meanwhile, we were doing over 100,000 copies of every album in Canada. It was all a bit strange."

It certainly was. With the possible exception of Bobby Curtola, Lightfoot was the only artist in Canadian show business history able to combat the traditional Canadian apathy towards domestic music.

"I always regarded Bobby Curtola as a stand up pop act, as Canada's answer to everybody in the States - Frankie Avalon, all of them. I didn't consider him part of my scene; I figured he'd been and gone when I arrived. He was on his way down."

Lightfoot talks of the old days, the early years of his career, with a strange air. You know it was as tough as hell, but he never admits it, and he occasionally alludes to an unusual and somewhat naive belief that talent always wins through.

"In 1958, I went out to California and studied music at the Westlake College for fourteen months. I came back to Orillia [his birthplace, a small town about eighty miles north of Toronto] and spent the summer working for my dad. Then I came down to Toronto, and worked at odd jobs, until I was able to make a living as a studio musician. I was a studio choral singer, doing lots of different TV shows, reading parts, working various vocal combinations, also some commercial work.

"In 1960, I was starting to listen to folk music, things by Pete Seeger and Bob Gibson. I quit the studio after three years. It was steady, good-paying work, but I just gave up the whole thing.

"By that time, I'd drifted over into the other scenes. I started playing guitar and singing in various folk clubs in the early sixties, with people like Bonnie Dobson, the Halifax Three [a third of which was Denny Doherty, later a member of the Mamas and Papas] and Ian and Sylvia. I made my living playing in bars, in London, Peterborough, all over the place.

"The two big folk clubs in Toronto at that time were the Purple Onion and the Village Corner. I really wanted to play them. Finally Shelly Abrams put me into the Village Corner when I couldn't draw anyone elsewhere. It was a big chance, but the club was on the skids — the Onion was getting all the business.

"I kept hitting on Al Lastman of the Onion to give me a shot. He was only bringing in heavy acts like Sonny and Brownie, Joe and Eddie, Judy Collins, Buffy St. Marie. But after eighteen months of bugging him, he called me two days before New Year's Eve to fill in for Brock Peters. We did a good show, and he booked me in later for a week.

"At about the same time, Ian and Sylvia had come to see me play at Steeles Tavern. They liked *Early Morning Rain* and *For Loving Me*, and they recorded both. They also played the songs for Peter, Paul and Mary, who cut *For Loving Me*. It was a top ten hit in the States; that got things started.

"Ian Tyson brought around producer John Court, who was then in partnership with Albert Grossman. I was into writing by that time, and Court asked me if I'd like to make an album with him. It looked like a good chance so I took it. I really didn't have enough material to do a whole LP, and had to work hard to get that together.

"The first album did fairly well. By the time the second one came, I was starting to get singles off in Canada. There was *I'm Not Sorry, Go Go Round, Spin Spin, Tom Thumb's Blues* - we were having singles released every three or four months. And they did well almost everywhere. Vancouver was the last market to fall. I started to think about doing a national tour, and I talked to Albert Grossman [by now his manager] about setting up a western tour. We hesitated for two or three months but Albert didn't work up too much enthusiasm about it.

"So we set up a deal with a promoter in Edmonton who pushed me through the West, one night in each town. He was getting a good-sized piece of the action for his trouble."

The first town they played was Winnipeg, where a 4,500 seat hall had been completely sold out. "I was quite surprised ... I'm always surprised at each new turn and development. I try to treat everything with reservation as far as my career is concerned.

"We played right across the country in 1967. The next year we decided to give it another shot. The promoter decided to book two nights in some places, and that went well, too. Trouble was that I couldn't get my money from the promoter for three months. The whole tour took three weeks, and if it hadn't been for the money hassles, it would have been really good."

Lightfoot repeated the cross-country tours in 1969 and 1970 (without the dubious help of that Edmonton promoter) and by 1971 the tour had reached immense proportions. There were two nights in Vancouver, four each in Edmonton and Winnipeg, three in Toronto, and three at Place des Arts in Montreal.

Even two years ago, a national tour by a Canadian artist was virtually unheard of. Lightfoot says he doesn't really know how or why he was able to achieve the formerly unachievable. "I guess I'm so 'Canadian' that I got everybody involved. My stuff was in such an unusual bag anyway. I didn't relate to any other person or type of music. But I had my doubts - I was always insecure about it.

"People would come up to me and say, 'You've got to have a drummer, or an electric guitar,' or whatever. I just didn't do it. There was no way it could have succeeded naturally.

"I guess there was a Canadian flavor, a Canadian feeling to my music. And the *Canadian Railroad Trilogy* exemplified it. There was also a little bit of mystique. In Canada, I'd tell people about my success in the U.S. I'd say I was doing really well down there, but that I didn't intend to live there. I was trying to play everyone for a while, but didn't deliberately try to make my songs more Canadian with obvious lyrics. I simply write the songs about where I am and where I'm from. I take situations and write poems about them. That's about all there is."

All of the songs for *Sit Down Young Stranger* (which Gordon considered to be his best album at the time) were composed in a four-week period in July 1969. "I wrote the songs in the house on Blythwood Avenue when it was still empty, before the family moved in. I came up every day for a month, and would spend twelve hours a day at it. I wrote about a song a day during that period, and then I picked out for the album the ten I liked best."

The rest, he said, were tucked away in a box with some one hundred and fifty other songs he'd "written along the way. There's also a few little bits and pieces of poetry tucked away behind the cobwebs in the back of the attic. There's another box with hundreds of ideas in the basement."

Although writing obviously plays a vital and frequent role in Lightfoot's creative life, he considers the live performance to be his most favored outlet.

"The studio is not my environment. It took me a long time to come to that realization. Where I really get off is in concerts. We always go on cold turkey - no booze, nothing. I get wiped out just being on the stage. You always enjoy a drink much more after you know you've been up and done the two hours."

Would the success of *If You Could Read My Mind* et al be likely to change his carefully worked out concert plans? "We don't really want to change the schedule. I wouldn't want to do more than sixty-five or seventy concerts a year, though. I suppose some of them will be more meaningful, because of the hits, but I don't want to play the really big places, the barns with audience capacities of ten or twenty thousand. Anything under five thousand seats is fine for me. I don't like to do more than one concert in one day, and I don't like using a supporting act. If we have another act, there's only half the time to sing the songs the people want to hear. We usually do twenty-five songs, with six albums to choose from, plus there's always some new material.

"I played the Peterborough Community Centre recently. It's something I do every year; makes one appreciate his roots. We did two hours and twenty minutes, and at the end, I felt as if I'd just gone on. They were still hollering when we quit, but there just wasn't time for everything."

Lightfoot usually goes on the road only at weekends, spending two eighteen-hour days a week writing new material. One rarely finds him in his old haunts; he grants few interviews. "It used to be a big thing to do an interview. But then I'd read them later and I'd always end up with a foot and a leg in my mouth.

"The trouble is that it's impossible to describe my art. That's why I stopped doing them. I just can't say anything about my work, I can't explain my music. Although I'm completely wrapped up in it and think about it almost all the time, even I can't describe it. You just have to listen to it for yourself, and understand it for what it is."

Early Morning Productions was formed in 1969. Lightfoot didn't attend the press opening. Al Mair says, with a tone of finality: "Gord just doesn't dig those sort of things. He'd rather spend the time writing."

Mair had worked for several years with Compo Records, concentrating mainly on Lightfoot product. "Compo did a good job promoting me in the early years," Lightfoot says. "Al was their field promotion manager."

Since its formation, Early Morning has been of invaluable assistance to a number of up-and-coming young folk artists such as Dee Higgins and Chris Kearney.

"We simply give people a little bit of guidance and arrange a few record deals," Lightfoot says. "We have no paper with them. I don't want to get any people under contract, nor do we have grand designs in that area. But if we can help with advice, we do.

"We have a lot of contacts in the States - publishers, booking agencies, management - so I have no trouble getting back and forth with those connections. The same people are able to help other Canadians."

Of his own songs, he prefers *The Last Time*, while "I think the public's favorite is the *Trilogy*." Those opinions were expressed before *If You Could Read My Mind*. Despite his caution on the subject, his hit single has and will have an influence on almost every aspect of his career. And he predicts more of the same.

"One thing I do believe is that we [he and Mair] didn't need the CRTC. My feelings about that scene are fairly straightahead. The CRTC had nothing to do with the success of my single. It broke out of Seattle and hit the U.S. charts first.

"I like to compete with everyone in the music business in general ... not necessarily with other Canadians. That's just how I feel." This is the comment of a gentleman who has stated that the CRTC legislation may bring him overexposure and a shortened career. Nevertheless there is no denying that his is a success based on nothing more than his own tremendous talent.

Lighthouse

Late in the sixties, rock music discovered and developed a new shot of adrenalin - the superstar musician. The spectacular sales of The Beatles' albums were falling off, the singles scene had sunk into mediocrity, and the kids were staying away from record stores in droves.

Up until this point, the rock musician as an individual celebrity had not meant a great deal. Certainly there was the odd well-recognized guitarist, drummer or horn player, but the mass idolatry which surrounds some of the top musicians in the early seventies was unheard of five years earlier.

Very few Canadians were caught up in this new pop wave (which was really only a mutation of the solo stars of the jazz era). Many Canadian musicians had the potential of standing in the most revered rock circles, but they were unrecognized in their own country and few had the drive or ambition to leave.

Drummer Skip Prokop, now with Lighthouse, was one of the handful who did, and probably the only one who was in on the early development of the super star musician. He played on the Super Session album with Mike Bloomfield, Al Kooper and Steve Stills. He was offered gigs with Janis Joplin, Steve Miller, and Mama Cass, but he ended up forming Lighthouse, an eleven-piece, predominantly Canadian band with as much potential as any ever assembled in this country.

As much as Prokop disdains the label of a super musician, there can be no doubt that he is one of the finest rock drummers the Canadian (or the American) scene has ever produced. He has sat in with the best of them and more than held up his hand in some pretty deadly contests. He tells his story - the rise through Yorkville, the hassles, the near hits, the expense account sprees - with understatement and honesty.

"I started on drums in 1963 with a couple of small bands playing legion halls for next to nothing. I formed a folk-singing trio called the Riverside Three in which I played guitar. We went down to Tip Top Tailors and got outfitted in these suits - the whole trip.

"We played banquets and more legion halls but it ended after about six months. I sat around for a while, then started gigging around Toronto with big bands. I was just getting that number together, when I decided I'd rather form a rock group.

"I got together with Bill Misener who I'd met back home in Hamilton. He introduced me to Chuck Beale and Chuck brought in Denny Gerrard on bass guitar. We bought old twelve-string guitars, put pickups in them and called ourselves the Paupers, which was a fairly appropriate name.

"We worked on some songs and went into Hallmark studios to cut three sides. Duff Roman [who is now program director of CKFH] was getting into management at the time. He had David Clayton-Thomas, and he wanted to manage us. We did without money for a while; then the record, *Never Send You Flowers*, came out and that helped. It got some play on CKEY.

"Not long after, we parted company with Duff. There had been a lot of hassles and uptightness. It was unfortunate for Duff; he had a lot of talent under his roof.

"We changed managers and took on Bernie Finkelstein who arrived with a lot of flashy ideas. At that point Bill Misener left the group and we found Adam Mitchell. Up until that time, we'd been into a goodtime Lovin' Spoonful sort of thing, but we fell into a new thing - everyone playing the drums at the same time, and that was sort of psychedelic and fitted in with what was doing down.

"Bernie had gone to New York and signed us to MGM Records with no front money. We went to New York and played at the Cafe au Go Go with the Jefferson Airplane. Suddenly, we were swamped with offers. When we signed a management deal with Albert Grossman, Bernie decided to split.

"Albert renegotiated our contract with MGM, and we did the *Magic People* album with Rick Shorter producing. MGM then sent us out on a $40,000 promotion trip across America. We were being pushed as the new Beatles or something and a tremendous amount of money was spent greasing us. For all that dough, our record could have been bought into the charts. We travelled first class everywhere; we were ordering shrimp cocktails up to our rooms in the best hotels at all hours of the day. It was all pretty far out.

"They sent us to Las Vegas to play four engagements and we had to stay over for a few days. We went crazy. Denny Gerrard made $3,500 on the poker machines, but the next day he lost it all, and his shirt as well. Really, he arrived back at the hotel one morning with no shirt on. He'd walked two miles from a casino because he'd lost every cent.

"There were no hit records, but it was one hell of a lot of fun. Afterwards, we played gigs in the States and a lot in Canada. Grossman got uptight about all the money that was being spent, and almost dropped us at one point. Albert had just hired Vinnie Fuscoe, and his first job was to fire us. Albert doesn't like to get rid of people, he just stops talking to you until you get the message. We managed to talk them into giving us another chance and we went on a money-saving spree. Went by road and rail - no air travel.

"We never did make any money as the Paupers. The most we could ever expect to see at the end of the week was fifty dollars. I'd gotten married and a baby was on the way and it was really hard. We cut ourselves down to two dollars a man on the road, and the fat guys, like equipment manager Bruce Bell, had to beg donations from the rest of the cats just so they could stay alive.

"This all built up to a gig in Chicago to open the Kinetic Circus. We took the train from New York - no sleepers - we sat up on the fucking train for twenty-six hours and the last few hours we were hassled by hard hats and other commuters in Illinois.

"The first night was a drag. The audience was full of super hip, groovy swingers. But the second night was a bit better. The third day, Martin Luther King was assassinated. That was incredible, man, really incredible.

"A cat we knew tipped us off that the club was going to be blown up because it was white establishment operation. We didn't want to play but the owner insisted we had to. In the middle of the evening everything fell apart. The cops locked everyone inside; there were people being shot outside. We finally got out, and one block up the road, we watched a cat get it between the eyes. The cops stuffed about fifteen of us into one cab and we were driven to the nearest hotel.

"There was no way the people with us were going to get home so we suggested they should just cool out in our rooms. We were getting into the elevator when these three heavies from a 1930 gangster movie hassled us. The city is burning, you can hear shots and screams, and we're being hassled about the number of people camping out in our rooms. There was no way these people could get home. What else could they do?

"We stayed in the rooms all through the next day and night, and then the following morning, caught a plane back to Toronto. Driving out of the city was an unbelievable experience - the National Guard was pouring in with machine guns and bayonets.

"Once home again, I figured it was just about time to forget the band. It just wasn't going anywhere. But we agreed to do a second album, *Ellis Island*, which, I thought, came off really well. It was cut by Elliot Mazer and we used strings and horns. It was the true start of the Lighthouse sound in my mind."

Prokop was becoming increasingly unsettled in the group, in spite of an encouraging second album. He moved between New York, Las Vegas and Toronto, doing session work with the Pozo Seco Singers and Richie Havens, backing Cass Elliot, and recording the Super Session album with Al Kooper. His return to Toronto in late 1969 sparked the reorganization of the group. Vinnie Fuscoe quit working with Albert Grossman and became the manager of Lighthouse. They were signed to RCA, and a huge promotion campaign was started. The gigs kept rolling in. The group played all over the U.S. to enthusiastic audiences. They went to Japan and to the Isle of Wight festival in 1970; the reviews were outstanding.

Yet for all its forceful attraction on the stage, Lighthouse simply didn't have it in the grooves. In February of 1971, Prokop was able to look back over those days with a new perspective. "I had a lot of trouble trying to figure out what we were doing wrong. We had all the talent there, but the records didn't seem to come together. I sat down around Christmas of 1970 and listened to all the records I'd made with the Paupers, Lighthouse, even an old demo of the first songs I'd written. It really turned me around. Even the earliest songs had a certain original essence - a simplicity - something which didn't come through on the Lighthouse records.

"Usually we'd give our new songs to Paul or Howard and they'd arrange them. We didn't have much to do with it. And so the songs came out with the same lyrics and melodies they'd started with, but lacking the feeling they'd had at first. It was a heavy trip for the band to go through, a lot of toes were trodden on. But it just hadn't worked and we had to change the approach.

"And we did. I can't really describe it. You'll notice it when you hear it. It just starts off and it flies. It was a big plateau which we'd finally gotten on top of."

Late in January 1971, Lighthouse hired a new producer, Jimmy Ienner. "We really need a commercial single, and Jimmy's the one who can do it for us. He's had about thirty top ten records in the States, a dozen of them reached number one. He's worked under a lot of different names - he was the high voice on all the Tokens' hits and did all the voices but the lead in *Duke of Earl*, worked on the first two Isaac Hayes' albums, and he was an original member of the Royal Teens."

The first Ienner-Lighthouse album, *One Fine Morning*, was released by GRT in May 1971, and turned into an immediate best seller. During one week in June, Sam the Record Man reported it as the fastest-selling album in his huge downtown Toronto store. In August, *One Fine Morning* received an RPM Gold Leaf award for sales in excess of 25,000 copies, a huge figure for the Canadian market. The change in producer and record company had proved to be a shrewd move.

Prokop feels the CRTC legislation will greatly help the group's acceptance on record in Canada. "It's already helping - not just us, but everybody. Some shit is being played, but you'll hear that anywhere.

Finally the guys who are great players will be able to make a living as rock musicians.

"I know that some of the most incredible musicians in the world are living in Canada. Now they're getting the exposure they didn't have in the old days. It can only help."

Mashmakhan

There have been few French Canadians able to break through to the English music scene, either in Canada or elsewhere. Crowbar's dynamic lead guitarist, Rheal Lanthier is one. Pierre Senecal, keyboards and horn player with Mashmakhan, is another.

The careers of Mashmakhan members extend back over a decade, yet it was only in 1970 that the soil was fertile enough for the group to bloom. A single by Mashmakhan, *As the Years Go By*, had sold over a million copies when the legislation era began, including a phenomenal 107,000 copies in Canada, 400,000 plus in the U.S., and another 750,000 in Japan, where the disc was number one for several weeks.

Pierre Senecal wrote *As the Years Go By*. He composes most of Mashmakhan's material. He is a French Canadian who thinks, reads and writes in English; the only way he can write a French song is by composing it in English and then translating.

"All the musicians I played with were English Canadians," Senecal explained recently during a stopover at Toronto Airport. The group was on its way from hometown Montreal to Detroit, where it was playing a gig at Cobo Hall with Three Dog Night. "I've always been the only Frenchman in the groups. I've always listened to English music and musicians. Of course. I've heard some French records, too, and I like Robert Charlebois and Jean Pierre Ferland. But I don't hear that many French records. It's hard to get into everything.

"I still have a very thick French accent. I haven't lost it, but I always think in English, especially in writing songs. The sound of the language is very important, as are the words you choose for each line."

Mashmakhan's origins date from 1960, when the four present members (Senecal, bass player-singer Brian Edwards, guitarist Ray Blake and drummer Jerry Mercer) were united behind an R & B singer. In the years that followed, several members split for other gigs. Senecal, for example, spent some time with an Afro-Cuban band from Miami, and toured the States.

In 1965, they were together again, this time to back up Trevor Payne, a singer with considerable R & B influence. "I guess we were fairly lucky. We always had a lot of work, on a small scale. It's when you try to go on a big scale while you're still small scale that you starve. We had no manager, no roadies, we did our own booking. We didn't expect anything more.

"We played with Trevor Payne for four years; at that time we were called the Triangle and started to do a bit of our own material before Trevor came on to sing. The stuff got better and eventually we were ready to go our own way.

"We were looking for a name for the new group. We asked our friends for some suggestions and told them to call us. One day a dope dealer I knew phoned and said he had some stuff called Mashmakhan. He thought it also might be a good name for the group. That was it.

"We signed with Columbia Records and they sent us to New York to cut an album at their studios with producer Billy Jackson. *As the Years Go By* was never meant to be a single. It was well over five minutes long, and it had been written about three years before. They cut it up - edited it or something."

Terry Flood, Mashmakhan's manager and a veteran of the Montreal English music scene, explained what went into making *As the Years Go By* one of the biggest selling Canadian-produced rock records ever.

"Roger Scott at CFOX in Montreal was playing the hell out of the album track, and he asked us to release it as a single. It was only brought out in Montreal initially, but the reaction was so strong that it spread across the country. Scott reported it on the MLS and it happened. The Maple Leaf System played a very big part in the acceptance of the single. And as the MLS was an indirect result of the CRTC ruling, then I suppose the CRTC is due some credit for this record.

"The national reaction was a great help in getting the record off in the U.S. We took ads in the American music magazines showing what the single had done in Canada, and claiming it therefore deserved to be heard in the States.

"If it hadn't been for one man, I think we could have reached the top ten in the U.S. with *As the Years Go By*. As it was, we sold over 400,000 and were on the charts for fourteen weeks. The problem was Paul Drew, who was then music director at CKLW, the big Windsor rock station which is heard in both Detroit and Cleveland. Paul didn't like the record and refused to play it [it wasn't the first time that Drew had not liked a proven Canadian hit]. This hurt a lot because CKLW is very important in the mid-west.

"Meanwhile, the record was doing well at a San Francisco station. Just as it was getting off there, Paul Drew was appointed their music director and he dropped the disc immediately. That was really a drag.

"We always thought the first album's success rested on how well the single did. We sold about 25,000 copies of the album in Canada, and approximately the same Stateside.

"We weren't overwhelmed by the first album," says Senecal, "but we weren't unhappy. The second album, which we did in Toronto at Thunder Sound Studios with producer David Briggs, has an entirely different sound. It's us entirely. We were free to do what we wanted, when we wanted. The second album is a rock group; the first was an orchestra. It wasn't a modern sound. It seemed far away, not right up close to you."

Manager Flood agrees. "David Briggs did a fabulous job with the group. We're confident that the new LP will establish Mashmakhan as an album group.

"We avoided playing the small clubs in the U.S. until we had a really big record. *As the Years Go By* did fairly well, but we waited. It was pointless going to the U.S. to play for $250 a night, when the group could earn big money in Canada. We want to be regarded as a concert act, not a bubblegum band. I think the second album, which by the way is called *The Family*, will do the job for us."

Flood has worked in the Montreal market with entrepreneur Donald K. Donald for the past four years. Donald looks after the booking and promotion; Flood is into management. Mashmakhan is the first act that has really happened for them, outside of Quebec.

Quebec, of course, has not been regarded as an important area for progressive English-language rock acts. But Flood detected a gradual change in the French Canadian scene in the summer of 1970, just as Mashmakhan was beginning to break in Montreal. "There have always been lots of French Canadian hits. The artists would steal U.S.

copyrights, make cover versions, anything to get a record out. It was possible to sell in French Canada, with a local act, as many records as a group like Blood, Sweat & Tears could sell right across Canada. That went on for eight or ten years. Then came Charlebois and the more creative French Canadian acts. That exposed the market to more progressive music.

"In the latter part of 1970, English acts had assumed amazing importance in French Canada. Not so much English Canadian acts, as the big U.S. and U.K. groups like Led Zeppelin. A whole underground scene developed, kids started turning on, listening to heavy music, and the old days went under the bridge. Folk artists like Donald Lautrec lost a lot of popularity; hard rock was happening. Only the creative French Canadians are still selling.

"The FLQ crisis hurt the music scene in Montreal for about six months, but it started to pick up as the CRTC rulings came in. The studios were getting better - RCA in Montreal is good - but there's a lack of engineers and producers here. That's why we cut the second album in Toronto.

"Things have been moving at a slow pace for Mashmakhan since the single. But it's been on the way up, just waiting and building. We expect to go to Japan in July, and we want to play in Europe."

Senecal, whose favorite composers include Leonard Cohen, Bob Dylan and Lennon-McCartney, believes the CRTC local content era has "got to be good. I don't think any of us are going to have to move away any more. I think Canada has become an international music country, from inside and outside."

Anne Murray

Canadian network television programmers and magazine editors seem to regard Anne Murray as the ideal girl-next-door, as a performer who possesses the sort of image which is unlikely to upset the most timid viewer or reader. Critics claim that the phenomenal amount of media coverage afforded Miss Murray is due to the fact that she fits the establishment's preconceived concept of what an all-Canadian pop star should look like.

Such critics actually tend to undersell the rather subtle talents of this young singer from Springhill, Nova Scotia. She is a natural for television and if some of her appearances have tended to project her with unexciting monotony, it is the failing of the medium rather than the performance.

Anne is the first by-product of the new Canadian star system which was clearly made possible by the advent of the CRTC domestic content ruling. It is logical that Canadians are going to want to see and hear more about any artist who can sell 50,000 albums in this country.

Whatever debate there may be over the relative merits of Anne Murray's style and that, say, of the Guess Who, it is enough for now to recognize the phenomenon she represents. For years, the cynics said it wasn't possible for a Canadian to be born and raised here, make records here, star on TV here or appear on the front cover of magazines here. Anne Murray destroyed that myth and in doing so has paved the way for what will likely be an endless stream of still unknown Canadian entertainers who will become household names. If she did not make another record or guest on another television special, it would not matter. Her most important contribution to Canadian show business has already been made.

For all this significance, Anne is surprisingly unaffected and unimpressed by the whole trip. For a start, she says that she never did have any dream or desire to become a show business celebrity. "All sorts of people say that I always wanted to be a star. But I never said that. I just go from day to day. You can't take it too seriously."

Anne claims she has no long-range ambitions. "When *Snowbird* hit 900,000 sales, my ambition was to have a gold single. When the *Snowbird* album got to 400,000, I wanted a gold album." A gold album is awarded to titles which sell in excess of 525,000 copies, which is $1,000,000 worth of discs at factory value. "My goals always seem to be immediately attainable. I don't think there's much sense in hoping for the sky until you're sure you can get there.

"One thing I do hope to do someday is travel. I'd like to travel the world without working. People think I'm seeing a lot of it now, but I'm not. All I usually see are hotel rooms, a stage or a recording studio when I'm on the road. You rarely get out to look around."

Anne admits that as a child she never contemplated her present life, although it all started at home. "There was always music around the house. I had five brothers and we all took music lessons. It was mainly classical music and theory. You'd be given one set piece and you'd practise it all year for the recital. We didn't take much notice of the music.

"I did a bit of singing in high school - the usual crap that you do. Then I took voice lessons for two years. I used to get up every Saturday morning at seven, travel fifty miles by bus to a place called Tatamagouche where my dad's parents lived, and then return by nine at night. That went on for two full years and it was rough.

"In my first year at university, I took more voice lessons. But I was being taught to be a soprano, which I could never understand since I talk like this [huskily] and I have to sing off the top of my head."

Two years later, Anne was persuaded by friends to appear in the university revue. "I'd checked it out the year before to see what went down," she admits, indicating a lack of the usual show business brashness.

"The summer before that, I'd also auditioned in Halifax for *Sing-along Jubilee*,' a CBC-TV show which featured Maritimes talent. I needed a summer job and it seemed ideal. But I didn't make the audition, and I went back to university.

"In my fourth year at university, I had a call from Bill Langstroth, the host and producer of *Jubilee*. He'd turned me down at the original audition but he'd remembered me and wanted me to come down and do another audition.

"I said no; my pride had been hurt at the first audition. But eventually he convinced me to do it, and they booked me for two solo spots that season.

"The following year I started teaching school, physical education, at Summerside, Prince Edward Island. I was beginning to get calls from all sorts of people. One of them was record producer Brian Ahern, who wanted me to make some records. He sent a special delivery letter every two weeks. But I just couldn't do it. Instead, I did a few TV and radio appearances."

In February of 1967, she faced a momentous decision - whether to return to teaching for a second year or go into the music business. "The principal gave me two weeks to decide, and I asked everyone I knew for their opinion. In the end, I called Bill Langstroth who said there really wasn't any decision to be made. That pushed me over the edge.

"I did the *Jubilee* show all that summer, and in the fall I went on the *Let's Go* teenybop show out of Halifax. It was kind of a boring year. Later on I appeared on *The Way It Is* and did a shot on the *Wayne and Shuster Show*. The next summer, I was back on *Jubilee*.

"At the end of the season, in the fall of '68, I decided to do some clubs. I cut a record for Arc with Brian Ahern called *What About Me* and it sold well in the Maritimes because of my club gigs.

"In the first few weeks of '69, I began doing concerts. I went all over the Maritimes and did fairly well because of the TV exposure. Once again I went back on Jubilee - the fourth season by then. I also signed a recording contract with Capitol."

To their eternal credit, Capitol's A & R department demonstrated much greater faith in Anne's talents than any of the other companies. Anne and producer Ahern were dispatched to the studios with a much larger than usual recording budget and the result was a debut album titled *This Way Is My Way.*

"We went a little overboard with some of the production. But we were really proud of that album. I am still very pleased with it. When I first heard it, I just flipped. Strings just break me up."

The album was issued late in 1969, and was received with little ardor or enthusiasm by Canada's still apathetic radio stations. "In February of 1970, Capitol wanted me to come into Toronto for a press conference. Apparently somebody at CFRB in Toronto had discovered the album - four months after it had been released. Nobody had touched it before that because of the miserable, rotten cover. It was a dollar jacket on a $4.29 album.

"After CFRB started playing it, the word got around. Everybody was saying 'Where the hell is she?' Well, I was in Halifax. Capitol whisked me into Toronto and I met all the usual people like Sam the Record Man. But I couldn't understand what all the fuss was about.

"The next month we recorded *Honey, Wheat and Laughter.* As well, I signed an exclusive contract with the CBC [the first in the corporation's history] and I began another series of *Singalong Jubilee.*"

Capitol Records in the U.S. had meanwhile heard the two Anne Murray albums, and decided to release *Biding My Time* backed with *Snowbird* as a single.

"I was first turned on to Gene Maclellan's songs by Bill Langstroth. He had called one afternoon in the spring of '69 and urged me to come over to the studio to hear some tunes by a guy he'd booked on one of his shows. I went over and Gene played me *Snowbird* and *The Call.*

"I thought *Snowbird* was hot from the moment I first heard it. Later on I found out that Gene had written the song a year before with my voice in mind. At that time we hadn't even met." Anne thought *Snowbird* was hot but she didn't think of it as a hit. "I'm a Maritimer and a Canadian, so there was no way it could be a hit song. Things like that just didn't happen here." Nor did Anne concern herself with the fact that *Snowbird* had been chosen as a B-side in the U.S.

"The first thing I heard was that *Snowbird* was bubbling under the U.S. charts. I didn't even know what 'bubbling under' meant. Capitol sent me out on a promotion trip to Cleveland, Pittsburg, Detroit and New York. The record started to take off from Cleveland and Pittsburg.

"It didn't really hit me until July when I was on vacation. Capitol called up and said that *Snowbird* was number forty-five in the U.S. I suddenly realized that it was almost in that legendary top forty, and I really started to get excited. It passed the million mark by November."

Paralleling the rise of *Snowbird* on the U.S. charts was the enthusiasm of CBC programming brass to get Anne's face on television as soon and often as possible. "The contract I signed with them originally called for a minimum of eight Tommy Hunter shows, ten *Singalong Jubilees*, and a minimum of one special a year. I was also supposed to do six *Nashville Norths* on CTV prior to signing the CBC contract." Nonetheless, Anne soon discovered the dangers of tube overexposure. Fortunately a new contract with CBC was negotiated.

At this juncture, Anne secured the services of a lawyer. Previously she had signed contracts with Capitol, Arc, the CBC, the William Morris agency, Glenco (the company which packages the Glen Campbell show) and her manager without any consultation or advice from a lawyer!

"I always deal with people on a personal basis. I suppose 1 could be very vulnerable. My lawyer couldn't believe that I'd signed all those contracts without professional opinion. It could have been a disaster, but fortunately nobody saw fit to screw me."

At the same time as Anne's Canadian TV career was booming, an executive of Capitol in Hollywood, Al Koury, persuaded two producer-writers of the Glen Campbell show to audition her. "I was too tired to be nervous when I got there so I just walked in and did five minutes with Glen on camera in front of about twenty people involved with the show. They proclaimed me a natural on TV, and I tried to explain that I'd had four years' experience on Canadian television. It worked out fine and they booked me on the Glen Campbell show, which was of immense help in the States."

While Anne's association with Glen Campbell was just beginning, the problem of a follow-up to *Snowbird* was a heavy burden. "Brian Ahern, Capitol in Canada and myself all wanted another Gene Maclellan song, *Put Your Hand in the Hand*, as the followup. But the U.S. Capitol people wouldn't hear of it. They said it wasn't enough like *Snowbird*. We were rather mad about it, but there was nothing I could do."

It has since been reliably reported that the real reason Anne's version of *Put Your Hand in the Hand* was not released as a single was because Capitol's now deposed president, Sal Ianucci, had felt she sounded too masculine on the record. In any case, *Sing High Sing Low* was the new single and *Put Your Hand in the Hand* remained in the can.

"I thought *Sing High* was a good record. We went in and recorded four songs and took the tape to Los Angeles for them to decide on the new single. They all agreed on *Sing High* but they didn't really believe in it. They didn't get behind it. I believe that if a record can be a big hit in Canada, which *Sing High* was, it can do the same anywhere else."

Ianucci's reluctance to release *Put Your Hand in the Hand* in its original version by Anne Murray proved to be a costly error. A later, less artistic version by Ocean sold more than two million copies! The Ocean disc is not a record likely to arouse Anne's enthusiasm, for more than personal reasons. "The production was atrocious," she says with candor. "I heard how Gene originally wanted it to be done. The only thing good about the Ocean version is the arrangement, which is a straight copy of my own.

Anne's next single was *A Stranger in My Place*. "It was a nice song, very middle-of-the-road, but it didn't have what they wanted. It did well in the country charts but nowhere else. I thought the next one, *It Takes Time*, was a great tune. But as soon as it was released, the U.S. Capitol brass cried 'We need a hit.' They didn't believe in that record either.

"Actually I've been getting a bit tired of all that 'we need a hit' nonsense. Any song can be a hit if the record company is behind it."

For all her participation in the star system syndrome, Anne has had her share of hassles with the music establishment. "After *Snowbird* was successful in the U.S., the record company down there decided to put my two Canadian albums [*This Way is My Way*, and *Honey, Wheat and Laughter*] together for an LP they planned to call *Snowbird*.

"They allowed Brian and I to program it and pick the cover, which was fine. But when we handed them an album with seven of the songs by Canadian composers, they were a little taken aback. Before they played the tape, they complained about the lack of recognizable songs [i.e. those by U.S. composers]."

"When they heard the stuff, they completely forgot their hasty judgment." Three of the songs were by Gene Maclellan - *The Call, Bidin' My Time*, and of course, *Snowbird*.

Anne has no desire to write songs herself. "I just don't want to do it. I'm not really very creative in that area. Vocally I might be but it doesn't seem that way to me. I just stand there and do it; it just happens. The same way as Gene doesn't sit down and say 'I'll write a song.' It just happens, too."

One advantage of writing her own songs would be the reduced necessity of making frequent TV appearances. "Gordon Lightfoot has stayed away from TV. People know him for his songs. All sorts of artists record them. But I have to be seen."

Anne was surprised when Lightfoot complained of radio overexposure a few months after the legislation era went into effect. "I don't think it's possible to be over-played on radio ... unless, of course, you're the only artist being played day and night. Television can mean overexposure. Believe me, I know.

"Both the CRTC legislation and my records came along at the same time - the right time, apparently. I don't know if I'd have been able to make it without the thirty percent business."

Anne believes that legislation is having a very positive effect. "In the beginning, a lot of radio people were pessimistic. They didn't want to play inferior records, and they did have a legitimate beef at first. But I don't think they have one any more. The record companies in Canada are now spending much more on production, and the product is improving."

Anne admits that her own success has changed her attitudes and way of life. "The farther I go, the more I want to retreat and be alone. When I'm not working, I never want to go out. I don't know if that's good or bad. I'd rather just sit at home on a night off and watch a movie or a hockey game.

"I like to get back to the Maritimes. I bought some property near

Peggy's Cove - about four acres with 1600 feet of water frontage. It's secluded; I'd like to build a home on it in the future.

"I always spend two weeks in the summer with my folks. I do the same things I did when I was sixteen - sunbathe, get fat and swim a lot. I want to keep in touch with that.

"As I said, you can't take show business too seriously. If you do, you're licked. When the people decide they don't want to hear you any more, you'll know and you just quit. That's all there is to it."

The Poppy Family

Terry Jacks, founder of the Poppy Family, named his publishing company Gone Fishing, but very few people realize its full significance.

When the Poppy Family's single of *Which Way You Goin' Billy?* was soaring into the number two position on the Billboard U.S. charts, where was Terry Jacks? He'd gone fishing. When TV producers, record company executives and potential managers were searching for Terry Jacks after the million plus sales of *Billy*, where was he? Gone fishing. When the whole world was waiting to find out about this new group from Vancouver which had stormed up the American and English charts, where was Terry Jacks? Gone fishing.

Jacks - who has made a small fortune out of three international hit singles and a big album - is Canada's first real rebel of the musical bigtime. In Ronnie Hawkins' inimitable words, Terry Jacks has been to the mountain top and messed with the lions. But Jacks didn't like what he saw. And he dropped out - went fishing at the most crucial period in the Poppy Family's career.

Terry Jacks is a singer-writer-producer extraordinary. He goes fishing with the only person in the world he still trusts, an eighty-one-year-old man called Charlie. You find Charlie's picture on the back of the jacket of the Poppy Family's first album, along with a picture of Jack's grandfather.

Of the few Canadians who have entered the global music scene, a small percentage have spoken out against what they saw. But none had the guts and audacity to turn their back on it. Many who get caught up in the whirlpool soon grow to hate it, but seldom do they have the nerve or financial security to opt out.

There isn't much about Terry Jacks which fits into the usual pop star mold. He's married to the only other member of the Poppy Family, lovely Susan. He couldn't care less about the vast sums of money which the act could be making in the U.S. clubs. And he disregards all the golden rules of rock success. He says precisely what he thinks. He dismisses Anne Murray as having "little depth"; he despises the sort of heavy publicity which surrounded the release of the Crowbar album *Bad Manors*. His frankness is often brittle, his candor, shocking. But one can't help but respect, admire and even feel sorry for him. Sorry because of the dilemma which has faced this young man from Vancouver ever since he first stumbled onto success.

"I worshipped Buddy Holly," he says. "When he died, I went out and bought a thirteen dollar guitar and joined a rock 'n' roll band to try and drown my grief. I was the worst musician in the group; I was sure they were going to throw me out of the band.

"So I decided to write some songs in the hope that they d keep me. Only trouble was that they expected me to sing them too. I'd never sung before but they forced me into doing it. We cut a record; the song was called *The Way You Fell* and it was a minor hit in the west. From there, we did some music hop gigs in other western towns, and in 1966,1 met Susan.

"Together we'd play up on Whistler Mountain for the skiers. They'd throw us nickels and dimes. It was fairly tough.

"Later on Susan and I were married and went out on the road. We added a lead guitarist, then a percussionist. We cut a couple of records as the Poppy Family. I found the name in a dictionary ... 'a varied species of flowering plant.' But at the time, nobody knew who we were. The name didn't mean a thing in B.C. If they knew who you were, and you happened to be a Canadian, you had no chance of getting your record played.

"We were lucky. Our first disc, *Beyond the Clouds*, did fairly well in B.C. but was ignored by the rest of Canada. The second record, *What Can the Matter Be*, was an ironic little nursery rhyme. It did all right in B.C. too. Some people still think it's better than the things we've done more recently."

Then came the third record. By the time the legislation era began, *Which Way You Goin' Billy?* had sold in excess of two million copies worldwide.

"*Billy* was cut for only $125. It was done as cheaply as possible; it was supposed to be a B-side. It was a strange record; only four musicians were used on it.

"Because we had little money, I gave the studio one-third interest in our record to help pay some of the costs. When I saw it happening in Canada, I bought the one-third interest back from the studio for $500. *Which Way You Goin' Billy?* has now earned us more than $150,000." The silence was deafening. With an investment of $625, Terry and Susan Jacks had made at least $150,000. Not surprisingly, Jacks has often attempted to analyze the reasons for the incredible success of *Billy*.

"Simple music, simple lyrics, a melody people could remember, a simple performance, a lot of sincerity - sincerity is the main thing - but spontaneity is also very important."

Billy (written, arranged and produced by Jacks) was released in Canada in 1969, and after early delays, became a huge Canadian hit, selling over 100,000 copies. Nine months later, it finally broke into the United States, and went on to sell more than 1,000,000 copies. And then, a few months further into 1970, it also broke open in England, thus rivalling the Guess Who's *American Woman* as one of the biggest Canadian discs of all time. A second single, *That's Where I Went Wrong*, went close to a million sales, and the debut *Poppy Family* album has sold more than 130,000 copies.

The whole sweep had been more accidental than carefully planned. The group wasn't out hyping itself, hardly anybody knew anything at all about the act other than that in publicity pictures. Susan Jacks appeared a fairly stunning blonde. One of the main reasons was the lack of TV exposure on the Poppy Family. "*Billy* had been number one in New York for six straight weeks, beating out the last Beatles single, *The Long and Winding Road* [and preventing it from reaching the top in the world's largest market] and we were offered an appearance on the final Ed Sullivan show of the season.

"But we'd already made plans to appear at Expo '70 in Osaka. Dub Albritten, Brenda Lee's manager who is also an old friend of mine, said we should do the Sullivan show. But we were really looking forward to Japan so we went there instead. By the time we got back, the Sullivan show had finished for the season, and when it resumed, we were between singles so it wasn't any use."

The Japanese trip had other influences on the Poppy Family's booming career. "When we came back I decided to disband the group and I went fishing for two or three months. I couldn't take it any more.

The pressure was incredible." Jacks paused at the thought of it. "I'm the kind of person who has to follow everything through himself. As a result, I was involved in managing, booking, promoting, producing, writing, performing and it seemed to get worse every day.

"When we started out, we were really struggling. When I decided to quit, our monthly expenses alone were $3,500. But we had enough money to retire for life. In two years, we'd gone from thirty dollars a night to six thousand. But we were losing touch with our music. I was losing interest; I wasn't even digging the music any more. So I went off fishing.

"They all freaked out. The record company kept telling us to go out on the road - if we could sell over a hundred thousand albums without exposure, they figured we'd be huge if we were working in the States. But the whole thing was a piss-off." So Jacks went fishing with old Charlie. He didn't even take along Susan.

"Susan always used to go fishing with me, but I wanted to be on my own. We'd been together twenty-four hours a day for almost four years, and it was just too much. Telling her what to wear, what to sing, how to sing it - instead of becoming closer, we were drifting farther apart. It was really affecting our marriage.

"I became paranoid about it all. Everyone was after me, wanting this, wanting that. The only one I still trusted was old Charlie. The whole thing was such an incredible drag."

Three months and a good rest later, Jacks decided to return to the bright lights. He and Susan went to England and cut an album with the string players of the London Philharmonic Orchestra. "We'd tried to do it in Vancouver, but the studios just don't make it."

Jacks spent the next nine months assembling a new backing group. Then he dissolved it early in 1970. "We were right back into it again. The last gig we played was New Year's at Disneyland with Blood, Sweat & Tears, before six thousand people. We received $5,200 for the gig, but ended up with only $1,800 after paying everyone. We just didn't want to do it any more. There was no satisfaction. And I'd gotten tired of writing for a chick; it's very hard writing from a chick's point of view. We decided to get out of the big money scene, and just enjoy the music.

"Susan has an incredible voice and great magnetism on stage. But it just wasn't happening for us at the gigs. People liked it, but we didn't. We wanted to get back to the real thing, forget about the plastic bullshit and just play the music.

"I saw Neil Young play in Vancouver, and I was really flabbergasted. He didn't need a heavy band. If you've got good songs, you can do it. Some people don't like Neil's voice but I dig it; it has sincerity. James Taylor is into a similar trip. I saw in both of them a step that we might be able to take. It gave me a good feeling inside."

Meanwhile, a solo single by Jacks, *I'm Gonna Capture You*, had also made its way onto the U.S. charts. "It was a song I'd written for Tommy Roe. I'm not a Tommy Roe fan, but I admired what he was doing in his field because he's a king at that. So I cut a demo tape of the song for him, but London Records liked it so much they wanted me to release it as a single. And they insisted that it be released under my name. It was embarassing."

Jacks also took a shot at producing the Beach Boys, U.S. superstars of the early and mid-sixties. "They wanted me to cut something with them. I had a Jacques Brel song which was a certain hit in my opinion. Al Jardine of the Beach Boys was a good friend of mine, so I went down for three days to get it together.

"I actually stayed for eight, and almost had a nervous breakdown. They were all unbelievably fucked up. Mike Love was on a watermelon fast, Brian Wilson wouldn't come into the studio before 4pm and he wouldn't sing high notes because of some old hang-up. The entire Los Angeles scene is decadent, a complete money thing. They've gotten out of the music."

Jacks says that he and Susan will probably go out on the road alone, eventually. "We'd much rather play to two hundred people who enjoyed our performance, then five thousand kids who are really out of it, and only there for the scene anyway. In the smaller places, you can reach the people.

"We've met some of the big stars in the States, like Janis Joplin. Those cats are terrified to walk out on stage. They're so insecure. Worried they can't live up to their image. They get to be stoned out all the time, not just occasionally, and sooner or later they do too much, and it kills them. The real murderers are the managers, the agents, the publicists. A lot of great artists are going under because of that. The strain is too much."

Another thing which disturbs Jacks is the tremendous amount of exposure granted to some artists, who seem to fit the media's preconceived idea of what a star should be like. "It really annoys me to see so many articles and TV coverage of people like Anne Murray. That just boils me up. Anne Murray gets TV specials, the whole works. She has a lot of front stuff in her act, but not much depth. Why all the fuss? The Guess Who had five times as many gold records in 1970 as Anne Murray.

"We've been offered so many Canadian TV shows I've lost count of them. But it's so pointless. Wayne and Shuster have been trying to get us to appear on their show. Did you see the last one? The sound was atrocious. You've got to use prerecorded backing tapes because they simply cannot get the sound together. People are used to really good sound on records, and they expect it on TV as well.

"So many people are left with the wrong impression of a group after seeing them on TV. We'd like to do a half-hour special which would show what we're really like. We'd sing and talk and entertain, but in our way, not the CBC's. We know our audience better than they do.

"I think Canada is going to go through the same super hype experience as the States. I know it's necessary but I think it hurts the acts in the long run. Because the Canadian thing is happening, there'll be a heavy sell on a lot of artists. Crowbar are getting it already. I think you should leave the decision to the masses; let them make their own evaluations, just present to them what's there.

"What really bugs me is the way every record company has to have a superstar. You know, like Emmit Rhodes. It's ridiculous. But one person who deserves the title is Gord Lightfoot. There's a cat who's gone the whole way.

"Gordon Lightfoot is a genuine Canadian superstar. And now there's a few more on the way."

4. THE ONES WHO WOULDN'T WAIT

For every one of the great Canadian artists who has achieved well-warranted international acclaim since the Guess Who breakthrough, there was an earlier artist who couldn't wait.

Confronted by a barrage of apathy and disinterest, a large number of Canadian musicians left their homeland in the sixties to pursue their careers in the United States. In most cases, they departed from Canada and entered the States as unknowns. Very few of them remained that way for long.

Most of the current top U.S. groups include a Canadian or two in their ranks due to this infiltration in the sixties. The list is virtually endless, but to mention a few: Mountain, the Rascals, the Mamas and Papas, Three Dog Night, the Union Gap, the Lovin' Spoonful and Rare Earth. These Canadian-American amalgamations have obviously produced stunning results.

Other Canadians arrived at the U.S. pop pinnacle unaided by Americans. Such artists as Joni Mitchell, David Clayton-Thomas, Neil Young and Andy Kim rose to the top in the States by a combination of talent and perseverance. Owing to their commitments, the majority of these expatriate Canadians now live in the United States. Faced with unsympathetic media and burning up with ambition to succeed (or at the very least, try to succeed), they simply turned their backs and headed southwards.

In this chapter, the expatriate Canadians tell of their trials and the unceasing battle to get on top and stay there in the jungle of American rock.

The Band

Of all the Canadians who left their homeland to pursue a musical career in the U.S., the Band were the first to infiltrate the American rock in-crowd. Neil Young did it later, so did Joni Mitchell; the Band were first and that is to their eternal credit.

The group was put together by Ronnie Hawkins (to his eternal credit) and after five years of playing the bar circuit as Ronnie Hawkins and the Hawks, the group split to Woodstock and became the vehicle through which Bob Dylan electrified himself. The Hawks played on what is probably the finest single Dylan ever released, *Like a Rolling Stone*. When Dylan went into an accident-enforced seclusion, the group emerged as The Band and surprised the entire musical world.

They were spoken of in hushed, reverent terms; they were worshipped by critics, who found their softer, gentler music a pleasant relief from the angry buzzing of heavy rock acts; and they built for themselves an image of lily-white virtue and social concern.

Yet their old mentor Rompin' Ronnie Hawkins couldn't understand the sudden switch in moral intent, and The Band couldn't understand why Ronnie would want to talk in public and in print about their rip-roaring days on the Ontario and southern U.S. bar circuits.

In late summer, 1969, a lengthy article appeared in *Rolling Stone*, in which Hawkins told all - in none too savory terms - about the old times with The Band. Some of it bears repetition. Firstly, Ronnie outlined how he assembled the Hawks.

"Levon Helm came up to Canada with me in 1958. We did our first Canadian gig in Hamilton at the Golden Rail. My entire band then was from Arkansas.

"We bumped into Robbie Robertson at one of the gigs and we made him our road manager. Later I worked him into the Hawks, first on bass, then rhythm and finally lead guitar.

"Richard Manuel came from Stratford, Ontario. He had a little group and I managed them for a while. Then it broke up and I brought Richard into my own group playing piano. That must have been 1962. We named Richard 'The Gobbler.' He's a house wrecker man, a working girl's favorite and a housewives' companion, if you know what I mean.

"Ricky Danko was an apprentice butcher in Simcoe [a small lakeside town fifty miles north of Toronto] and we picked him up from a poker band. He was a good lookin' boy with plenty of potential.

"The boys must have worked for me for four or five years. And they were hard years. By God, I made them rehearse every damn day. We played some real tough places - the people didn't come to hear you, they came to mess with you. They'd flick cigarette butts, throw coins, steal your equipment and if you still kept right on a-playin', well, maybe they'd sit down and listen to you.

"I remember one time in West Helena, Arkansas, when we actually had to stop playing when a brawl started. Three rednecks started tuggin' this young guy, and well-dressed he was, too. He up and took after them with a plugged in chain saw. Wow, he damn near sawed the whole place down before the fuzz arrived. The guys that had started hassling him ended up tearing the back wall out of the club and jumpin' into the Mississippi River.

"Yes sir, they was rough times, but they were good times too. Musicians nowadays don't know what it's like to have hard times. Back in the fifties, rough times were when you didn't have a darn thing to put in your mouth but a woman's tit. Man, you didn't eat until after you got up there and played. That's what I call paying dues; the band paid them, man, they sure did pay them.

"They were boys when they started with me, but they were men when they finished. They've seen damn near everything there is to see. They practised, played and screwed in every town you care to name."

But five years of even the wildest good times are apparently enough for anyone. "After a while, the Hawks wanted to play more blues than I could let them. John Hammond came to Toronto and he really impressed the boys. This Hammond fellow knew Bob Dylan and he told them Dylan was ready to go in a blues direction. He told them to go and see Bobby.

"So the boys went down and played a gig in New Jersey without me, and met up with Dylan and settled down with him. Then later, when Dylan decided to quit the road and recording, the boys either had to break up, come back with me or go out by themselves."

They went out by themselves, and as rock history records it, they created a minor sensation. Their first album, *Music From Big Pink*, was greeted with enthusiasm by the critics, and it sold reasonably well. Even Hawkins liked it.

"There were two or three cuts that I really liked. But I'm not really a good enough musician to understand all that stuff. I do understand the lyrics though ... understand them better than most people.

"That one about Caledonia Mission and being surrounded by the Mounties; that was that time they got busted at the border. They're writing about true things, the things that happened to us along the way."

Members of the Band were reportedly so disgusted at Hawkins' disclosures of their past that they threatened to sue the Hawk for his remarks. "I don't know what came over those boys ... they never pretended they were somethin' they're not when I was around 'em. The pure image just doesn't suit them."

A couple of months later, the Band was able to get a strike off in retaliation. In an amazing cover story in *Time* magazine late in 1969, a couple of Band members took the opportunity to take a few scathing shots at Ronnie. From then on, Hawkins was careful not to say a word which might in any way imply that the Band members were anything more than straitlaced, musical-minded young men with never an immoral thought in their minds.

Despite many sound amplification difficulties on tour, the Band's reputation grew and their second album. The Band, cemented their place in contemporary music. But little is known of the group after it left Hawkins. The Band give very few interviews. They seldom talk of the old days on Yonge Street in Toronto. Canadian musicians are unanimous in their contention that the Hawks influenced more local groups in the mid-sixties than any rock act, then or since. Hawkins has very little to add about his boys.

In an interview with Robbie Robertson published in *Rolling Stone* in December of 1969, the Band guitarist said: "Success has changed nearly everything. It's changed the music a little bit. It's an incredible thing. I don't even know if we're successful; it's crazy, it really is.

"There's just a few groups that have been together as long as we have. One is Creedence Clearwater. They've been trying to make it now for eight or nine years, and finally did it and are right up there. Now I've just heard they're splitting up. That has a lot to do with success too. Everybody gets to be a different person and it's not as tight as it should be."

In 1970, The Band recorded their third album, *Stage Fright*, which did not achieve either the sales or critical success of the first two albums. But it did not matter.

The Band had already left their stamp on North American music in the late sixties, as they had on the Toronto scene in the mid-sixties.

As they say themselves, their music says it all.

David Clayton-Thomas

If you wanted to put together a documentation of discrimination in the Canadian pop scene of the mid-sixties, you could find no better or more bitter witness than David Clayton-Thomas, the big, ballsy bull of a lead singer with Blood, Sweat & Tears. If we are to believe Clayton-Thomas, no Canadian musician in history was treated so badly or accorded so many bad breaks.

A lot of people still believe that Clayton-Thomas suffered incredibly at the hands of music manipulators and crooked promoters, and at the feet of Canadian radio stations. Ronnie Hawkins agrees about the radio stations, but believes that Clayton-Thomas asked for at least a portion of the ill treatment he received.

"He was a rough, tough punk. He played every little skid row bar in Canada. But he got into fights a lot. He would pop off real quick. He seemed to have a grudge against everyone.

"David once worked with me at Le Coq D'Or for a couple of weeks. He had a fine band. Matter of fact, he always had a fine band. He had a couple that could have made it world-wide if they'd been given a chance by the local radio stations and if he'd been pushed properly.

"But his success with Blood, Sweat & Tears has mellowed him a lot. He always had tons of talent, but now he's down to earth. Success spoils most kids, but it has helped David Clayton-Thomas."

Personally, I've never found Clayton-Thomas to be rough or tough. He's always been a perfect gentleman. Certainly he's militant. He's outspoken. He's intensely critical of the "good" old days in Canadian music. No one can ever deny that he had a hard time. And nobody remembers those times better than Thomas himself.

"I worked for ten years in Toronto, and I had hit records - five of them. But I didn't make any money and I wasn't able to make any sort of a living. I was lucky to pull in $125 a week, and that doesn't give you much incentive. Scuffling around the country like starving rats, begging agents for an extra fifty bucks a week so that we could get some new strings for the bass guitar, or a new drum skin.

"The only way you could survive was to join the bar circuit, and that completely stifled any creativity you might have had. I recall one time when we were working at Friar's Tavern in Toronto for $130 a week (that's all I got after the band had been paid) and we had a top five record. Up the road at Le Coq D'Or, some crummy group from Boston who had not even made a record were pulling in twice as much as we were. There was a complete and total lack of acceptance of Canadians by Canadians. It didn't matter how bad you were ... as long as you were American or English, the crowds still thought you were great. But try wearing a maple leaf on your sleeve ... "We had a few hits but I don't remember getting any royalties. Then, when I finally made it in B, S & T, you should have seen the Canadian leeches coming out of the woodwork claiming they had old contracts with me. I'd like to name a few names, the bastards.

"I'll never forget one Canadian record company man who flew into New York to try and stop Columbia Records from releasing the second B, S & T album. Columbia wheeled in a few of their attorneys and soon had that creep running up the wall. All he wanted was money to buy him off."

I remembered another veteran Toronto record man who'd told me confidentially (i.e. he didn't want to be named) that Clayton-Thomas was "just a troublemaker, a bad kid, he wouldn't leave things the way they had always been running comfortably. He had an ego problem and he got into a lot of trouble and he deserved every bit of it ..."

Opinions on the Thomas of the old days vary considerably. Scott Richard, who is one of Canada's best known pro-Canadian promotion men (he works for RCA), was a member of the Boss Men, probably the best group Thomas ever put together. He speaks fondly of the gig. "David has to be one of the most loyal people you could meet. He totally committed himself to the group. There is always conflict within any group, but David worked hard to overcome them. As a performer, he was absolutely great. And I value his opinion as a critic and as a musician. I'm glad I had the chance of working with him."

Nevertheless, says Clayton-Thomas, "I didn't survive in Canada. The only way you could do that was to join those walking jukeboxes at Friars Tavern. I had to leave but I proved they were wrong and I was right.

"It was ironic that I wound up with B, S & T. While I was still in Canada, quite a few offers came in from the U.S. But I never found out about them. One of my managers decided that if I wandered off southwards, he might lose his twenty percent. So I wasn't told about the offers, and I had to wait, not knowing that anyone in the U.S. was interested. It really pisses me off to remember that small-time thinking.

"My dream was always to have a big band. The Boss Men were the first of the jazz-rock music mergers. Our first hit single, *Brain-*

104

washed, had a rock guitar section with jazz piano.

"I always believed in myself, the music I was writing, and the bands I had. The trouble was that I wouldn't accept anything less than the best of what Canada had to offer at the time. It wasn't much but I felt strongly that we deserved it anyway. We worked out of Yorkville in Toronto for six years, and we never earned more than $25 a night, two or three nights a week. That was about $75 a week ... wow, really heavy bread."

The bitterness of his sarcasm does not escape notice. Nor does the emotion which is stirring up inside him. "But we didn't cop out, man. Looking back, I'm glad about that. We could have easily gone the cop out route ... we could have done the Top Forty on TV, we could have bought mohair suits and looked like finks. But we didn't. And it was tough. You had the conservative establishment of Toronto at your back, and the U.S. border at your nose. There wasn't much you could do about things you didn't dig.

"I always hoped to combine classics, jazz and rock into one band. Rock needed some sort of validity. It was always my ambition to help it happen. But you needed really top-line musicians to do it. The cats in B, S & T have approached it as jazz and classical musicians playing rock. But we are still a rock 'n' roll band. Our unified aim is to legitimize rock."

Though Thomas thinks he'll be with Blood, Sweat & Tears for quite a while, he doesn't discount the continual rumor that he's going solo. "It's my eventual ambition," he freely admits.

Thomas spent a year pounding the pavements of New York's lower East side before finally getting the vocal gig with B, S & T after the original singer, Al Kooper, had split because of ego hassles. "He wanted it to be his band, they wanted it to be everybody's band," says Thomas. Despite the fact that a Toronto vocal coach had once told Thomas that his voice was "beyond help," the forceful singer shot to world fame at the front of the freewheeling B, S & T horn section.

"I'm just a Canadian kid who loves the blues," says Thomas, with a one-phrase dismissal of his success. He still maintains close ties with Canada. The songs he has written for B, S & T, for example - Spinning Wheel and *Lucretia Macevil* - are published by a company in Toronto with "one of those old contracts." Several companies did very little for Thomas when he most needed it, but they haven't spared any effort to get in on the action now that there is some.

"I left Canada because I realized it couldn't be done from there. Yet I eventually want to return. I'm still a Canadian, my best and oldest friends are in Toronto. Occasionally I take a day off and sneak back home. The lack of uptightness in the people is something I didn't become aware of until after I'd left."

But Thomas says there is no way he'd return to work in the Canadian music business. "All the backbiting and petty bullshit that goes on in the music business - you can accept it for ten grand a night, but for a lousy couple of hundred bucks, man, you can forget it. It just ain't worth it."

Andy Kim

Andy Kim always believed that eventually he would become a star. He told a lot of people about it over the past nine years, and his only problem was that most of them took longer than they should to realize he was right.

Andy Kim is a star, in every sense of the word. But he is an American star. He is a Canadian citizen but the U.S. has become his home. The sad thing is that the choice wasn't his. He seizes every opportunity he can to inform the world that he is Canadian, and that he was forced to leave Canada because there were no opportunities for a young man who started out "wanting to become a star."

Andy Kim is candid and forthright. He has staggering determination; very few unknown artists could have endured the rigors of the New York music scene and somehow survived to finally emerge on top. Kim did it.

The battle he fought is one that Canadians may never have to fight again; Canadian talent shall overcome.

"I knew nothing about the music industry when I started, but I wanted to get into it. I was a young boy in Montreal and found to my disgust that I couldn't really get anywhere in Canada. I talked to a local disc jockey, George Kirby, and he told me as much as he could about the Canadian music scene. He said that people weren't interested in Canadians ... they wanted the Nashville sound; Floyd Cramer was big then. I came home - it was Thanksgiving Day - and I told my parents I was going to New York to become a star. I was going to try and find the roots in New York, because they certainly weren't in Canada.

"My folks were kind of surprised. I'd never sung professionally and they really had no idea of my ambitions. I took a week off school and bought a train ticket to New York with my brother Joe [who now managers Andy].

"So there we were in New York, staying at the YMCA. I had $35 in my pocket, and I bought a copy of *Cashbox*, the music magazine. I looked through the charts and it took me a day to organize myself. I started with 'A' and was going to visit all the record companies.

"ABC Paramount was first on the list, and I went up to their offices. In the reception, I asked to see the director. The girl asked if I had an appointment, and I said no, but I told her I had appointments with Capitol at 2:30 and Columbia at four, and I was just passing, and you know ...

"I didn't even know if Capitol had an office in New York. The girl then asked me if I had a demo, and I said yes. So she picked up the phone, and told me to go in. Turn right, and through the mailroom - I'll never forget it.

"The man was sitting in his office with the record player running, and I told him I had no idea what a demo was, but that I was from Montreal and I was going to be a star and make hit records.

"The guy asked me if I wrote songs. 'No.' He asked me if I played guitar. 'No.' He then explained to me just what I was up against. That was in 1962."

Kim returned to Montreal, quit school, and spent the next four and a half years in New York, with occasional visits home. "I kept on making demos and taking them to record companies and producers. I often needed money to make the demos so I had to go out and work. I sold lawnmowers in New York, flogged candy-floss in amusement parks, sold nails and hammers at Eatons in Montreal - anything to get enough bread to keep making the demos.

"I was also trying to rearrange songs. I'd take a ballad and do it up-tempo, change the vocal phrasing, the whole number. I picked up *Cashbox* again and saw that it was only a handful of people who wrote almost all the hit songs.

"I visited as many of them as I could. Most of the time I couldn't even get a foot in the door. They only wanted to write for established artists. They couldn't care about the kids who were trying to become established. I came back to Montreal.

"My brother played guitar, and I wanted to learn how to play because I needed something on which to write songs. He fell over laughing. But he taught me two chords - C and F. I sat down and wrote a song called *How'd We Ever Get This Way?* It had only two chords, C and F, because they were all I knew.

"I returned to New York and went to see Jeff Barry, who was just winding up his interest in Red Bird Records. I'd met him a few times before, and I went in and told him that if he wanted to make a million dollars, he should sign me up. For the next twelve months, I kept going to see him. I really hounded him. He would promise to make my record when he had 'some spare time'.

"One afternoon I went around on my usual visit to Jeff, and again asked, 'When are you going to record me.' He said he'd have to find some material, so I played him *How'd We Ever Get This Way?* He liked it.

"We cut a record of the song on December 21, 1967. It didn't come out until the following March, but it sold 800,000 copies soon after. It confirmed what I'd been trying to tell people for quite a time."

Andy Kim had waited almost six years for his time to come. "Since then. I've been writing and improving a talent that had been hidden for a long time, I guess."

His second single was *Shoot 'Em Up Baby*. The timing of its release could not have been worse. "The U.S. racial riots had just begun, and the big urban cities with large Negro populations refused to play the disc because they thought it might incite further violence. Then in some other places, they thought it was a drug song, and banned it as well. So I wound up only getting play in the South, and a few smaller northern cities."

Nevertheless, *Shoot 'Em Up Baby* (which Kim says was his description of the go-out-and-have-a-good-time philosophy) managed to sell over 500,000 copies.

"Then came *Rainbow Ride*, which didn't do as well as the first two. I wrote a song called *Tricia Tell Your Daddy*, which was about Tricia Nixon. But nobody seemed to catch on, so it went nowhere.

"In 1969, I had *Baby I Love You*, which sold 1,500,000 copies. In that year, I also wrote *Sugar, Sugar, Jingle Jangle* and *So Good Together*, all of which were monster hits for the Archies." *Sugar Sugar*, which sold about six million copies worldwide, will probably earn Kim more than $100,000. He wrote it over the phone in twenty minutes.

At the start of the legislation era, Kim was preparing to return to the studios for the first time in eighteen months. "Everything had been so rushed before. They'd say you've got a week to write and record a new album. I was a little bit naive, but I learned from it. I cut a new song of mine called *I Wish I Were*. It's very original, quite a change for me."

While in Montreal recently, Kim had taken a close look at the local music scene. "There is getting to be more and more Canadian product. Some if it's good, some of it is bad. But there's still an unfortunate attitude towards records in Canada. It doesn't matter if it's Canadian content, American content or Japanese content - a record is good if it's good. A programmer shouldn't have to play something merely because it comes from his own backyard. It's a pretty sad statement that it had to be done in Canada.

"If the CRTC ruling had been in effect when I started out in 1962, I don't think I'd have gone to the States. I'd probably have stayed here, cut a record, and waited to see what happened. It would be groovy to be able to record here ... really, nobody likes to have to leave their country, and I like Montreal a lot.

"I think eventually Americans will want to record in Canada. They go through a series of places - Nashville, Muscle Shoals, New York, Los Angeles, Detroit, Chicago. Sooner or later a producer will come along and have a lot of hits from one Canadian studio. Then everyone will want to record there.

"But there's a lack of producers in Canada. We have the talent, that's obvious, but we need the producers. What Canada needs more than anything else is for the people who are in a position to do something - the radio programmers, the writers, critics, magazines, the entire media - to get off their butts and do it. It's their fault that it took so long for things to start happening."

Joni Mitchell

Joni Mitchell is one of three great folk idols born in Canada and now living in the United States. The others are Neil Young and Leonard Cohen.

The internationally acclaimed songwriter-singer left Canada six years ago with memories of gigs in church basements and of washing dishes to earn enough money to eat.

"Many things took me to the States," she says, in matter-of-fact tones. "For one thing, I married an American. I also went for recognition. The masses receive their information through American newspapers, magazines, radio and television. In Canada, there were only three major centres - Vancouver, Toronto and Montreal - and that's just not enough publicity.

"Exposure is vital to success. Nightclub owners wouldn't hire you unless you had a name to guarantee a full house. So I packed my bags and went where I could get a name."

Joni Mitchell, that wistful girl from the Canadian prairies, has become a composer and lyricist of world stature. Her songs can be heard in a dozen different languages in fifty countries. Judy Collins sold a million copies of the poignant Joni Mitchell love ballad, *Both Sides Now*. Miss Collins has since gone on record as saying: "I sing Joni's songs because I like them immensely. There doesn't seem to be anyone quite as good. Her lyrics are exquisite and it all fits together."

Joni Mitchell now lives, a golden goddess, in Laurel Canyon, California. She is one of west coast folk's elite, respected and often loved by her contemporaries, admired and emulated by thousands of young girls with long, brown hair and a guitar.

But not all her songs are about the sunny haven she has built in California. She writes of things and people she knew while young, growing up in Saskatoon. *Michael from Mountains*, one of her best-loved ballads, was dedicated to her grade seven teacher, Mr. Kratzman. "Most of my songs are written from personal experiences. The Michael in *Michael from Mountains* is a real person. He was a child-man always showing you his treasures, like a boy.

"Mr. Kratzman taught me how to write about the simple things in life, things that I knew about - like gathering tadpoles in an empty mayonnaise jar after the rain. I still remember playing dress-up in the attic of the house in Saskatoon with trunks of old clothes in a world of make believe."

Joni Mitchell is now into a second era of composing. Her first was often lonely and loveless, like an old person without a friend. Now she's more intent on bringing people up.

"I do a lot of night writing," she once told Larry LeBlanc, a Canadian free-lance writer. "I need solitude to write. I used to be able to write under almost any condition but not any more. I have to go inside myself so far, to search through a theme. Writing is more than simply arranging a pleasant combination of sounds.

"When I write a new song, I take it and play it for my friends, who are fine musicians and writers. I'm largely influenced by their reaction to it. If they like it, I'm knocked out. I guess I write for those people. They're really my audience."

That audience includes such notable contemporaries as James Taylor, Neil Young and Graham Nash. I still remember one late summer's night in 1969 at the Laurel Canyon home of Stephen Stills. Joni had been playing a gig in the east and Nash had driven out to the Los Angeles airport to meet her. He had clearly been pining for her all day; their close relationship was obvious. They drove back to the house, where Joni was received joyously. An hour or so later, she was seated at the piano playing one of her new songs. Stills, Dave Crosby, Neil Young and of course, Nash, were mesmerized.

The annual Mariposa Folk Festival took place the following weekend and I was back in Toronto covering it for the *Globe and Mail*. I went out to the city's Centre Island on a small boat with Joni and Graham Nash, and during the concert, Joni started to sing a new song she's written for him. It was a tune about Willie, a nickname of Nash's. She found herself unable to finish the song; clearly, Joni Mitchell feels her feelings deeply.

She gave up performing for a year in 1970, not long after the end of her affair with Nash. "I needed new material," she said. "I need new things to say in order to perform, so there's something in it for me. You just can't sing the same songs.

"I was being isolated, starting to feel like a bird in a gilded cage, I wasn't getting a chance to meet people. A certain amount of success cuts you off in a lot of ways. You can't move freely. I like to live, to be on the streets, to be in a crowd and move freely."

Joni learned to play ukelele while attending art college, and taught herself guitar from a Pete Seegar instruction book. She left Saskatoon in 1961 to appear at the Mariposa Festival in Orillia, Lightfoot's birth place. Martin Onrot, one of the organizers of the event (which was forced by injunction to change location a few hours before it began) recalls: "Joni had come in with some people from the west, and she helped us load trucks and move the entire festival. She really chipped in.

"The first time I heard her sing was in a downtown Toronto rooming house. She had a soft, beautiful voice, and an easy, melodic style. It was nice, but I had no idea that she would become a superstar."

She returned to Toronto in 1965 and stayed for a couple of summers. Finally she left when it became obvious that the world would never have the chance to appreciate her unique abilities while she remained in Toronto, unknown, undiscovered and misunderstood.

"I still feel a Canadian at heart and with the U.S. being under such peculiar circumstances I may come back, perhaps to Vancouver. Most of my friends are in the U.S. and that's why I'll stay a little longer."

There were years of dues-paying on the east coast U.S. folk circuit, but eventually, Joni's songs began to turn up on prominent folk albums. Her early compositions such as *Urge for Going, The Circle Game* and *Chelsea Morning* are now rightly regarded as classics of the folk idiom. From there, it became easier. She gradually gained acceptance as a singer as well as writer, and began making concert tours. Her popularity grows daily, and the chances of her returning to Canada are slim despite her protestations.

Steppenwolf

John Kay was fourteen years old when he arrived in Canada after emigrating from West Germany in 1958. He couldn't speak a word of English, and he suffered from bad eyesight. Thirteen years later Kay, who's now the lead singer and writer with Steppenwolf, speaks more eloquently, persuasively and compassionately about the Toronto music scene of the mid-sixties than almost any Canadian-born musician. His understanding of the Toronto scene vis-a-vis the rest of the music world in that period surpasses almost anything you'll ever read on the subject.

"The music scene in Canada was remarkable. Everyone in the media was looking to the United States and Great Britain for leadership, direction, hit product. Canadian acts were glossed over, and I couldn't understand that. I'd been to Buffalo a few times and found nothing but terrible bar bands.

"Yet Toronto had the most incredible groups. I'll always remember the first time I went to see the Hawks. I didn't leave the ceiling for two or three hours afterwards. I could not believe what Robbie Robertson and Garth Hudson were doing on stage. It was unbelievable.

"Later on I went to the U.S. and was confronted with all the leftover surf groups. I was appalled that this incredible band back in Toronto, the Hawks, should be feeling around playing in Ontario when these American groups with the big gigs were so rotten. The U.S. was not necessarily looking for anything better, but the Hawks were just so far ahead of what was happening in the States. It really infuriated me. The Hawks had so much raw energy it was frightening. I think a lot of that power has gone now, but back in '65, it was not to be believed. When they were playing the Hawk's Nest, they were a fantastic, super-energy band. If only the rest of the country had been ready for them.

"Everyone used to go to the Saturday matinees to see the Hawks. Even when the Hawks split, Hawkins still used to play the matinees. A bunch of other good musicians turned up with him - Bobby Starr, Freddy Keeler, Jay Smith. I often wondered why none of them tried to make it in the States.

"I confronted Jay about that one afternoon. I asked him why he was working for Hawkins for $150 a week, when he could be down in the States making much more. He had virtually no interest in it. They all considered it the pinnacle of their career to be a member of a Hawkins band. They seemed scared to strike out on their own. Hawkins was the end of the road and the top of the class for them.

"My second view of the Toronto scene came after I'd been away to the States and came back as a solo artist playing guitar. I was astounded by the way Yorkville had developed into a great breeding ground for folk talent. The level of expertise surpassed anything you'd see at the clubs in Greenwich Village, with the exception of only the biggest clubs. There was Elyse Weinberg, Ian and Sylvia, Gordie Lightfoot, David Rae, Joni Mitchell ... it was incredible.

"I thought to myself at the time, 'Here's a country with only nineteen million people yet in one town there was more real talent than New York and Los Angeles combined, as far as popular music was concerned. But it wasn't until The Beatles era that anything happened in Toronto.

"Canadian talent has since snuck into the U.S. music mainstream through the back door. It took a while to get together. When better musicianship became expected in the U.S., Canadians were able to break through. In general, Canadian bands were always better than their American counterparts. Take the Sparrow - we were just one of a dozen bands from Yorkville, yet when we went to play in New York, every musician in the city would come to see us. There had to be something there for Butterfield, the Byrds, the Blues Magoos and even the Stones to come and dig you.

"The Toronto city council should have realized that a rare phenomenon was taking place in the city in Yorkville. Even in physical eye appeal, it was vastly superior to Greenwich Village. There may have only been a small area covered - Cumberland, Yorkville and a bit of Avenue Road - but it was incredible. I'm absolutely amazed that the city deliberately helped to kill the scene - went out of their way to destroy something that happened by accident. There was tremendous energy and originality to it.

"It was the home of something very valuable. There were two kinds of bands at the time - imitators of the Hawks, and the long-haired groups. If it hadn't happened that we all lived together within a few blocks, none of us would have strived for the musical standards that we did. We lived on top of each other, and we were exposed to constant talk of what each band was doing.

"We were all involved with each other. For example, prior to joining the Sparrow, I had been living with a Toronto folk singer, Vicki Taylor. When I joined the group, I wanted to submerge myself in it totally and I decided to move out. The day I left, Neil Young moved in.

"In the States, all the bands were doing versions of the same numbers. There was no spirit of competition. In Yorkville, we saw the first roots of the new sub-culture. That in itself produced an incredible artistic breeding ground, with tremendous incentive. It was so far ahead of what was happening musically in the States at the time."

Yet Toronto media chose either to ignore it, or to regard the phenomenon as a bunch of kids making an unintelligible noise. The radio stations, in particular, ignored it. And the studios remained years behind the rest of the world. It was impossible for hit records to come from these incredible groups in Yorkville Village. The growth of a viable youth sub-culture, later seized upon by San Francisco, was cruelly destroyed like a clumsy foot on a tiny seedling, left to die because of apathy. The cream of the Toronto sound crop had to leave to find the acclaim and reward they so justly deserved. Canada is much the poorer for it.

John Kay was one of them. "I'm grateful to Canada because of what it taught me, but I didn't really care when we went to the States. I'd left my home years before. Canada was just another stop.

"I started school in Toronto at Humberside Collegiate near High Park. But because of my eyesight, they sent me to the sight saving classes at the Canadian Institute for the Blind. There wasn't too much work to do, so I learned to play guitar - Hank Williams stuff mainly.

"Then I went to Buffalo for a few months, and I picked up on the folk revival thing. I got into Robert Johnson and the country blues scene. I was very much influenced by country blues."

Kay stayed in the States for two years, spending much of that time in Los Angeles. He returned to Toronto in June of 1965, and was booked into the Half Beat Club. Next door, in the Devil's Drum, a group called Jack London and the Sparrow was playing. One night, there was an impromptu jam session which was attended by a couple of members of the Sparrow, Lonnie Johnson and John Kay. Kay played harmonica. One of the Sparrow was so intrigued by the harp that he suggested Kay should stop in the next afternoon and play some licks for Nick St. Nicholas, another member of the Sparrow. "We had lots of fun playing together. They suggested I should drop by between sets and sit in with them. We did this for several nights in a row."

A member of the audience was Bill Benson, a visiting Englishman who was unsuccessfully trying to persuade the Sparrow to tour England. Before he left, disappointed, Benson suggested that Kay should join the group.

"I joined the Sparrow the same day as Goldie McJohn, the keyboards player. Two nights later, we were scheduled to play our biggest gig up to that time - Waterloo Lutheran University for $1,000. We stayed up all night and learned twenty-five songs at the Jubilee in Oshawa, an auditorium owned by Jerry Edmonton's father.

"The Sparrow had been formed by Jack London, Dennis and Jerry Edmonton and Bruce Palmer on bass. Shortly after, we traded Bruce Palmer for Nick St. Nicholas, who was a member of the Mynah Birds. It's interesting that Bruce was instrumental in having Neil Young join the Mynah Birds a few months later."

The Sparrow played in Toronto's Yorkville Village from September 1965 through May of the next year. "We managed to sustain our-selves by playing clubs like the El Patio, Charlie Brown's and Jocks, none which paid that much but which allowed us to rehearse on the premises during the week days.

"It paid sufficiently for us to rent two apartments in Yorkville. There were no expenses, and we often used to work at the Hawk's Nest and at other out of town clubs. We learned all the U.S. hit parade songs and slipped our original goodies in between."

Kay's experience in California convinced him that the group would have to leave Canada to have any chance of big-time success. "Not having any family ties with Canada, I tried to talk the band into moving to the west coast. Canada had been good to me - I was introduced to the North American life style, I learned to speak English, I got started in music. I regarded Buffalo as a toilet, but California was the first place that geographically attracted me.

"When I'd been in Los Angeles, I'd seen the beginnings of the Byrds era, when local radio stations would play L.A. demo records by the group every hour, as though they'd been paid to. It was the same sort of city spirit with the Rising Sons, the group which included Taj Mahal and Ry Cooder. The local attention was incredible and I figured that if I could get the Sparrow out there, we would probably be in the right spot to get that sort of exposure.

"Then we met Stanton S. Freeman, who'd been the vice-president of Clairtone and who was a friend of Sybil Burton's husband, Jordon Christopher, who owned Arthur's in New York. He became our manager. In March of 1963, Freeman took us to New York to cut some demo records.

"There was just no way we could have done them in Toronto. The engineers at the studios were afraid to let the needles run into the red, and very few had had any real recording experience. We tried Hallmark, which was the best then. They had the same sort of equipment as I have now in my home in Los Angeles - a four- track Ampex recorder.

"We talked Freeman into spending some money on demos, and we cut four sides [which ended up later on Columbia's *John Kay and the Sparrow* album]. A guy called David Kapralik [who discovered Streisand and Mathis and now manages Sly and the Family Stone) heard us playing at Arthur's one night, and took our tape and his opinions to Columbia Records. The stuff we were playing at Arthur's was like nothing they'd ever heard before. Only Butterfield was playing that kind of material back then."

The Sparrow returned to Toronto to await further news. A deal was negotiated with Columbia, with Itapralik's company greased in as producers. The Sparrow flew back to New York for a month at Arthur's. Then came the Downtown Club in the west Village.

"The audience was mainly black. You really had to play. The crowd at Arthur's knew nothing about rock, but the Downtown was a real disco for people. They'd yell to have a record put on if you weren't getting it together. We really developed some stamina at that club."

A month later, the Sparrow was booked into The Barge on Long Island, a club which is located on a genuine barge. "One night there was a huge thunder storm and water poured in onto the stage. There were three power failures in an hour, we were getting shocks from everything, and there were only twenty people in the audience. We quit before we were all electrocuted."

The next day, the group received a telegram stating that their six week contract had been cancelled because they'd refused to play. Things were frankly, grim.

"I worked on Freeman's head and convinced him we should take a shot at California. We set off in a '65 Chevie wagon with a U-haul trailer full of equipment. After three days, everyone was convinced there was no California. I mean, we drove along Route 66 for days."

Eventually they reached Los Angeles, and landed two bookings one at the It's Boss Club (now Ciro's) and the other at the Whisky a Go Go. They were well received but their return gig at the Whisky took place on the same night as the Sunset Strip riots. Afterwards, the Whisky switched to an R & B booking policy and most of the other clubs closed down.

A friend convinced the Sparrow that they should move up to San Francisco. The friend also secured a booking for them at another barge-bound rock club, the Arc in Sausalito, which had recently booked in Moby Grape and Janis Joplin with little success. "We played on a strictly percentage basis," Kay recalls, "but we had a following within three weeks. There were Hell's Angels tripped out on acid, kids from San Francisco, locals. We had a more polished stage act than most of the Frisco bands, and more presence because of the New York experience."

One evening the group, just for fun, did a fifteen minute sound effect introduction to *The Pusher*. ("It wasn't going to be *The Pusher* but it just happened that way") and it tore the place up. The next night, Steve Miller was there; the group had to repeat their new version of *The Pusher*.

"It was non-musical music, but no one cared. Actually it developed into a blend of rock and the early twenties experimental electronic-symphonic stuff from Europe. The audiences took it to be a re-construction of the act of shooting dope. It evoked emotions."

The group's fame spread and it wasn't long before the Sparrow were being booked into the Fillmore and Avalon Ballrooms. On one particular night at the Avalon, the light show presented a special effects routine to go with *The Pusher* and it brought down the house. The Sparrow had been third on the bill. "It was the biggest success we'd had," says Kay.

At about this point, Columbia's interest in the group returned. They sent David Rubinson (who'd produced *The Time Has Come Today* for the Chambers Brothers) up to San Francisco to see where the group was at, musically and personally. "We later spent forty-eight hours in Columbia's studio getting nothing together. All we got were a few demos, which made up the rest of the *John Kay and the Sparrow* album."

To further confuse the issue, a rift developed within the group on what direction should be taken to gain recognition. Dennis Edmonton and Nick St. Nicholas wanted to do "a commercial thing"; Kay and the rest wanted to go wherever the music led, be it commercial or otherwise. There were also financial problems.

"In June of 1967, we split up. Dennis changed his name to Mars Bondfire and made solo records; Nick joined a Los Angeles group called Time."

And Kay? He got married and moved into an apartment in Los Angeles. Living next door was a friend of his wife (both girls had been cocktail waitresses in Toronto) who had just married Gabriel Mekler, a struggling record producer who'd worked with David Blue and the Lamp of Childhood.

"Gabriel wanted to get into a funkier thing. I played him some of the tapes we'd done and he said that if we could put together a group and rehearse ten songs, we could probably cut a demo album which he'd take up to Dunhill Records."

Kay had kept in close contact with Jerry Edmonton and Goldie McJohn, and they advertised for two other players. Kay selected the strongest songs from the Sparrow days, and they cut the demo album. Mekler took the tapes to Dunhill, who were suitably impressed. "We signed with them for a small monetary advance and a guarantee of two albums a year. They also said they'd release an album first. We'd worry about singles later.

118

"We cut the first album in only four days - eleven basic tracks were put down in the first two days; on the third I did the vocals and some percussion overdubs, and we mixed on the fourth day."

While all this was happening, the group had been thinking of a new name for itself. "We'd gotten a contract release from Columbia, but we didn't really want to use the Sparrow again. We went through all sorts of strange names - things like the Humble Fumbles because the lead singer was almost blind." After several fruitless weeks, Gabriel Mekler suggested that Steppenwolf might be a possibility. He'd just finished reading the outstanding Herman Hesse novel of the same name. The group liked the name, but it was six months later before Kay got around to reading the book himself.

"I had no inkling of what the book was all about when we first agreed to use the name. It was really strange - the main character of the novel is strangely representative of the same kind of alienation that people are going through now, even though the book was written long ago. The character drifts into a no man's land— between the establishment and total isolation. No side will accept him unless he conforms completely to their scene. The book has a great deal of relevance. And the name has been good to us, despite the fact that people in Tulsa, Oklahoma, still come up and ask which one of us is Stephen Wolf."

The first album came out and soon after, a single called *Born to Be Wild* roared to the top of the charts. It sold over 2,000,000 copies. There have been many other hits since - *Magic Carpet Ride, Move Over, Monster, Who Needs Ya?* There have also been six gold albums. Everything seemed smooth sailing for Steppenwolf. But late in 1970, a conflict developed between the group and its record company, Dunhill.

"We felt that *Steppenwolf 7* was the best album we'd done since the first LP and the *Monster* album. We really wanted to follow it with something even better, but it takes times to do that - time to rewrite songs, change parts, re-examine the processes.

"Then, completely without our knowledge, the company released an album of golden hits. The cover was designed by a company man. The group itself had designed the three previous covers, and then along came this abortion ... it was like a second rate New Orleans hooker covered in Woolworths' jewellery.

"We had no plans for a golden hits album. *Steppenwolf Live* had been something along those lines, but we didn't want another greatest hits thing out for at least a year.

"The company is paying dearly for that mistake. We worked out a new deal and we hit 'em where it hurts the most - in the accounting department.

"The main thing is that we've survived all the problems we've run into since leaving Yorkville. We've been through three bass players, the current man is George Biondo, two guitarists, (Larry Byrom joined the group late in 1970) three lawyers, two business managers, four road managers, six equipment men, and two sound men. Many times we had to start all over again. But now we've got it together. Our managers are our friends and we trust them. We have our own corporation, our own publishing companies, and we have one of the finest travelling road teams in the business. Ask any of the leading acts about that. We've also got a great PR man in Gary Stromberg, who really understands us."

Today Kay is far removed from the Canadian and Toronto music scenes by both time and space, yet he senses the situation. "It's weird, but to this day, I still picture Toronto as having lots of incredible groups who have yet to be discovered. It's sad that so many fine groups disappeared because of local apathy."

R. Dean Taylor

There are two sides to every tale, and this story is no different. R. Dean Taylor, Rare Earth recording artist, holds the minority view. He considers the CRTC local content legislation all wrong; he doesn't think Canadian radio stations should be made to play anything except what they want to. He believes CHUM is doing a great job for Canadian talent (his, anyway) and that most Canadian-made records are garbage.

He thinks there is a lot of talent in Canada but that no one knows how to record it. He is concerned about the long-term results of radio station reaction to the legislation.

All of this he says from Detroit, his home for the past seven years. Canadian radio stations play his records enthusiastically. Shortly after the legislation era began, CHUM was playing two of his singles. They qualified as Canadian content. R. Dean Taylor has had some U.S. success and he is therefore regarded as a real talent by Canadian broadcasters.

But it wasn't always that way. Indiana may want him now, but there was a time when nobody in Canada gave a damn whether he was alive or dead.

"I started out in 1961 playing piano and singing with various groups. We played Le Coq D'Or, the Edison, all the places. I made a couple of records for the Audiomaster label, which is out of business now, but was once distributed by Quality. The records didn't do anything. The studios were bad, there were no producers; they didn't get played.

"In early 1962, I went down to New York and cut a demo for Amy-Mala Records. It was a horrible record, but it received some attention. I came back to Toronto, and Amy-Mala wanted to sign me to a long-term contract.

"But a friend of mine in a Toronto advertising agency suggested I should try Detroit. He later went to work in Detroit himself, so I stopped off in the Motor City on my way to New York.

"I got to talk with Holland, Dozier and Holland, who were the top producers in the world before they left Motown in 1969. Brian Holland took a liking to me. As a result, I moved to Detroit and went to work with Motown.

"I was the ghost writer on many, many of the Holland-Dozier-Holland hits which came later. My name did appear on a couple of them - *I'll Turn to Stone* [Four Tops], *Love Child* [the Supremes], and that real bummer, *I'm Living in Shame* [the Supremes]. I used to go into the office everyday and write songs. It was a real drag."

Strange words, indeed, from an artist with Motown, a company whose acts have traditionally had absolutely nothing to say. The company had a strict policy in the sixties that its artists were forbidden to make any public comment on any subject of a controversial nature. This included the Vietnam war, even after Gallup polls had revealed that the majority of Americans were against the war.

With a little coaxing, Taylor has even more to lay down on the subject. "I think I was taken advantage of by Eddie Holland. I only got $800 for *You Keep Turning Away* [the Temptations], they gave me a third of the song on *I'll Turn to Stone*.

"But they took me when I had nothing. They gave me money and allowed me to go home occasionally. I wrote an enormous amount of songs for them. Some I was paid for; others I wasn't. Now I feel like I was shafted. But it was like going to school. The price I paid for the schooling was enormous [some of those copyrights are worth a small fortune now] but I still love them dearly.

"Brian Holland was the greatest record producer in the world.

I learned everything I know from Brian. He was better than Phil Spector or any of them. He was simply the best in the business."

Taylor had originally gone to Motown with the hope of becoming an artist-producer - not a ghost writer and odd session player. Eventually he was given his chance. "I'd been telling them for years that I wanted to be an artist, but no one took me seriously. Motown wasn't interested in white acts at that time; they wanted me to keep writing. I finally got a producer's contract in 1968 after a long battle.

"My experience with Brian Holland had given me the know-how to cut my own record, so I did a thing called *There's a Ghost in My House*, with help from Holland-Dozier-Holland. I think it was like a gratuity for having worked for them. My second single was *Let's Go Somewhere*, which in fact went nowhere because Motown just wasn't promoting white artists.

"But the third single, *Gotta See Jane*, which I produced by myself, did extremely well in England. It reached number six and was a gigantic record all through Europe. That made Berry Gordy Jr., the president of Motown, take notice of me as an artist. He got serious about white artists. They formed the Rare Earth label and put out *Indiana Wants Me*."

Despite a complete lack of critical acclaim from the rock press, *Indiana Wants Me* climbed to the number one spot on the U.S. charts, becoming the first white act from Motown to do so. "Berry Gordy says it's the most important breakthrough for Motown since its inception," claims Taylor. "Motown has always been labelled a black company; now it's a record company, full stop. It's another dimension.

"Rare Earth is only the first step into white talent at Motown. White artist tapes from all over the world have flooded the company since my record hit.

"Now Berry Gordy Jr. is personally handling my career. I'm going to be doing a TV special with the Jackson Five in the summer of 1971 and I'm working on a movie called *Tears on a Golden Circle*."

It's a new way of life for R. Dean Taylor, and a far cry from his old days in Toronto in the early sixties, pounding the Yonge Street pavements, trying to get help from Harold Moon of BMI, the performance rights association. Taylor admits it was "frustrating." He says he had a couple of bad managers but that the main problem was simply a case of "nothing happening".

Seven long years later, Taylor looks upon the Canadian scene with a somewhat jaundiced eye. He views the CRTC content ruling with much reservation, in fact he appears to think it is a bad omen for the future.

"I believe that if Canadian records were or are good records, they will be played. Anyone with any sense can see that it's not a good situation."

Taylor thinks most Canadian discs are not good ones. "I get between fifteen and twenty Canadian records a week coming across my desk and the majority of them are terrible - garbage. These people don't know the first thing about recording, about equalization, about setting up of microphones, about producing. But the Canadian theory is that if you throw enough shit against the wall, some of it must stick.

"Stations are being forced to play records they don't like. I know. I speak with them all the time. Guys in Toronto, Montreal, Winnipeg, Calgary, Vancouver. Do you know that for the first time even disc jockeys are turning off the studio monitors when some of these Canadian records have to be played? CKLW in Windsor is playing records that make you want to change stations.

"Canadian music directors have the Canadian flag jammed up their asses. American record company people are laughing at the lousy quality of Canadian records. Not one out of a thousand can stand up to American records. Look at the number of Canadian records released and how many make it? It's a joke."

I considered mentioning to Taylor that something like four hundred new records come out weekly in the U.S. and less than ten make the charts. I also considered asking him if he thought such U.S. hits as *Yummy Yummy Yummy*, *Gypsy Woman*, *Rose Garden* and even his own *Indiana Wants Me* were of such high artistic standards. But Taylor persisted.

"You can't take guys off the street and expect them to produce an international hit record. The market, the money, the facilities - they're all down here in the States. They can sell more records in Detroit and Chicago than the whole of Canada.

"Don't get me wrong though, I think Canadian talent is great. I always have. But I don't think it needs a crutch like government legislation to bring it to the surface. If it's good, it will make it."

When the subject of CHUM's initial refusal to play the Guess Who's *These Eyes* came up, Taylor dismissed it as an exception.

"I think CHUM is great. They've been good to me. But like a lot of other stations in Canada, they're very bitter about legislation. They don't want to be told what to play." Taylor admitted that CHUM might not have played them if they'd been recorded in Canada and had first release in the States. He agreed that if legislation would change this traditional inferiority thinking of many Canadians in the media, it would have done some good.

"I'd like to see a Canadian scene happen. But the way it's happening is a bad thing.

"The trouble is that there are no studios and no producers. They can't make records as good as we can in Detroit. What is needed is for producers from here to go up there and show people what to do. Capitol for instance should bring in some top U.S. producers, make it worth their while, let them show Canadians how it's done. That's the only way there'll ever be any good product coming out of Canada."

Import your technicians along with your tastes? Establish the branch plant and stifle the home grown? Where does that put the development of the Canadian music industry, the realization of its economic and artistic potentialities? How would Taylor solve a fifteen-year drought without seeding the clouds?

"I don't know. I really haven't got any answers," he says.

Whether one agrees or disagrees with the principle behind government legislation in the field of pop music, one has to admit that the CRTC is at least proposing some answers.

Neil Young

Just one day after the Canadian content regulations went into effect, Neil Young rolled into Toronto to play his first major concert at Massey Hall.

Of course, Neil had appeared in concert in Toronto many times before, but always as a second stringer. His last appearance, for example, had been a week's stay at the Riverboat Coffee House in Yorkville, in February 1969. In the two years since, Neil Young has become a major rock star and a cult hero in his own right.

His Massey Hall concert in January 1971 sparked an incredible audience response. After two standing ovations, Young - clearly suffering from a slipped disc which he'd somehow acquired on his ranch near San Francisco - returned backstage. The applause which followed was unlike anything I had ever witnessed in three years of covering rock concerts at Massey Hall. For at least ten long minutes, the packed audience cheered, shouted, stomped, clapped and roared for more.

Never had a Canadian been granted such enthusiastic acclaim by fellow Canadians. And the mere mention of Canada from the stage (in his song, *Helpless*, which refers to "a town in North Ontario") was greeted by a fierce howl of recognition and appreciation not characteristic of young Canadians in general. The concert was a highly rewarding and stimulating experience, in more than one way. Apart from Young's fine solo performance given under difficult personal conditions, I doubt if I'll ever forget the degree to which Canadians had at last shown they could support a Canadian rock artist.

Still, it was difficult to escape the irony that Young had only succeeded in gaining this acceptance by moving south. If Young had stayed in Canada, it is very likely that he would not have been heard of by record buyers to this day.

In the late summer of 1969, I had talked to Young about his early days in Canada. At the time, Young had just joined David Crosby, Stephen Stills and Graham Nash, and the group was to become known as Crosby, Stills, Nash and Young. Their success with only two albums was so immense that many people expected them to actually replace the fast-waning Beatles.

"I was brought up in Winnipeg," Young said, "and I quit school after failing grade nine. I'd failed once every two years for the past six years.

"As soon as I left school, I took off with a couple of guys to do a musical number. We made our first stop about four hundred miles from Winnipeg and we didn't have any bread or anything. We struggled along and did the number, like everyone does the number. I mean we toured around and tried to get gigs and couldn't get gigs and got fired and just went through the general bummer of it.

"I did that for about two years, and then settled in Toronto because that was where the music scene was supposed to be happening in

Canada. It sure wasn't happening in Winnipeg.

"I spent some time in Toronto training myself as a folk singer. But I soon realized that nothing was ever going to happen in Toronto. I split and went to Los Angeles. I was just completely fed up with the Canadian scene."

Within three days of arriving in California, Young met Steve Stills and joined a group which was being assembled by Stills. Known as the Buffalo Springfield, the group spent two years fighting management hassles. And then, just as the Springfield were starting to make their presence felt in the front guard of pop, they split up.

"The best things we did in the Springfield," Young told me "were on the *Buffalo Springfield Again* album: *Expecting to Fly, Hung Upside Down* and *Broken Arrow*. At times there was so much joy in the group that we'd embrace one another on stage. But there were bad things too.

"I couldn't go through the group thing again - the gigs at the Fillmore and so on. Too much noise, too many people around, the groupies, the creeps. When I wanted peace and quiet, I had to consult four other guys."

The management problems didn't help. Young recalled that one composer's $25,000 royalty check was whittled down to $1,000 after various people, managers and the like, had scooped out their share. But Young did come out on top with the Buffalo Springfield. He said he'd made $100,000 over the two years, of which $75,000 had been invested for him.

At the time Young decided to go solo, I remember writing that solo stars were as much in demand as a winter vacation on Baffin Island. But neither Young nor myself could have dreamed of what the future would hold in store for the tall, lean and unlikely pop star.

A few weeks later, Young announced that he had linked up with a back-up group called Crazy Horse. "There's three guys - guitar, bass and drums - and I'm playing lead guitar. I'm the boss. I wouldn't work as a member of a group again." Young and his Crazy Horse cut an album soon after which met with minor success. In July of 1969, his second album, *Everybody Knows This is Nowhere*, was released. The next month, Young made world music headlines with his decision to team up with Crosby, Stills and Nash.

Young used to drive up to Stills' house in Laurel Canyon every afternoon, more often than not with his old lady and daughter. They'd swim in the pool, talk, sit around sometimes, play incredible music.

On one occasion, the four superstars got together in a wing of Stills' house and jammed up a storm. The emotion in that soundproofed room was almost delirious - their personalities as well as their instruments spilled over into one another with a reckless abandon not usually associated with folk-oriented players such as these.

An hour later, Crosby was off brooding in a corner, Stills was clearly depressed by the current woman in his life, and Nash was rapping to a guy about guitars. I seized the opportunity to talk to Young about why he had joined up with another group, after vowing a year before that he was done with groups forever.

"The reason I was the last to join Crosby, Stills and Nash was because I really didn't think about it until after everybody else had already started. Then they came out and asked me to do it. I was doing my own thing, and they were doing their thing. When it didn't look like my joining the group would interfere too much with what I was already doing, I decided to give it a try. And I've learned a lot from those three cats. Just as I did from Steve Stills the first time around in the Springfield."

I asked Young what Crosby, Stills and Nash meant to him. "I don't know, I really don't know," he answered. "All I know is that everyday I get up and come up here and play and the music is groovy. The music is the only thing that keeps me in it.

"I'm not going to say that I don't like the money. I do like the money and it's going to make me a lot of money and that definitely plays a part in my being here. I think that's the way it is with everybody. If we weren't getting paid, we'd obviously be doing something else."

Although somewhat reserved about his role in Crosby, Stills, Nash and Young, he did reveal a strong affinity to the group's music. "This is the best band I've ever worked with. Definitely better than the Buffalo Springfield. Crazy Horse, the group that I did my second album with, is a great band in a different way. It's much more relaxing to play with Crazy Horse, but the music isn't as stimulating."

Only two LPs have so far been released with the Crosby, Stills, Nash and Young line-up. The first was titled *Deja Vu*; the second, *Four Way Street*. The former sold close to three million copies internationally. Cut in a marathon eight hundred hours of studio time, it was also hailed as one of the finest rock albums ever recorded. Young wrote two of the tracks *Helpless* and *Country Girl*, and co-wrote *Everybody I Love You* with Stills.

"I don't really know what it is that I'm giving these guys. *Deja Vu* is going to be funkier than the first Crosby, Stills and Nash album. It's going to have more of a down-home feeling about it than the first album. I don't know if that's because of me, or because of everybody playing together or what. It's really hard to say.

Young wasn't too sure of his composing role within the framework of the group. "There'll be two or three of my songs on *Deja Vu*," he said, "but I serve an instrumental function. On the first Crosby, Stills and Nash album, Steve Stills played organ, guitar and bass, but everybody knows that Stevie can't play organ, guitar and bass on stage all at once, and sing too. They had to get somebody else as an instrumentalist, and it happened that I was the only one they could get to do it. I'm not the only one that can do it, but I am the only one they could get at the time.

"I write songs; I consider myself more of a writer than a guitar player, but in this band, I think I'm more of a guitar player than a writer."

The others speak of Neil with apparent love and respect. Says David Crosby, "I've known Neil for the past four years and I've watched him the whole time. I first met him when he was in the Springfield. Neil and Steve could make their guitars sing a duet.

"Neil writes really incredible songs. He has written some of my personal favorites, and there are some of his tunes which I rate as classics. He has two of them on one album - *Broken Arrow* and *Expecting to Fly*. Those two tunes absolutely floored me. *Mr. Soul* isn't exactly bad either. He's a fine writer, that's all I can say."

Graham Nash: "Neil at first comes on negative, but you realize that his negativity is in fact, positive, but expressed in a matter of fact way. Neil is very direct."

Stephen Stills: "Neil is just about my best friend in the whole world. If you really want to know what I think of Neil, there's a song he wrote about what he thinks of me called *On The Way Home*. That's pretty much where it's at. "We know each other and we're both people that grew up where our whole clan was kind of different from everyone else. There was always a certain kind of alienation to the people around us, and there are old things that no amount of analysing and psychotherapy and all of that stuff can wash away. The scars stay. You have to fight it yourself and we both see and understand it in each other. I mean, we can look each other in the eye."

It was within the framework of Crosby, Stills, Nash and Young that one finally began to realize some of the reasons behind Neil Young's musical accomplishments. When Young goes in, he goes in with all he's got. He becomes totally involved. And paradoxically, the price of musical perfection is personality hassles. Neil has proved on several occasions that he can go through in one year what it takes most people a lifetime to experience.

Less than a year after these conversations took place, Crosby, Stills, Nash and Young was no longer. There was no formal announcement of a disintegration, nor was there need for one. After one North American tour, Stills split to London to cut a solo album. Nash and Crosby went off on a sailing cruise. Young was left to his own devices.

He cut an album, *After the Gold Rush* (his third as a solo artist), which became a million seller within two weeks of release in the fall of 1970. Later in the year, he undertook his final concert tour (without Crazy Horse) before retiring for twelve months.

Parts of the tour, which included New York's Carnegie Hall, gigs in Vancouver, Edmonton and Winnipeg, and also the aforementioned Massey Hall concert in Toronto, were recorded as sections of Young's fourth solo album.

"It's going to be a chronology of my songs, starting from the Buffalo Springfield days," Young told me in a Los Angeles hospital, where he was being treated for the slipped disc. "I really want to get this tour together. I've done three tours with Crazy Horse, two with the bigger band and now I'm ready to just wrap it up. I want to bring it back to the roots again, and then I'm going to take a year off the road." He had also planned to write and direct a movie, in which he would likely have a small walk-on part.

Danny Whitton, the leader of Young's old group Crazy Horse which was planning to go out on the road without Neil, had an interesting comment to make on Young's future. "Neil likes to play in groups, but basically he's a solo artist. I don't think he'll ever stay with any group for very long. Deep down, he knows that he has to do the gig himself."

And very likely he will. Young has already demonstrated, on more than one occasion, tremendous determination. He survived the barren environment of the Canadian music scene in the sixties, and he continued to prosper through the expiration of two globally recognized groups. Though now an American citizen, he has taken Canada to the far distant corners of the world. It is likely that several hundred thousand people heard the word "Ontario" for the first time in the context of Neil's *Helpless* song on the *Deja Vu* album.

Neil perhaps best describes the real Neil Young when he talks of his ambitions. "I don't think about that very much. I just go from day to day. I don't really have any artistic goals other than trying to do a good job and play what I think is right. My music is not sophisticated. In some ways, it used to be in the second Springfield album. I was into a whole sophistication trip, but I'm not on that any more. I'm just as comfortable playing with someone who doesn't even know how to play, as long as they have the feeling.

'That's all that matters to me. That's why it's pleasing for me to play by myself. I have a good time playing by myself."

5. THE HORIZON

At the same moment as you read this sentence, thousands of Canadian artists from Victoria to Newfoundland are contemplating world fame in the light of an era when domestic records are daily becoming hits at home and abroad.

No longer do our young musicians think of Los Angeles and New York as the only places where records are made. No longer are discs beyond the scope of a Canadian group. Every day there is a producer cutting a world-standard record somewhere in Canada. There are now at least two hundred Canadian acts actively recording in this country, and many of them are turning out hits.

Of course there is still no guarantee that every record will be a hit. There is no automatic assumption that every band which finds itself on disc will ultimately become a super group. But there are records, and when there are records and radio stations who will play those records, there will be hits.

In this chapter, we cross this huge country and rap with many of the acts most likely to succeed and a few who already have. These are just some of the names which will transmit Canadian music to the globe tomorrow, next year, and in the years to come.

Aarons and Ackley

You wouldn't normally expect a young man who had gone on the road with the Beach Boys and had written material for Don Ellis to turn up in Toronto. If it hadn't been for the Vietnam war, it may never have happened.

Jim Ackley arrived in Toronto in February 1969 "to avoid the draft". His musical partner, Chuck Aarons, had been to Canada several times prior to 1969; he liked it here, and he kept coming back.

Chance played a hand in the meeting of the two in August of 1970. Says Ackley: "Chuck had come up to Toronto to work with Rolf Kempf, who I think is probably the best songwriter in North America, on an album for A & M. When he arrived he had no money and nowhere to stay. I met him through a mutual friend, producer Dennis

Murphy, and I suggested he should spend some time at my place.

"I'd been very much into music in my hometown, Los Angeles. I worked with the Beach Boys on the road for a couple of years, and I wrote *Diamond Head* on their *Friends* album. I did a lot of writing for Don Ellis, and arranged and played on a really fine P. F. Sloan single, *I Can't Help But Wonder Elizabeth*. I don't think it was ever released, which is a pity.

"When I first arrived in Canada, I hoped to get into something musically. But because of a lack of bread, I took a job sorting out books for a publisher. Later on, I got a job at Capitol Records. It wasn't what I really wanted to do but I was meeting people and starting to get my own lifestyle in order."

One of the people he met in December 1969 was John Lennon. Ackley acted as Capitol's man-on-the-spot at Ronnie Hawkins' Mississauga farm while the Lennons were in residence. Apart from the fact that he accidentally set fire to a shed while burning waste paper for Lennon, he performed his duties well.

But Aarons and Ackley was still nine months away. "When Chuck came to stay, we didn't talk about music at all. But after a few days, we sat down and played a bit. It was terrific ... I was as nervous as hell because I hadn't played the piano for ages. In any case, I was always primarily a jazz musician; I got into rock because of economics, but I became more interested as the music developed after The Beatles.

"Chuck and I played just those songs we both knew, things like *Old Man River*. We did this for a few nights and then Chuck brought out a song he'd written a year earlier. It was called *Willy Boy*, and it needed a bridge, I came up with a chord sequence. That's how the songwriting thing happened."

Two weeks later, Aarons and Ackley were considering a return to the music scene as a duo. "Nobody was working with just a piano and guitar. Within three weeks, we had written five songs for a possible album."

The album project began after Capitol's A & R chief, Paul White, had shown interest in a "very rough demo" that the duo had cut. "We did five songs in forty minutes - all very 'untogether.' But Paul felt there was something there." After consulting with the New York A & R people, Capitol decided to sign Aarons and Ackley for international release.

The first album was cut with Dennis Murphy, who'd returned to his hometown of Toronto after working with Elektra Records in New York. "He did a fine job on the album," says Ackley. "Actually, we were very, very pleased with it. There's some straightahead electrical stuff, some down acoustic things, some heavy vocal numbers and some laid back stuff. I think the LP offers a lot of variety."

The album was released in the spring of 1971. It was cut at Eastern Studios in Toronto.

Aarons and Ackley planned to go on the road, but in a highly selective manner. "It might sound crazy, but we want to pick and choose the gigs. The money is of little concern - we want the concerts to have some integrity to them. I've been on the road in the past as a sideman, and I don't really dig it that much."

Chuck Aarons has also paid his road dues. Born in the midwest, he moved to New York and studied classical guitar. He played with a lot of people on a lot of records, and his background was "rock 'n' roll, with folk thrown in".

But, says Ackley, "the time had to come when I wanted to find out if I had anything to offer as an entertainer in my own right." Aarons is free to travel back and forth to the U.S. because of a 4-F draft classification. Ackley, however, cannot return. "I left Los Angeles with the knowledge that it was never going to be my home again. I came here and went through the bad times, but to come up with something like this — wow, it's more than an accident.

"I think too that people are starting to wake up to the fact that there's a hell of a lot happening in Canada, more originality, more excitement than in the U.S."

Bush

Don Troiano, lead guitarist with Bush, was talking about the Toronto music scene in the mid-sixties.

"The tragedy is that so many really first class musicians went down the spout; some went heavy into dope, others split because of the futility of it all. Some of those cats are pumping gas and mending roofs now, man, and many of them were super fine musicians. A lot of us got fucked up and some will never forget it. And you can't blame them."

Troiano, a veteran of that scene himself and one of the very few that survived, speaks with concern on the subject of Canadian music. He is especially bitter about radio stations in Canada, and the disinterest they showed in the Mandala, of which Troiano was an integral member. The Mandala were the closest Canada ever got to achieving international music recognition in the mid-sixties. Had a couple of breaks gone their way, it might well have been the Mandala who opened the U.S. chart door to the Guess Who.

"It's hard to be objective," says Troiano frankly, "but the Mandala were doing better musical things five years ago than most bands are doing now. If we'd been given a chance on radio in Canada, I think we might have had a good shot at the U.S, scene. That was always the problem - the radio stations in America always wanted to know how your record was doing in Canada. When you said 'nothing,' they automatically figured you weren't any good. They had no understanding of the domestic situation in Canada then."

The history of Troiano, who came to Toronto from Italy when he was fifteen, and his fight for survival in the music jungle is typical.

"I started playing guitar in 1961. There wasn't much of a scene then, but someone gave me a guitar, and two weeks later I was out playing with a band.

"At that time, there were only about six popular local bands in Ontario. There was Johnny Rhythm and the Suedes, Bobby Dean and the Gems, Little Caesar and the Consuls, the Silhouettes, and Little Anthony and the Road Runners. They had the clubs locked up tight.

"They were all seven or eight piece groups, very R & B oriented musicians who used horns. I was headed in that direction early in my career. Every group in those days had the same basic lineup so they could play this hard stuff - bass, guitar, drums, piano, two horns and a singer.

"I was always lucky. I was usually in good bands, and we influenced a lot of other groups. The bands that were really popular in live performance were not doing commercial material. Some of them could draw a thousand people to a dance, which is unheard of now. The band I was in with Robbie Lane got to be pretty good, but I was still in school."

Considering that Toronto groups had been able to draw fans to performances, one wonders why it did not naturally follow that they would make records. This is the usual process of events in England, the U.S. and most other places.

"I thought recording was for superstars only. I mean, one just didn't think of ever making a record. That was always synonomous with the U.S. business; if you were in Los Angeles, you'd make a record. But in Toronto, never. It just didn't happen."

Ronnie Hawkins zoomed into Toronto shortly after that, bringing with him U.S. ideas and money. "He was talking about starting a record company, so we worked with him for a while. But then he decided he wanted to do a really commercial number, and we weren't into that at all."

Then came The Beatles; any hope of creating a music scene in Canada was squashed under the massive weight of the English invasion. Radio stations developed an attitude to English records which approached idolatry.

Don Troiano, happily, was one of the people who (with inside knowledge of the U.S. blues scene) thought the early Beatles records were atrocious. "The guitar work was sloppy and amateurish. I said to myself, 'I've spent two years trying to get something good happening on my instrument. Now we've got to turn around and do something like that?'

"A few months later, Ronnie Hawkins brought up a guy from Nashville, guitar player Fred Carter, to cut some records with Toronto groups. It was awful. All of those people had a fixed idea in their minds of what the group had to play. You had no choice - record it their way or don't record at all. The rules were ridiculous: the bass player had to use a pick, the guitarist had to play on the second and fourth beats. It just didn't seem right to go about it the way we did.

"The records came out nonetheless, and they received a little airplay. Ronnie had a better chance than most people. He'd have all the disc jockeys down to Le Coq D'Or, and he'd buy them booze, take them to parties, get them broads. It was pretty far out.

"But nothing really happened with the records, so I split over to the Blue Note, which was becoming an important club for rock cats. The recording scene stagnated for a few years; the only things you ever heard were by Bobby Curtola.

"An additional problem in Canada was that all the bands were into rhythm 'n' blues, but the radio stations wouldn't play black songs if they were anywhere near funky. The music directors would do anything to keep R & B off the air. So we all tuned into a station in Buffalo and picked up on the real stuff.

"We formed a group called the Rogues [Crowbar keyboards player

Joey Chirowski was a member at one point] and played the Blue Note. All the agencies said we didn't stand a chance because people weren't ready for that kind of music. They didn't hear it on the local radio, so they figured it would never be popular with kids. I don't believe it yet."

In 1966, the Rogues changed their name to the Mandala. Soon after, they cut a demo record, more for their own amusement than anything else. "It must have been the first bootleg record. Some cat got hold of one of the demos, and pressed up two hundred copies. Kids would come up to us at dances and say they'd bought a copy of our record for ten dollars. It was incredible."

At that time the Mandala consisted of Troiano, drummer Whitey Gian and singer and ex-choir boy Roy Kenner. "We got a manager, Randy Markowitz, who was dynamite compared to the other rock managers in Canada. Randy changed the whole scene. He made the act professional; he was aggressive. He put our price at $1000 per gig.

"We cut a record, *Opportunity*, and it was released in Canada. CHUM wouldn't play it because of some old hassles with the music director. But they couldn't ignore the number of fans we had built up over the previous four years. Those kids had come to see us every weekend, and they really wanted to hear our first record. When CHUM refused to play it, almost two hundred Mandala freaks picketed the station. It shocked the hell out of them.

"You wouldn't believe the kind of things Randy had to do to get CHUM to play our records. I began to realize that you couldn't be what you wanted to be, and still be popular with everyone.

"We were desperately keen to do our number as a Canadian thing. But you got tired of that when everybody in the media was trying to screw you. We couldn't get any space in any of the papers except with sensational stuff, like girls ripping off their clothes or fainting at our gigs. Nobody would write about our music - they refused to believe that a Canadian band could actually make music.

"In the fall of 1968, we went out west for the first time. Our records hadn't even been played there. It was the same in Montreal. But we drew fairly well due to word-of-mouth and Randy's hustling.

"Eventually we decided that we had to go to the States. You just couldn't keep playing to a thousand people a night and hope to reach the world ... it would take all of your life."

The Mandala caused a commotion in the States. "In the U.S. they couldn't believe what we were doing. In Canada, they wouldn't believe that we were doing anything." But they started to take notice when the American rock pundits started to rave about the Mandala. Quite possibly, if they'd had the right record company working for them at the time, the Mandala would have conquered the world. But depressed by poor record company promotion, the group became homesick and returned to Toronto.

"Despite the press we'd had from the States, Toronto was still the same. People would tell you to your face that you weren't good enough. Music directors would tell you to beat it because they'd never play your records. We changed record companies, and had a near-hit in the U.S. with *Love-Itis*. But it was the last straw, and we finally quit."

The group travelled to Arizona, where they spent a summer reorganizing. They emerged from the desert sun as a new group, Bush, with a new bass player, Prakash. Signed by Reb Foster in Los Angeles, who also manages Steppenwolf and Three Dog Night, they cut an album for Dunhill in 1970. As good as it was, the album was lost in the plethora of new releases in the U.S.

Midway through 1971, Bush broke up. Troiano was more determined than ever to succeed in the States. He teamed up with some other musicians and started work on a solo album. There was also widespread talk that the new group would be doing some work with David Clayton-Thomas, including session gigs for his solo album.

"I'm interested in being a musician," says Troiano. "As long as that scene keeps getting better, I'm happy. There's two things in the music game - the music and the business. Music is my gig; the business, thank god, doesn't get in my way."

Terry Bush

Terry Bush is not the average Canadian rock star. He is married and has three kids. He owns an extremely successful commercial jingle company. And he's been playing guitar for more than fifteen years.

Bush was twelve years old when he first picked up a guitar, and the rock 'n' roll era was still two years' distant. "When rock came along, like everybody else, I just jumped in. But I had the advantage of two years of playing experience, which was more than most of the guys around."

Early in the rock era, Bush joined a band which toured the U.S. for nine months. He returned to Toronto, unimpressed, and went back to college.

In the early sixties, he teamed up with singer Robbie Lane and went to work with Ronnie Hawkins for a year. "It was the best road experience I ever got" Bush recalls. "Ronnie could enthuse a group. He might have underpaid them but they were always enthusiastic."

Guitarist Don Troiano was a member of Hawkins' band at that time. It was the first group Hawkins had assembled since the Hawks left him, and Bush says there was tremendous incentive for the group to play well. "We were filling in after a really fine group and that made us try all the harder."

When Robbie Lane split to do the national TV series, *It's Happening* (originally called *A Go Go '66*), Bush went with him. "After three years with the show, I decided to split. I got into writing and recording commercial jingles." Bush's amazing versatility on several instruments enabled him to gain quickly a foothold in the fiercely competitive jingle business.

Early in 1970, he got together with record producer Terry Brown to rap about making some rock 'n' roll records. Brown was enthusiastic, and the two decided to cut a commercial version of a song which Bush had written for the Council on Drug Abuse (CODA).

"The song had been played all over the country in the anti-drug commercials, and stations had been receiving requests for a rock version. So we went in and cut one." The song was called *Do You Know What You're Doing?* and Bush played everything on the disc except drums. It received extensive airplay just prior to the legislation period, and RCA in the U.S. picked it up for international release.

Meanwhile, Bush was working with Terry Brown on his first album, which from first indications, looked like a real barnstormer. "It's so nice to be working in a world class studio," Bush said. "That's what I think prevented the development of the Canadian music scene in the sixties. Sure the radio stations were rough on local talent, but the lack of studios didn't help either.

"It was frustrating when you'd get something nice happening in a band, and then you just couldn't get it down in the studio. About five years ago, there were only three good studios in Toronto, all three-track. It was the big thing then. A while after came four-track, just as the Americans moved up to eight-track. When Canada finally reached that, the States were into sixteen- track.

"But it wasn't only equipment. Often they had adequate equipment but no one knew how to work it properly. Canada was always behind the times in the old days. It's great to see that changed. Toronto Sound, for example, is as good as any studio I've seen anywhere in the world, and Terry Brown is, of course, an internationally famous engineer."

Bush has no plans to go on the road, should he achieve record success. "I'm not a good entertainer. I know it and I don't fool myself. But I'm at home in the studio. That's where I do my road work.

"With the jingle business going so well, I'm in no great panic to make it. I'll just wait until the right thing comes along and hope it's a hit. But I must admit I'm starting to get a little excited about it all."

Christmas

Of all the strangely named rock groups in Canada - and there are quite a few - no one has yet come up with a name quite as mysterious as Christmas. But an unusual name is the least impressive of this Oshawa group's many qualifications.

Christmas boasts the youngest membership of any rock group in the upper strata of Canadian bands. It is without doubt the hardest rock act in the country. After hearing the group's *Heritage* album one critic was moved to write, "England has Led Zeppelin; America has Grand Funk Railroad; and Canada has Christmas."

When the *Heritage* album arrived on the market in late 1970, two members of Christmas were still sixteen - drummer Rich Richter and bass player Tyler Reizanne. Lead guitarist Robert Bulger was a mere eighteen and the group's leader-writer-singer, Bob Bryden, nineteen.

Many radio stations shied away from such a hard group. Others were highly impressed and devoted lengthy amounts of airtime to two of the longest cuts on the *Heritage* album. One of the tunes, *Zephyr Song*, probably shows more than anything else just how advanced Christmas music is to the Canadian contemporary scene.

"We wrote the song late in 1969," explains Bob Bryden, "and it often reaches as long as twenty minutes in concert. It consists of seven sections, and it tells a science fiction story about Red China causing World War III. A group of children escape in a space ship and live among the stars while the earth is destroyed." Another track, *April Mountain*, features graceful, surrealistic lyrics. Clearly, Christmas is not just another rock group bashing out twelve-bar blues tunes from an old Muddy Waters album.

Bob Bryden, for example, spent four years in the Oshawa music scene before the legislation era began. Most of his friends think of him as a genius. It's no surprise to learn he didn't last long in school; the pressure to conform was too great for such a sensitive poet, lyricist and musician as Bryden.

"I just up and quit," he says with some pride. "I got fed up with it. They're flogging a dead horse. They'd say learn your schoolwork and you'll always have something to fall back on. But I'd rather have it the other way around. Music is the thing I am going to fall back on. In any case, I hate regimentation of any kind, which rules out school."

The three other Christmas members feel the same way. All are school system drop-outs. All have worked hard to raise the money to pay monthly instalments on instruments. Music is all they live for. Christmas' dedication is the sort which in the end brings rewarding results. One does not need any crystal balls to see that Christmas is going to be one of the most important hard rock groups ever to take up guitars in Canada.

"I was never into bright lights music and the stage suits," Bryden says. "San Francisco epitomized what I wanted to do musically with my life."

Christmas had been together for a year when the *Heritage* album came out. "For the first couple of years in music," Bryden recalls, "I fooled around with a lot of different groups. Then in the middle of 1969, I got into writing and that changed my whole outlook on being a musician. From then on, I wanted to put together a group which could express what I wanted to say in the most positive and professional terms."

Christmas came about during the Christmas of 1969 - at least the name did. "Christmas struck me as being one of the most savagely original names you could imagine for a rock group."

At the time Bryden was in a band called Reign Ghost. The singer with the group was Linda Squires, who also starred in the Toronto production of *Hair*. Reign Ghost cut one album for the Allied Company. "We did it with two mikes on a two-track tape recorder.

It was strictly a one-take-per-song production but the experience in the studio environment just blew my mind. From then on, I became fanatical about music. It became my whole life."

Linda Squires split for the *Hair* role, and Bryden looked around for a lead guitarist. A few days later he found Robert Bulger and the group was renamed Christmas. "I'd finally found the group I was looking for. The name Christmas was very representative. Although our music is heavy, it is optimistic. In part, it's also peaceful. And Christmas is something to get into the spirit of."

Christmas rehearsed for several months in an abandoned air force barracks at the Oshawa airport before being discovered by Love Productions.

"In one year, we'd seen a whole era of Canadian music slip by. We went from a two-track studio to a sixteen-tract studio with plenty of time in which to get the right sound, and from an Ontario release to an international release."

Rapping with Bryden, you get the feeling that he is one of a rare breed - a musician who puts practicality before whim, honesty before dream. "I suffer from an inferiority complex, but I'm really a perfectionist. I can be very impatient. What I'm trying to do is create the highest quality music. My ambition is to have my songs evolve to a high standard and to keep them there."

After a lack of any large sales success on the debut Christmas album, the group went back into the studio and compromised somewhat with a thoroughly commercial version of a Neil Sedaka tune, *Sing Me (I'm a Song)*.

Bryden says he'll use almost any method to project the group to the masses. "What I've always wanted to do musically is what The Beatles did - to take all forms of music, poetry and art, and combine them into a new music."

You could hardly deny that he and Christmas have made a strong start in that direction.

Bobby Curtola

Bobby Curtola, Canada's only teen idol of the early sixties, always refers to himself with the royal plural. "It was something else when we started," he recalls. "We had to find our own way. They told us that you couldn't do it in Canada. You needed a U.S. hit.

"But coming from the sticks - compared with the U.S. or Toronto - we didn't know any better. So we just went ahead and tried to do it without knowing you couldn't, and in the end we succeeded."

Curtola takes a deep breath. "We were like the first Dairy Queen in Canada. We started a lot of trends. We had thirty-two top ten records out of forty-six records we released. We opened the west and other tour routes to all Canadian artists. We had to rub shoulders with Elvis Presley and Roy Orbison and Bobby Rydell to do it. But the kids went crazy for us.

"We never paid anybody, we never bought anybody. We just had a lot of grassroots support. Nobody was hotter than we were in Canada. I always say 'we' because we're a team: everyone has their role. I just get up on the stage and entertain. That's my part. "

That's how Bobby Curtola, at the ripe old age of twenty-six (he swears it), describes how it was between 1960 and 1965, when he was Canada's only answer to the American rock 'n' roll idol invasion. His success is living testimony to the music business adage that if at first you don't succeed, you should keep punching anyway.

Bobby Curtola, Gordon Lightfoot and Ronnie Hawkins were the only three Canadians who not only survived, but succeeded in the wasteland that was Canadian music in the sixties. Curtola's story is one that will probably never be repeated, now that the legislation era has arrived. The obstacles which he overcame in both Canada and the U.S. during the period of dominence are quite literally, extraordinary. The fact that he continued to prosper into the seventies, albeit in a different area of music, says more for Curtola's working knowledge of the industry and his rapport with old fans, than any essay on his ability could hope to achieve.

His first professional engagement - a high school assembly in his home town of Thunder Bay, Ontario - took place in 1959. "Before then, I'd only sung for my family, to earn a quarter now and then.

"We did well at the assembly. I don't know whether it was fate or luck but the kids in Thunder Bay seemed to like us. We got lots of newspaper space and we had a lot of work in the area.

"I went to school with the son of a local songwriter, Dyer Hurton. He wanted to get some of his songs out before he died. One day he called and asked if I wanted to sing on a record. I just couldn't believe it.

"The record, *Hand in Hand With You*, was cut on a mono tape recorder at a local radio station. We had to do all of the record in one take - there were no spare tracks for over-dubbing. Hurton got some of his relatives to sing the background parts, and after about twenty-five tries, we had a good take ... the sound was unbelievable.

"We took it to some of the record companies in Toronto, but they weren't interested. We decided that the only way to get the record out was to start our own record company, which we did. It was called Tartan Records.

"The Toronto companies advised us not to press more than a thousand copies; we sold that many the first day it came out. It was first released in February 1960. In July, a couple of Toronto stations played it.

"It wasn't until the fifth record, *Don't You Sweetheart Me*, that we started to get real national radio action. Getting on those charts was just hell. If they think it's hard now, they should have been around then. It was virtually impossible.

"*Cashbox* was the bible. If you were on the *Cashbox* charts, the radio stations would play your record. Otherwise, forget it."

Finally, Bobby's persistence - and the angry phone calls of his fans - brought some major market plans for his records. It was around that time that Gordon Lightfoot asked him, "How the hell did you get such a fan club going for you?"

In 1964, two of Curtola's singles, *Fortune Teller* and *Aladdin*, made both the Canadian and U.S. charts. But the U.S. company offered little support. "We had no promotion. Ask Bobby Vinton about it. I was competing with his *Roses are Red* in many places in the States. But we couldn't get out of the contract.

"With our next two records, *Indian Giver* and *Three Rows Over* we tried to handle the distribution from Canada. We were shipping into the States and getting lots of airplay, but the U.S. Government put an embargo on Canadian records being exported to the States. Export of Canadian discs into the U.S. was impossible. So we just had to sit it out, and wait until the contract ended.

"As a result, I wasn't really able to take advantage of the success I'd gained with hit records in the States. I did a few tours, but nothing significant. The contract ran out late in 1964, and Dick Clark, the American disc jockey, was all set to get me signed to Capitol Records when The Beatles hit. That ended that. I often talk to Dick and we laugh about it now.

"In a way, I'm glad that we didn't do too much in the States. American teen idols were managed and manipulated; one was only as good as one's last hit. Nowadays, people dig you for what you are, and what you can do on stage. If we had a Stateside hit now, we would be able to take full advantage of it."

One thing which initially boosted Curtola's career was his involvement with Coca-Cola. "We were the first people to record a jingle that didn't sound like a jingle, one that actually sounded like a song. That started a world trend. Coke did all their jingles with artists after that.

"I have fond memories of my association with Coke. They used me to promote their product all over Canada. They figured that they couldn't get a better salesman that Bobby-on-the-spot, and the Coke promotion tied in with all my appearances. We even pioneered playing shopping plazas. Coke followed us wherever we went, and we went everywhere. Only ourselves and Revene the Hypnotist were covering the entire country from Vancouver to Newfoundland in those days."

Curtola has visited every province in Canada and has missed playing only the Yukon - and he and booking agent-friend Maria Martell are working on that one.

"In the end, the association with Coke hurt us a bit. We had a lot of trouble getting some of our records played because radio stations didn't want to seem to be favoring one product over others."

But Curtola the teen idol was faced with a tough decision by 1967. He'd cooled off at dances and in the record stores, and it was necessary to make the transition to an adult artist - no easy task for a former rock star. "We went through hell; it was the crossroads of my life. I'm not really religious but I realized at that time there was more to life than a new car and a motel room ... you need a spiritual purpose. My own real purpose is to help those who need help."

Curtola made the transition with ease, and became even more popular in nightclubs across Canada than almost any American artist. Perhaps because of jealousy, perhaps for other reasons, Curtola's changeover caused a lot of bitter comment from other Canadian artists. This is probably why he now speaks out strongly against the lack of respect and cooperation within the Canadian music industry. "As far as the future of the Canadian music business is concerned, we badly need to get together in the artistic ranks. We should brag about each other. The Americans are great at that. We need a sense of comradeship, a love for each other, more co-operation among ourselves. There is room enough for all of us. We should not put each other down; that will never bring more recognition to Canada.

"The Americans are starting to look up here with watering mouths. But so many Canadian performers are small. You can say I'm old hat or whatever you like but we've got to team together. I'm the last one to blow my own horn, but I've done a lot for Canadians. Others have done a lot for me, and I really appreciate it. Dammit ... all the possibilities are here.

"We've got to start a star system, we've got to get the CBC to plug more than just one Canadian artist. Far too many people do not get the recognition they deserve in Canada. Gordon Lightfoot, Ronnie Hawkins, Gene Maclellan, Tommy Hunter, Walt Grealis - they should be recognized and given credit for their contributions."

Curtola recently signed a record distribution deal with Capitol Records, and had a new album planned for spring of 1971. "We're going after something new. There's a shortage of good original material so we're taking the best of the contemporary standards from everywhere. We believe it could happen all over again for us."

Curtola is the first to admit that things are a lot easier now than when he started, mainly due to the CRTC. "Finally everyone is realizing that this is a business. It operates on dollars and cents. In the old days, the record companies only put out U.S. hits; it was a simple process and a sure money-maker. Radio stations played only U.S. hits; they thought it would bring them the highest ratings.

"The record companies were affiliates of the U.S. companies, and they couldn't imagine Canadian talent making them any money so they stayed out of it. Now, of course, they are investing in local talent. But only because now it's likely to make them money - it's a damn good investment.

"It's a pity that we weren't able to get a music scene together without the government having to step in. But all I can say is, 'Mr. Juneau, God Bless you'."

The Dorians

Kingsville is a sedate little town of 3,500 people, situated about thirty miles from Windsor, Ontario. It's not the sort of place one would normally expect to produce a hit rock group, but in the case of the Dorians, that is exactly what has happened.

John Unger, twenty-one, is the lead singer and writer of some of the Dorians' material. He's been in the music business since he was eight years old.

"I studied violin for six years, and then I picked up guitar. Lately I've been doing some violin. I think there's a place for it in rock music, I really do."

Unger worked in a couple of local bands (the Small Town Boys and the Living Ends) before starting up the Dorians with bass player Bob Nixon, who had also played in the Living Ends. Nixon is another composer in the group. "Our manager gave us the name Dorians, because we're heavily into progressive music. We play in three-quarter time, and we jam a lot. The Dorian mode in music implies free form." My dictionary says 'of or having to do with Doris or its inhabitants.' In any event, says Unger, "We liked the name, and we've stuck with it, even when we added another member." The complete Dorians lineup is John Unger, Bob Nixon, lead guitarist Bill Loop and drummer Mike Bets.

"We were in Windsor a couple of years ago, just fooling around in an attic which had been converted into a studio. While we were there, this man from Detroit, Floyd Jones, walked in and said we had something happening. He'd been in the Ray Charles band, and was an arranger and session man at Motown Records. He said he'd like to produce us and we were interested."

The first record they cut, *Psychedelic Lipstick*, was issued in several overseas markets but not in North America. The second single, *Help for My Waiting*, was a completely different story. Released in early winter, 1970, the record did not arouse immediate attention, but when the legislation era began, it was on the chart at CKLW, the powerful Windsor station which rates number one in both Detroit and Cleveland.

At the same time, the group was working on its first album. "We've been in the studio continually since *Help for My Waiting* came out. Floyd Jones has a fascinating concept of making the music. We play electric guitars without amplifiers. It's really good for getting the vocals together. The rehearsals last longer, but it's easier on your nerves, and you can get into some better things. Floyd doesn't believe in leaving a stone unturned."

Prior to the start of the legislation era, the group hadn't even been to Toronto. "If the Windsor thing hadn't worked out, I guess we would have gone to Toronto to try and get something happening. But as it did happen, we didn't need to. Detroit is only forty miles away and they've got everything we need there."

Edward Bear

Edward Bear auditioned more than 150 different drummers, and actually jammed with fifteen of them, before deciding that Larry Evoy was the player they wanted. It proved to be a wise decision. Evoy not only became Edward Bear's drummer, but also its lead voice and original songwriter.

One of his songs, *You Me and Mexico*, written about a girl he'd still loved when she left for Mexico, became one of the biggest hits to rise from Canada in 1970, and elevated the group to international prominence.

But a second single was not the hit that the first had been. By January 1971 it appeared as though Edward Bear had sunk back into the woods. They had grievances with their U.S. record company; they lost almost every cent they had in a premature western Canadian tour, and there were differences of opinion between the group and its local record company on material.

Edward Bear had lumbered into the charts with what most people called a bubblegum record, but they later decided that bubblegum music wasn't where they were at. There were a couple of cuts on their second album, *Eclipse*, which would have probably been suitable follow-ups to *You Me and Mexico* (*Four Months Out to Africa* likely would have surpassed the 125,000 sales of the first Edward Bear single). But the band insisted that they wanted their second disc to be a reflection of what music the group is really into. They chose *You Can't Deny It*.

Says Evoy: "We tried to release a record that was more representative of Edward Bear. But it didn't work because of the success formula in music - with the second record, you have to duplicate what put you up there originally. You just can't violate that formula. People wanted another *You Me and Mexico*. When we didn't give it to them, they didn't want to know and they didn't understand. The song was fine, but the timing was wrong. So we missed. That's about all you can say."

On the strength of *You Me and Mexico*, Edward Bear (named after the Winnie the Pooh character) went out on a full-scale tour of western Canada in the summer of 1970. "There's traditionally no work in Ontario during the summer, so we figured it would be an idea to get out and play across the country.

"We had all sorts of gigs booked, but many of them fell through by the time we reached them because of agency mix-ups and general apathy. It was really a pity. We lost all the money we had on that tour - about $4,000."

In December 1970, Capitol Records flew the group into New York and Los Angeles for promotional gigs, but the company had delayed too long. Somehow it seemed that Edward Bear's chance had come and gone. The most remarkable thing was that their initial impact had been so immense in Canada. The first Bear album, *Bearings*, sold in excess of 10,000 units, a huge figure for the Canadian market.

"It was an honest evaluation of what we knew at the time. It was a case of getting a lot of songs we had on tape," says Paul Weldon, organist-bass player with the group, and a practising architect and art designer.

Edward Bear's success caused Weldon to reduce his professional hours from forty a week to less than ten. "The architect game is a strange one," he says, "You need to have a lot of contacts and you need to join golf clubs and fraternities and all that stuff. I'm not really into that scene. The only people I know can't afford to get a house built for them."

In May 1971, the Bear replaced their lead guitarist, Danny Marks, with Roger Ellis. They also announced their intention of reverting to the commercial style which had originally launched them. It appeared to be a timely and sensible decision, in the circumstances.

Larry Evoy is an ardent fan of the Guess Who. "I don't think any of us could have made it if the Guess Who hadn't blasted open the doors. But even they've been completely mistreated in Canada. Half the country doesn't even know who they are.

"It's a pity Canadian radio stations are so tightly formatted. They should be more willing to get things happening. They should want to make Canada an important record market for domestic product."

Evoy allows, however, that things have improved through the years he's been a participant in Canadian rock battles. "Just by sheer volume of records, the scene will get better. What I want to see is Canada becoming a music power in its own right; not a mere extension of the U.S. contemporary scene."

Everyday People

Everyday People had just returned from a month of gigs in the Maritimes, and lead guitarist Bruce Wheaton (a native of Amherst, Nova Scotia) wasn't happy to be back in Toronto. "All the good Canadian records were being played down east ... not the shitty ones, just the good ones. You get the sort of treatment you deserve down there. The stations play your records and the kids come out to see you perform - even if it's only to hear the one song the stations have been playing.

"You come back to Toronto and melt into the crowd. It makes you feel like going back home. But we've got to conquer Toronto somehow."

Wheaton almost did it once before, as a member of the Stitch in Time, a prominent Toronto group in the late sixties at the height of Yorkville's brief reign as Canada's hip district. "I was in the group for two and a half years. We were in a fairly unique position. I think we had more going for us than anybody and might have gone far if it hadn't been for an awful record scene.

"We were with Arc Records, and we were looking for something better. But the people at Arc wrote letters to all the record companies threatening to sue them if they tried to sign us. So there were continuous lawyer hassles for two years, and nothing happening. In the end, we packed it up. "

For a while, Wheaton wandered around wondering what to do with himself. He worked in a bar band for a couple of months, made some bread, quit, ran out of money and put an ad in a Toronto paper in the spring of 1970 to get some players together to form another bar group, "just to make a little bread to keep living," he says.

A drummer and an organist from Markham replied to the ad. A vocalist, Pamela Marsh, joined at Wheaton's request and another musician was found through a second ad.

Four months later, the bass player decided to split the gig, and the group almost disintegrated. "We were having such a hard time getting started. We were down the Village one day and an old friend from Halifax was driving past. We raced out on the road and asked him if he was looking for a gig. He was."

That was in July, and soon after Everyday People were signed to Terry Brown's Dr. Music Productions. An English producer with an outstanding track record, Brown set about cutting a single with the group. A song called *You Make Me Wonder* was released in the fall.

It was a hit in some areas, completely ignored in others, particularly in Toronto. The B-side, *Nova Scotia Home Blues*, also met with success in the east.

Three of the six members come from the Maritimes; Wheaton is from Amherst, Pamela Marsh and bass guitarist, Carson Richards, are from Halifax. Drummer Alan Muggeridge is from Barrie, Ontario, where he played with a local group, Cathedral; keyboard player David Hare is from Oshawa, Ontario, and once played with the Sparrow, the forerunner to Steppenwolf; guitarist Christ Paputts, a Greek immigrant now based in Toronto, was in the New Breed.

On the strength of the first single, and the second release, *I Get That Feeling*, Paramount Records in the U.S. and England's Island label was anxious to sign the group. In Canada, their material is released on GRT.

Although Everyday People are not dazzled by the Toronto scene, they say they'll stick around until opportunity knocks. "There's got to be a time when this thing breaks and people realize that Canadian records are good enough to get played with records from anywhere.

"Our ambition is to write our own music, play it the way we feel it and have people get off on it. We're not so far out that people can't get into it. We think it feels better if the audience understands what you're doing.

"A record that gets no radio play is discouraging. You can only conclude that it was a lousy record. But we've had a big hit in some areas with *You Make Me Wonder*. Stations all around Toronto were playing it; not one in Toronto was. When that sort of thing happens, it's time for government to step in."

Five Man Electrical Band

Nobody had an easy time of it in the early days of Canadian music. Naturally enough, some artists had a rougher scene than others. Some had it so bad that it's amazing they were able to stand the strain and lack of encouragement for more than a few months.

The Five Man Electrical Band was one notable exception to this particular rock rule. Based in Ottawa, the band traces its beginnings back eight years.

Considering the number of disastrously bad breaks which somehow came their way, it is quite a feat that they're still in there battling.

If one piece of bad luck had been worth a musical instrument, the Five Man Electrical Band would boast the largest orchestra in the country.

The group has five members - Rick Bell, Mike Bell, Ted Geron, Les Emmerson and Brian Reding. Les Emmerson is the writer of almost all the band's material, and he's usually its spokesman.

"It's been a long battle. When we started, the belief was that if you could make it in Toronto you had the world at your feet. But we never even tried Toronto. Instead we went to Montreal. Dave Boxer was the big disc jockey down there then.

"I saw a TV commercial in Ottawa a few days ago, and there was Dave Boxer trying to sell windshield wipers. Perhaps there is some justice. We used to have to do everything but kiss his ass to get one play on any of our records back then. He'd get us to perform for not much more than scale at his Montreal dances. There were times when 8,000 kids would turn out for those dances.

"But it still wasn't as bad as Toronto. Trying to get onto CHUM was literally impossible. Eventually we went and played in Toronto, did some gigs in the Village, but it took us nowhere.

"We'd all been playing in various bands when we decided to get together under the name of the Staccatos. I'd been playing in a country group. A little later, disc jockey Dean Hagopian - one of our few friends in radio in those days - suggested that we should go to Buffalo and cut a record. Can you believe that? Buffalo!

"We spent about twenty-four hours cutting a stack of tunes. Our old manager, Sandy Gardiner [entertainment editor of the *Ottawa Journal* and long a patriot in the Canadian talent struggle] even wrote one of them. Apart from that, the session was just awful.

"We took the tape to Capitol who turned us down. We eventually got the record out on Allied, and it sold reasonably well in Ottawa. You could barely hope to get a Canadian record played in your home town, let alone anywhere else. So that was one down, at least.

"Then we went to Montreal with David Britten [singer-writer-opportunist] and helped him cut some tracks. We had enough time left after one of the sessions to cut the first song I'd written, *Small Town Girl*. We ripped off a B-side, and Capitol agreed to release it.

"Again, its success was restricted to Ottawa. We went back to Montreal and cut some more tracks at that poor little four-track RCA studio. We were just getting into the Beach Boys music, the incredible harmonies and all, and we cut *Do You Mind If I Dance With You, Girl*. The next single was *Move to California*.

"All of this led up to *Half Past Midnight*, which was also done at RCA in Montreal. The technical people at RCA could never believe us - we actually wanted distortion. The engineers had no idea at all of how to make a commercial record. Jingles were the extent of their musical feel for rock 'n' roll.

"By law, you were not allowed to overdub strings on records, unless you paid the players double time. We didn't have much bread, but we persuaded them to do a couple of takes for us to choose from. We used both.

"That was in 1966. *Half Past Midnight* did really well; probably it was one of the biggest ever Canadian rock singles at that stage. Capitol was thrilled to death. Capitol in the U.S. began releasing our records. But soon after entered an awkward situation in which all communication was lost between Capitol in Canada and Capitol U.S. Capitol here couldn't tell the parent company what to do, and as usual, we lost out.

"Capitol U.S. was just losing the Beach Boys' contract and they thought they might need another falsetto-styled group. We cut all sorts of records with them. There was a wheelbarrow full of tapes, including one completed album. We were just jammed up in the corporate squeeze between Hollywood and Toronto at Capitol. We went through a lot of compromises." Nevertheless, several of their singles came close to reaching the U.S. charts.

At about this time, the group decided to change its name to the Five Man Electrical Band. They felt the Staccatos was worn out, and that it didn't seem to have much luck attached to it anyway.

"We were in the process of getting away from Capitol. We were impressed by a young producer, Dallas Smith, who was just leaving Liberty Records and was setting up a deal with Canopy, a company which U.S. writer Jim Webb [*By the Time I Get to Phoenix, Up Up and Away* and *MacArthur Park*] had started.

"The company was run by Jim's father, Bob, a former minister. He's a real nice guy but he was pretty naive about the music business. Jim Webb was holding out on several companies trying to get a bigger deal.

"Again we were kind of caught in between. We cut a lot of tapes with Dallas Smith but they weren't getting out. Eventually Canopy made a deal with MGM ... we had no choice or say in the decision. You might say we've made some classic errors in those areas."

Late in 1970, an album titled *Goodbyes and Butterflies* was released in the U.S. One of the cuts, *Hello Melinda Goodbye*, was a regional hit in Canada. Then an American station flipped the record and began playing a song called *Signs*. It spread from the south and eventually became a national top ten smash. Meantime, the group shifted its base of operations from Ottawa to Los Angeles.

Emmerson isn't too keen to predict on how the group's fifteen-odd singles (prior to *Signs*) would have fared in a more favorable Canadian radio climate.

"I've listened to most of our old things recently, and I can see now where they were missing - just not commercial enough." Emmerson can, however, see in the light of hindsight that bad luck haunted the group. "When we cut that Coke album *A Wild Pair* with the Guess Who, we were really impressed by Jack Richardson. He was a professional - something we'd never seen before in Canada. He knew how to talk music because he was a musician himself. He was commercially oriented, but he had enough balls to hang in there. If we hadn't been tied down with Capitol, I think we'd have tried to work something out with Jack. We really liked him. So, apparently, did Burton Cummings and the guys."

Emmerson makes special mention of *RPM* publisher, Walt Grealis, as a supporter of Canadian talent through the sixties. "It must have been discouraging for Walt. He plugged away for so long and he was laughed at by so many people. But now he's enjoying the last laugh."

Emmerson readily admits that some Canadian product in earlier years wasn't really that great. "The stations were always so U.S.-conscious. But the stuff coming out of Canada was often so bad that it paled in comparison with the U.S. product.

"I think it boils down to one thing; once you've gained fair access to the airwaves, nothing can stop a genuine hit record, Canadian or otherwise."

Tommy Graham

Tommy Graham is a sensitive, soft-spoken young man with longish hair and a fondness for turtlenecks. He is also a veteran of the early years of the Toronto non-rock scene. He joined his first rock group in 1958, a point in time when rock musicians had more chance of aspiring to fame and fortune if they resided elsewhere. He went through the high school rock band number, and gigged at the Blue Note Club for two years after it opened in 1960. In 1962, he went to Los Angeles and spent a year there, just hanging out.

"I came back to Toronto in 1963, and got involved with Shirley Matthews. I was a member of the Big Town Boys, and we used to back up Shirley. We also cut a few records of our own - even an album. We started out playing R & B, but after a while, we couldn't get any gigs playing that kind of music.

"Eventually, the Big Town Boys switched to an extremely commercial bag, and we were booked steadily. Very few people knew the evolution we'd been through, from R & B to pop. It gave us a lot of experience though, both in TV and recording work. It was small time though, compared with what it must have been like right at the top.

"At the end of 1968, the Big Town Boys split up, and I used what little money I'd made to buy a round-the-world air ticket. I spent the next couple of years just travelling. I lived in India for a year, and the immersion into another culture really did it to me. I stayed in Calcutta most of the time, but I spent three months touring all over India, East and West Pakistan and Afghanistan."

Graham returned to Toronto in late 1969. "Shortly after I got back, I bumped into Brian Ahern. He'd just come in from Halifax and he was working as a staff producer at Arc Sound. The Big Town Boys had worked with him some years earlier when we cut a theme jingle for Big G. Walters, the disc jockey.

"Brian was just getting ready to record Anne Murray, and I became involved. I played a couple of instruments on *Snowbird*."

He doesn't volunteer which instruments, so you ask. "Tamborine, a bass drum, and rhythm guitar. I didn't think *Snowbird* was a hit record. I wasn't really hip to the kind of music it represented. But Brian seemed to have a lot of confidence in it."

Despite his rugged experiences with recording in Canada as one of the Big Town Boys, Graham decided to make a record as a solo artist after the Anne Murray sessions. "When the Big Town Boys were going, there just wasn't a record scene happening in Canada. It was hard enough to get a disc jockey to listen to your record, let alone play it. The only half-decent studio was Hallmark. Management hassles, which all groups seemed to have in Toronto then, were another drag. Infighting only brings everyone down.

"When I came back from India, I went to see Paul White at Capitol Records. I'd known Paul when the Big Town Boys recorded for Capitol. He suggested we should cut some sides. I did four singles and Paul liked them, so we decided to go ahead with an album."

The LP, which Graham produced himself, was called *Planet Earth*, and was released by Capitol in December 1970.

"I don't really know if it's done well. I can't be bothered ringing up for sales figures or anything. I've always thought the album's success depended on a single coming from it; it is mainly a pop-oriented album."

Graham survives by session musician work. "I'm very fortunate in that Brian Ahern has used me on most of his sessions. That bread really helps out. Things have been getting a little tight financially in recent months. I can only hope that something happens soon."

Joey Gregorash

Joey Gregorash was a willing product of the new era in Canadian rock music. He was promoted, publicized and treated like a star by Polydor Records; he was whisked across the country on a promotional tour; and he was rewarded with several hit singles prior to January 18, 1971.

In short, he was granted the rights and privileges which had been denied his predecessors in Canadian rock. In 1970, record companies began to feel the unprecedented effects of radio exposure of Canadian productions, and they had started to plough some of their large profits on foreign discs back into the homeland.

Gregorash, who had started out in music in 1964, was signed by Polydor in the summer of 1970. He was only twenty years old, and he'd gone to Minneapolis and cut some sides with a big band sound. The results included two hit singles, *Jodie* and *Down By the River*, and a successful album, *North Country Funk*.

Gregorash's father was a violin player. "I wanted to make music somehow ... because of his influence. I tried violin for two months, but just couldn't get into it. So I took up drums and when I was fourteen, I started a group called the Mongrels. I played drums for them for two years.

"Then one night, the parents of the lead singer said he had to leave the band and do some studying. I filled in for him at the next gig; the next day, the group got another drummer and I remained as singer. I stayed with the Mongrels for another couple of years and really got into singing. We even cut a couple of records, but they went nowhere."

In 1969, Gregorash left the Mongrels, and the group continued on its own merry way. A single, *Ivy in Her Eyes*, drew some attention in 1970. Later that year, Gregorash was selected as host of a weekly one-hour Winnipeg TV show called *Young As You Are*.

"The experience was fantastic. It gave me some confidence. The promotion tour was so much easier because of the show."

In the spring of 1970, Joey flew to Minneapolis (many Winnipeg acts have used the Minneapolis recording facilities) and cut two singles. "The first one was *Stay*, and it sold about 2,000 copies. The second, *Tomorrow, Tomorrow*, did much better. But I'm looking forward to the material from Memphis hitting the market. I'm glad I dropped the horns and big band stuff we used in Minneapolis - that should be left to groups like Chicago.

"We spent one day rehearsing the songs in Memphis, and then cut them. Half the songs were tremendously changed from the original concept." Gregorash wrote most of the songs on the album. He was also responsible, along with lyricist Norm Lampe, for the first two singles.

Success goes down well with Joey Gregorash. He may be benefitting from the CRTC ruling, but he hasn't forgotten his roots.

"There were some hard times. You'd go fifty miles out into the sticks to play in some one-horse town. Greaseballs would be out to get your head, and you weren't in much of a mood to play music. Matter of fact, it was enough to make you want to quit. But, for some reason we didn't."

Dee Higgins

Dee Higgins is a pretty, blonde girl with a flair for writing songs and singing them in rather special fashion. By the start of the legislation era, she had three years' experience as a solo artist behind her, but the battle was far from over.

The lack of a coffee house circuit in Canada outside of Toronto and Ottawa forces artists like Dee Higgins to play taverns and sometimes even bars, hardly the ideal environment for a folksinger. Mariposa, the Ontario folk festival, has done much to bring people like Dee to the attention of the folk fraternity, but even Mariposa's endurance record (the festival celebrated its eleventh year in 1971) has not made an impression with most Canadian radio stations. They have generally ignored its discoveries.

Joni Mitchell was discovered at Mariposa, but she still had to leave Canada to gain wider recognition. Dee Higgins doesn't plan to follow Joni's lead, but you can see that she's growing weary of the Canadian folk scene.

Her first record, *The Song Singer*, came out in the summer of 1970, but received little Top Forty play. It was a nice song, deserving much greater attention than it actually received. Later in 1970, Dee spent some months working in Japan. She returned to Canada just prior to the legislation era, and a tie up with producer, Dennis Murphy, (arranged by Early Morning Productions), suggested that things might be on the upswing.

Dee has certainly paid her dues with overtime. She spent five years with the Seaway Singers, before breaking away to go solo in 1968. After three years of trying to make it on her own, she remains perennially optimistic. "It's all a matter of fate – you're meant to do it or you're not. The people who have made it - the Jose Felicianos, the Joni Mitchells, the Gordon Lightfoots - they all say you just have to keep on trying. You can't set deadlines or goals, you simply keep doing your best and sooner or later, it happens for you."

Leigh Ashford

As Joe Agnello tells it, Leigh Ashford was a sixteenth century English prostitute. But Miss Ashford was no run-of-the-mill lady of ill repute. As legend has it, Leigh Ashford used to do her thing for the benefit of London's many starving musicians. The compassion of Leigh Ashford's calling led Agnello and friends to name a rock group after her. That was back in 1967.

Agnello's closest friend in the part-time, non-union band was guitarist Gord Waszek. When the band went full-time, Agnello decided to quit and go to college. He lasted only one term. "Gord called me one day and said the group was looking for a bass player," recalls Agnello. Four days later, he'd quit school, returned to Toronto and was rehearsing with the group.

Shortly after, the band teamed up with another Toronto group, the Spirit, and named themselves the Spirit Revue. "It was a thirteen-piece band - we hated each other - but we made a lot of money. We didn't get to see too much of it after managers and agents, though. We were royally screwed."

After the large group split up, the Leigh Ashford members reunited and went out as a soul band. When they found only sparse popularity coming their way, they switched to commercial rock and became one of the most demanded bands on the Yorkville strip, circa 1968.

Heavily influenced by the Vanilla Fudge, Leigh Ashford produced a powerhouse, polished sound which would have been snatched up by a dozen record companies if the band had been working in New York. Yet when the club at which the group had been playing, the Flick, closed down, Leigh Ashford kept itself alive playing high schools and colleges. In the fall of 1969, a recording contract was signed with Nimbus 9. By then, the band had changed its style again, and was into a "heavy, original bag".

"We went to New York to cut the album, but it just didn't come together. Frankly, it was the shits. It wasn't a very good record; I don't think five cents was spent promoting it. It died."

A couple of months later, Leigh Ashford was in danger of breaking up. "We kept losing our drummers, and no one was happy because things had been going so bad. Just as things were really the worst, we met Roland Paquin who became our manager and has been responsible for all the good things which have happened since."

Pacquin, who was running an instruments store in Yorkville and had been closely involved with the Mandala, managed to get the group a gig at the Strawberry Fields Festival at Mosport in early fall of 1970. Despite having to use a stand-in guitarist, Leigh Ashford fared well at Strawberry Fields. In September, Paquin obtained a release from Nimbus for the group, and they were signed to Revolution Records.

Agnello thinks the CRTC played a big role in the acceptance of the group's first big single, *Dickens*. "We wouldn't have had half the airplay without the CRTC. It was the only way we were able to have the record on CHUM for two weeks."

In June 1970, Leigh Ashford's first album, *Kinfolk*, was released simultaneously in Canada and the U.S.A. The Nimbus album was never issued. Since then they have written even better material and have a certain future among Canada's top groups.

Mainline

"Our music is like nothing you've ever heard," says Mainline's Joe Mendelson, and he may be right.

"We started out as a blues group when blues was having a boom. Then we evolved; blues also evolved. We now play blues better than ever. But the whole thing has widened considerably."

Formed in the summer of 1968, Mainline became one of the most successful concert groups in Ontario. At the start of the legislation era, the group could command higher gig prices than almost any other Canadian band - without the obvious benefit of U.S. success.

Mainline had already been to England, lived there for six months, and cut an album. In 1970, they toured Australia with Frijid Pink, hardly competition for any Canadian band worth its salt. In many cities, the Pink had a lot of trouble following Mainline.

They may lack some of the technical mastery of the blues as possessed by King Biscuit Boy, but Mainline has a unique aura -a dynamic stage presence which possibly accounts for the group's tremendous popularity in concerts.

Joe Mendelson always was the leader and firebrand of Mainline, but he says he has stepped back from the spotlight recently. "In the old days, when the group was called the McKenna Mendelson Mainline, I was the over-riding musical influence. But it's not that way any more. Everybody - Zeke Sheppard, Tony Nolasco and Michael McKenna - plays a key part. Our music covers a lot of ground; it has evolved into something very political and very weird."

Of course, it wasn't always that way. "In 1968, I got together with Mike McKenna, who'd been playing with the Ugly Ducklings. We put an ad in the paper to form a band."

The ad brought results in the shape of ex-Paupers' bass player, Denny Gerrard. But Gerrard split after three months to get another gig together, and Mendelson and McKenna brought in Mike Harrison, who had worked with the Power.

"We played around Ontario for a while, and then went to England in December of 1968. It was there we cut our first album, *Stink*. We came back here in the summer of '69."

Stink, without the assistance of a genuine hit single, sold some 30,000 copies, according to Mainline manager, Wayne Thompson.

"Most of which was in Canada," adds Joe.

"The music isn't what it used to be. It's more mature, more of an original sound." Mainline completed a second album (this time for Capitol) in Los Angeles mid-way through 1971. Mendelson says his ambition is "to play better and to come out on top despite all the bullshit."

Nolasco would like to be "recognized by a lot of musicians as being a good player. The public's opinion is not as important as the feelings of our competitors."

"That's the ultimate," agrees Mendelson, "winning the respect of other musicians."

Motherlode

Six months after the Guess Who's *These Eyes* in the spring of 1969, a second Canadian group made it into the U.S. charts. The band was Motherlode, a four-piece Toronto group whose single of *When I Die* sold some 500,000 copies in the U.S. A second single, *Memories of a Broken Appearance*, made a very brief showing at the bottom of the American charts, and the *When I Die* album also saw some fleeting success.

Our hopes were raised that a trend of Canadian hits might be beginning, and we looked to Motherlode to sustain its initial American action. But the band broke up - victims of the excesses of success - and it was left to Edward Bear and the Poppy Family and, of course, the Guess Who to man the front line of Canadian music.

Steve Kennedy, veteran saxophone player and co-writer of *When I Die*, looks back on those days with understandable regret. "One of the problems was that the record company wanted us to keep on writing *When I Die* over and over. Another beef was the concept. Some people stifled the creativity of the band."

Motherlode disbanded in January of 1970, none the richer (financially) for their success, but a lot better off for the experience. There was an attempt to revive the band around organist-singer William Smith in the summer of 1970, but it proved unsuccessful.

The Motherlode disintegration was made even more tragic by the wealth of playing experience which had been gathered by the band. Few Canadian bands in the late sixties could boast the proven talent which Motherlode represented.

Kennedy for example began blowing saxophone professionally back in 1959. "I bought a sax when I was twelve, but I didn't do anything with it until the Blue Note Club opened in Toronto. I worked semi-professionally with a group called Kay Taylor and the Regents—the only band in Toronto with a black singer.

"In 1964, Doug Riley, Terry Bush, Howard Glen, Fred Theriault and myself formed a group called the Silhouettes, and we did a lot of gigs outside the Blue Note. Our two singers were Dianne Brooks and Jack Hardin.

"We didn't do too well in 1966, but the following year we reformed and named ourselves Eric Mercury, Dianne Brooks and the Soul Searchers. The band lasted for two years. We had a lot of gigs but no records. We worked all the joints - North Bay, Timmins, all over. Cliches aside, it was rough being a black group. A lot of clubs wouldn't book us, and the ones that would didn't pay too much." Kennedy was the only white in the group.

"We were very much into R & B. Personally I'd been brought up on the rock records of the fifties - Little Willie John, Chuck Berry, Little Richard - I knew all their bands and every saxophone lick they had.

"Things didn't improve; finally I joined Kenny Marco, Wayne Stone and William Smith at the Image club in London, Ontario. We called ourselves Motherlode."

They were heard by Doug Riley and Mort Ross of Revolution Records and it was decided that Motherlode should cut some tapes as soon as possible. "We got about twenty-five songs together, and then went in and recorded *When I Die* and *Livin' Life*, which were two of our early originals.

"Neil Bogart of Buddah Records came down to see us play when he was in Toronto and he flipped. Buddah agreed to release *When I Die* in the U.S. and it broke out of the west coast."

Initially, this fine single was given little airplay in Canada, even though it was a locally produced record coming hot on the heels of the Guess Who's *Laughing* and *These Eyes*. It was only after the record had broken in the U.S. that Canadian stations turned onto it.

The business hassles which followed bewildered Kennedy. It was really his first confrontation with the cold dollars aspect of the music scene. "It's frightening actually," he says, "but I see in Neil Young and artists like that the emergence of a new scene. It may not be slick, in tune or even recorded that well, but it's honest. That's what matters."

David Clayton-Thomas once told Kennedy not to be afraid of success: "Come down here to the States and do it," he advised. But Kennedy resisted the temptation and Canadian music is much the richer for it. He has been studying music theory, harmony and composition with Gordon Delamont for a year, and he's been writing songs for the new group, Doctor Music - a sixteen-member all-star aggregation of some of the finest singers and players in Canada. The group is led by Doug Riley, himself one of Canada's most outstanding musical talents. Riley is a versatile arranger (his work runs the gamut of a Ray Charles album to an Edward Bear single), an accomplished pianist, and a remarkable songwriter. Riley penned the first Doctor Music single, *Try A Little Harder*, which somehow seems to be the battlecry of the group.

The second Doctor Music single, *One More Mountain To Climb*, came from a different source. It had been written by Neil Sedaka, the noted U.S. singer-composer, and the group were turned on to it by the highly respected Canadian record producer, Frank Davies. The group was signed to Bell Records in the U.S. and Doctor Music had already taken the first few steps towards stardom.

Meantime, Kennedy and his compatriots kept the wolves from the door with a series of jingles, radio shows and background session work. Kennedy's ambition is to make money "but not to sacrifice in order to make it. I don't want to sell out. I want to keep working at Toronto Sound Studios and become a good writer and arranger."

He received several lucrative TV singing offers in 1970, but most of them would have meant moving to California, something which he's determined not to do.

"I've realized you can't do it all in one day. It takes a long time. But I've got a lot of little pieces of paper with ideas I've written down. One day I'd like to put together an album of my own; it'll take at least a year before I've got all that settled in my own head. But I'm working on it and it's feeling good."

Tom Northcott

Tom Northcott is as familiar as sub-zero weather to western Canada, yet his name means very little in the east. For some reason, Northcott's name is almost a household word between Winnipeg and Vancouver but he has never been able to break through in Toronto or Montreal.

Despite eight years of professional gigs and hit records in British Columbia, Northcott had not made an appearance in Toronto prior to the start of the legislation era. He did turn up, a month later, for a week at the Riverboat Coffee House in Toronto and was given a long overdue welcome in Canada's supposed capital of folk music.

Tom Northcott is extremely sensitive, but at the same time, appears to be practical and honest with himself. He has worked with some of the top names in the international music scene, people like Leon Russell, producer Tony Hatch, Glen Campbell, Jim Gordon and producer Lenny Waronker, yet he always returned to Vancouver. He is a partner in Studio 3, one of the finest studios on the Canadian west coast; he is a recording artist with international releases; he is a record producer, and his compositions are so highly regarded that he has performed them with the Vancouver Symphony Orchestra.

In the course of an interview, he is alternately eloquent and emotional. He tells his own story with precision, professionalism and mature wit.

"The music started for me when I was a little kid. My dad was a cellist, and I loved to listen to him play. He would make up little things for the kids - *The Bear, The Gorilla*, and so on. We really got into sound, things with pitch and rhythm. I soon saw how it transmitted effect, how it moved the spirit. I mean, a cello can really growl when you're four years old. It had a very strong effect on me.

"In school, I found that I could sing better than most of the kids. I had an ear for tone - I could tell who wasn't singing the right part in the right key.

"I took up the trumpet but hated the lessons. I refused to learn how to read music. So when I joined the school band, I had to learn the parts from the guy next to me as they ran through the song the first two or three times. That helped develop a really good ear for sound."

When he was fifteen years old, Northcott picked up his first guitar. "I worked on a B.C. ranch one summer. It was a guest ranch as well as cattle - they'd get seventy head of guests there in the summer. In the daytime, I'd do odd jobs and in the evenings, I would sing for the guests.

"After that, I got a gig with a Canadian Legion group. We played hospitals and prisons, which was tremendous experience. I gained a sense of empathy and of what music can do for invalids, for people in pain, for people in trouble. I didn't really understand it then but I was learning some lessons in humanity. I saw how much entertainment means to people."

In 1963, Northcott obtained his first professional folk singing gig in Vancouver. "It was at the Inquisition Coffee House for $50 a week, and while I was still at school. I went to university for six months, but had no idea what I was there for. One day I decided it was all bullshit and quit. My family thought I was completely irresponsible."

The next few years were spent scraping a living out of the numerous, low-paying folk clubs between Vancouver and San Francisco. Northcott also made an entry into the rock field with appearances on several CBC-TV musical shows.

He started his own record company, New Syndrome, because Capitol Records had refused to put out a record he'd made. "Paul White, the A & R manager, turned down my tape, and because I'm a very proud person, I couldn't stand to be refused and I did something about it."

The song *Cry Tomorrow* came out and sold about 1,800 copies in Vancouver. "Considering the mediocre playing and the small studio, it was a good record for its time," he says. He made two more singles for New Syndrome, before some newly found but at that time, little known friends, the Jefferson Airplane, arranged for Northcott to appear at a small folk club in San Francisco.

Several record companies put in offers for his services, and he decided to sign with Warner Brothers, "because their producer, Lenny Waronker, seemed sincerely interested in me." Unfortunately that scene never did work out. Northcott discovered it was Waronker's material that he would be cutting and that Waronker wasn't too keen about Northcott's original tunes. It was temporarily resolved by Leon Russell, who offered to produce Northcott doing his own songs. But then Russell decided that he wanted to cut Northcott's songs, rather than Tom himself, and at that point, the Vancouver singer split to England.

"I went to see the producers I'd heard of - people like George Martin, Tony Hatch and Mickie Most. I was still naive; I didn't realize when I did a record with Tony Hatch that he had a certain mold. So he cut some Petula Clark songs with me. At this point, I really didn't know what to do. I'd worked with some of the best people in the business, and I still wasn't satisfied. I realized then that I had to do it myself."

Several of the records Northcott had made while away from Canada had met with minor success. His *1941*, for example, reached the lower rungs of the U.S. charts in 1968. *Sunny Goodge Street* was a smash in several big cities. *Girl From the North Country* scored in Australia and Italy.

"They were spotty records; they did well in parts but not the whole. *Rainmaker* was the same. It took all of six months to run its course in Canada."

In 1969, Northcott returned to Vancouver. "I came back, like the ad says. Mainly because I dig being in Canada making music. I'd rather be here than in Los Angeles or New York. I love this ground, this ocean; it's all so much a part of me. I want all my music to be part of that. I feel that I'm the middle man between my environment and the music coming out the other side."

Within a year of his return from England, Northcott appeared in concert with the Vancouver Symphony Orchestra, performing his original composition, *And God Created Woman*. The unlikely combination drew healthy critical acclaim in the west coast press - underground and establishment.

"It was a great opportunity to feature a song I had, on a fairly grand scale. The song lent itself to a symphonic interpretation. I'd like to write another one, but the trouble is, I usually only write when I'm on the road, and I haven't been on the road too much lately. When I'm in Vancouver, I have all these things to do. There's always a pile of tapes to listen to, someone to see; it robs you of a lot of the whatever it is - creative energy or something."

Northcott is a partner with Ralph Harding and Andy Finneran in Studio 3 Productions, probably the largest independent production company on the west coast. In the latter part of 1970, Studio 3 signed an important production deal with MCA Records in New York. The contract called for advances of $600,000 over five years, on yearly options renewable by MCA.

"As long as they've earned more than they've paid out to us in the previous year, they'll stick with us. We've been busting our asses trying to find something great. But it's not that easy. It's not even easy finding something that will sell $25,000 worth of records."

Northcott spent much of the winter of '70-'71 working on a new album he called *Upside Downside.* A great deal of the work involves selection: sifting through material, his own and that of others.

"I'll record a song for one of two reasons - if it's my own, or if I can make it my own. So the new album will consist of my songs plus other people's songs which I believe I can sing better than they've been sung before. The ratio is half and half."

Northcott is a supporter of legislated local content. "It's an excellent idea. I don't claim that programming won't suffer initially; you can really get bogged down when you consider all the ramifications of it. But after all the water that has already gone under the bridge, I think it's good. Nobody will be hurt by it.

"Most of the people who listen to radio have a love-hate relationship with the records they hear. They don't listen to music the way we do. So radio is not doing them a disservice by playing Canadian records; to them it doesn't really matter where the records come from."

One thing which the CRTC ruling is likely to affect is Northcott's own broadcasting exposure. It seems likely that Toronto and Montreal radio stations will join their western counterparts in allowing his considerable talent access to the airwaves.

"I don't know if I've really encountered the eastern bias against western music. All I know is that people all around Canada played my records, but Toronto didn't. And talking about Toronto, you are obviously discussing CHUM. I believe that CHUM doesn't think of itself as Canada's biggest rock station; I think they consider the station as another major market U.S. broadcaster ... they're not too concerned with Canadian music and Canadian problems."

Ocean

Gene Maclellan was well established as a foremost Canadian composer when the legislation era began, and some of his most significant work had been done in the six months previous. He wrote *Snowbird* for Anne Murray, and it sold a million copies. He was also responsible for a song called *Put Your Hand in the Hand.* There were several versions of it out as singles in January 1971; the most successful was by a Toronto group called Ocean.

It was Ocean's first record, and a great many people were surprised at the unusual exposure afforded it by Toronto's CHUM. Later it was learned that the record had been produced by CHUM disc jockey Johnny Mitchell.

"The group was formed at the end of the 1970 summer," explains Greg Brown, Ocean's keyboards player and vocalist. "Dave Tamblyn, our lead guitarist, and I had originally played together in a weekend group. In 1970, we got together and I brought along singer Janice Morgan, with whom I'd been working for the previous eighteen months.

"I just wanted to get off the road for a while. I really wanted to form a concert group. We had Tom Wilson, the booking agent, looking for other players. Primarily we were searching for a bunch of people that we liked. Ocean is more of a people thing than anything else.

"We were signed by Arc Records in the fall after we'd spent a couple of months rehearsing. But we had very little original material to record. Someone suggested that we should think about doing *Put Your Hand in the Hand*. We thought about it, liked the idea, changed the song around a bit, and produced the record ourselves.

"We cut the B-side first. It was our first time in the studio and it didn't go too well. But *Put Your Hand* more than made up for it. I wouldn't say that we feel strongly about the religious angle of the song, we were concerned that it might give the group a 'gospel' image."

The group enjoys working with Gene Maclellan material, and was thinking of including another of his songs on the first album. "His stuff is very natural. It's simple but not boring. He uses basic forms; it's wide open as to what you can do with it from there."

Brown, originally from London, has played in five different bands in his ten-year career. He likes the Guess Who, but says "they're into a very commercial, top forty thing."

As for Ocean, Brown hopes to see the group move into the field of albums, where they will be freer to experiment and try on a variety of styles.

PepperTree

The members of Pepper Tree were gathered around a huge ten-ton school bus, which was stuck in a deep snowdrift, a characteristic feature of winter in the snow belt of southern Ontario.

Shovels in hand, they were trying to push and dig their bus out of the snow to get to a gig. The farmhouse which they had rented since leaving the Maritimes in October of 1970 was only a few hundred yards away.

"This sort of thing keeps happening to us," Doug Hirschfeld was explaining. "The generator and the battery need to be replaced but we can't afford it right now, so we have to keep pushing. "

Money has been tight for Pepper Tree since they left the relative security of a big following and regular bookings in the Maritimes. "There are two reasons why we have to stick it out. First, we want to be close to Capitol, our record company, so as to maintain effective communication. Second, we've got to break through in this area, and the only way to do that is to be here," observes Hirschfeld.

Most groups from eastern Canada have found it necessary to pay some Ontario dues before they had any chance of cracking the national market. Everyday People also moved west from Halifax and found themselves in a similar position to Pepper Tree. Both bands kept with it and by early 1971 had made considerable progress and appeared likely contenders for national and perhaps international acclaim before that year had drawn to a close.

Like many Canadian groups, the members of Pepper Tree have a wealth of experience behind them. All have been playing for at least eight or nine years. The beginnings of the group can be traced back to a band called Central Nervous System, which cut an album in New York for MGM in 1964. There were six members of the System - vocalist Doug Billard, Jack Harris on drums, Keith Jollimore on saxophone, trumpeter Bruce Cassidy, guitarist Richie Oakley and Jim White on lead guitar.

The Central Nervous System broke up before the album had a chance to try itself in the marketplace. Says Hirschfeld: "If the guys had stayed together just another two days, they might have made it. The manager had gotten together a bunch of U.S. dates for them." Harris and Oakley wound up in Soma, Jollimore went with Lighthouse, and Billard and White later became part of Pepper Tree.

In the summer of 1969, Capitol's eastern promotion man, Alex Clark, saw the group play, was impressed by what went down and suggested they should make a demo tape for his company.

"We'd never even thought of recording before that. Down in the rear end of Canada, there was no such thing as making records. But we made a tape and brought it up to Toronto. After two days of running around trying to find Capitol's A & R director, Paul White, we finally made a deal with him.

"Early in 1970, we cut four sides for Capitol in Toronto with Jack Richardson producing. We weren't overjoyed with the results; they weren't overly exciting songs. But the company had insisted that we cut original material.

"We were still living in the Maritimes at this time. The morale of the group was going down fast, and a change had to be made. Three members of the group had to either change their ideas or leave. In the end, they left. One of them was Doug Billard, who had been our lead vocalist."

During this period of readjustment, Pepper Tree's recording career had taken a nose dive. The decision to move to Toronto was easily arrived at.

"We spent the first three weeks trying to live right in Toronto. It almost drove us mad. We were used to a slower, easier way of life. We then got the farm and now we're really digging the country. There hasn't been much money but we've enjoyed ourselves."

Although the group did not starve during the first few months in Ontario, they came about as close as you can get. "We often had to make do with a $30 food budget for twelve people each week. It was rough. We could have made more money by getting day jobs. But we wanted to work on new material and we were getting one or two gigs a week ... there wasn't much time left after that."

The group's persistence in writing new original material proved to be a shrewd move. Capitol's Wayne Patton arranged for Jack Richardson to cut the first Pepper Tree album shortly after the legislation era began.

"The material represents our confrontation with the Toronto scene. Jack Richardson did a fantastic job. I don't think we'd have been able to get it together with any other producer. He's genuinely interested in the group - he doesn't make any money unless we do, and the only way any of us can is to come up with a good album."

The group's personal on the first album included Tim Garagan on drums and lead vocals, organist Bob Quinn, Jim White on lead guitar and bass player Chris Brockway. Most of the material was written by Garagan, Quinn and White.

"I think they are well above average for Canadian originals," says Hirschfeld. "And they can compete favorably with most of the stuff coming out in the States," - an appraisal that bodes well for Pepper Tree and Canadian music in general.

The Stampeders

The Stampeders had been fighting a losing battle on two fronts for seven years; then came the CRTC decision which at last and at least made it a fair fight. Not only are the Stampeders Canadian, they were also western Canadian. So they had to fight the national apathy, as well as the eastern disinterest in western talent.

"The first few years were real tight," recalls Stampeder drummer Kim Berly. "But it was a development period. What else could we expect but a few hard times?"

The then six-piece group, which had formed in Calgary in 1964, battled on against all odds. "We worked all the local clubs, and finally we made a record. It was called *Don't Look at Her*, and it got a little play in the local area.

"Things went on in much the same manner until the summer of 1966, when we decided to come east. There was so little happening in the west; we came to Toronto with the intention of staying for quite a while."

They played all the Ontario bars for a year, and although there wasn't much work, they somehow survived. One of the reasons for this was the loyal and sustained effort of their manager, Mel Shaw, who had come east with both his group and his family. Mel organized a record release in 1967 of a song called *Morning Magic*. It won a BMI Certificate of Honor (for songwriting) and was a minor Canadian hit. It gave the group a name.

In the next year, the Stampeders signed a one-record deal with MGM in the States. "We went to New York and recorded *Be a Woman*. It didn't come out for six months, and by then, we weren't as happy with it anymore. It did nothing at all in the States, but it went fairly well in Canada." The group kept working in Ontario, then cut another single, the B-side of which, *I Don't Believe*, was played by CHUM for two weeks.

At the end of 1968, growing animosity within the group resulted in the departure of three members. "They were the three oldest guys in the group and they just got tired of it all; they sort of gave up." When Race Holiday, Van Lewis and Brent Little left, the Stampeders were left with three players - lead guitarist Richard Dodson, bass man Ronnie King and drummer Kim Berly.

"We decided to go out as a trio. Within six months, we were more heavily booked than we had ever been. People seemed to recognize the new energy and purpose in the group. In the summer, we headlined at the Ottawa Exhibition with the Guess Who, and I think we were well received."

The group ceased recording for eighteen months and wrote a lot of original material. "We went back into the studios in the fall of 1970 and worked on and off for eight months. *Carry Me* was one of the tracks we cut. Another was *Sweet City Woman*. *Carry Me* was a national hit, but next to the massive success of *Sweet City Woman*, most people forgot the former. The warmer climate of the legislation era had brought forth direct results in the long-overdue acclaim and success of the Stampeders, who finally began to live up to their name.

"The scene for us is rapidly improving. I still see a lot of good groups not working, but the whole gig scene was always very tight in Canada. We don't have any pressing financial problems any more. I can say that we're realistically optimistic about our future. Our association with Mel Shaw has been of immense benefit. Good management is really lacking in Canada, but the creation of a music scene here will change that."

"I think the heavy thing - down music - has just about run its course. Come to think of it, I think the old Canadian music scene that we came up in has just about run its course, too. I really believe the time has come. So many people are hitting from Canada; it looks like we're getting there, all of us."

Steel River

Although Steel River didn't make the U.S. charts in 1970, this Toronto band came as close as you can get.

The first single by the group, *Ten Pound Note*, reached the so-called "Bubbling Under" list on the *Billboard* Hot One Hundred in the States after achieving tremendous success in Canada in the early winter of 1970. Three months before the release the members of Steel River were only part-time musicians. One worked with a paper company, another in a hardware store; another made tea kettles.

"Ten Pound Note changed a lot of things for us," says organist Bob Forrester. "After it had become a hit our bookings tripled, in quality, quantity and price. We'd been together for six years previous but our recent success makes it feel like much less.

"We started as weekend musicians and turned professional about a year ago. We used to play small clubs and high schools - went through all the usual changes, the R & B double-breasted suit bit and all the rest."

Despite a lack of originality in early years, Steel River had been into writing songs since 1965. By the time they met up with Greg Hamble-ton, who produces the band for his own Tuesday label, the group had six of its own songs completely arranged and ready to record. They decided to make a demo disc. Stan Klees, veteran record producer, supervised the session, and Greg Hambleton was the engineer. "I don't think Stan liked us very much," Forrester recalls, "but apparently Greg did."

Forrester mentions that not just one but several record companies expressed interest in signing the group. "There has been a big upsurge in interest in Canadian music recently. It hasn't reached its peak yet, either."

Forrester and the rest of the group worked right through the height of Toronto's underground rock popularity in the mid-sixties. These were the days when local groups could draw more than a thousand kids to a concert. If there had been a record industry happening at that point, this book would likely have presented a very different story.

"Most of the groups were rhythm 'n' blues-oriented; there was a definite Toronto sound, one heavily influenced by the Motown sound. Toronto is musically very close to Detroit. A lot of Toronto bands worked hard at getting that funky sound with tight bass and drum work.

"Then Toronto went into a whole chicken rock thing. You had to keep the guitar work down to nice jazz chords. But that's not a sixteen year-old's music; the kids don't get off on it.

"Now we're getting back to the old way - music with balls, driving, exciting stuff; raw, and at the same time, a little sloppy. That's what Steel River is all about - it's emotional; we don't care if we make a few mistakes."

"*Ten Pound Note* brought the group a great deal of national attention and even though the disc made some forty Canadian charts, CHUM did not play it.

Still the group's Canadian success did not greatly change its basic outlook. "We're not looking to make it in the Rolls-Royce sense. It would mean much more to us to be accepted as musicians by other musicians, the way Eric Clapton has been.

"We're not really worried about whether our singles make it. A group makes it, in our opinion, in terms of its live performance. If that scene is together, a group doesn't need hit records."

Tundra

As is by now obvious, almost all of the top Canadian groups came up through the bars. There is no more gruelling training school for young musicians. Bar bands rarely get to play the sort of music they would like to play; if they don't please the patrons the word soon gets around and the group is out of work.

It is an especially rough experience on a girl. Considering that prior to joining the bar circuit in the summer of 1970, Tundra's Lisa Garber had never even sung professionally, the tales she has to tell of her bar gigs are especially intriguing.

"The bars were incredible. I remember one place where the owner suggested we take a day off and learn some nice country and western songs. I hate country and western! Nobody in the band is into that scene.

"Another club manager told me to buy a long, black slinky dress, put on some make-up and get my hair done, bouffant style. At other clubs the audiences were really rowdy. They'd yell at me to take off my clothes. I just couldn't believe it."

Little wonder then that the members of Tundra greeted record producer, Harry Hinde, with open arms when he arrived one day to rescue them from the bars. "Harry supported us while we got an act together for high schools, and while we cut our first record, *Band Bandit*." Hinde, a veteran music businessman, had worked in Canada for several years before moving to Detroit. Says Hinde, "I got so tired of beating my head against a brick wall that I just had to split. When I heard about the CRTC decision, I decided to return home."

Hinde's first production and Tundra's debut record became a national hit. It was a success due in no small part to the phenomenal publicity job performed by Liam Mullan, national promotion director of A & M Records, which had leased *Band Bandit* from Hinde.

Lisa Garber had joined Tundra early in the summer of 1970 on a whim more than anything else. She was staying with a musician friend in Toronto while travelling across the country to Vancouver. The musician was Bruce Manning; his brother Al was putting together a band to make some money playing bars. A drummer was added and the foursome went out under the name of Manning. Less than half-a-dozen bars later, Manning was ready to quit. But at this point, piano player Scott Cushnie (who once played with Ronnie Hawkins and The Band) joined the Manning lineup.

"We considered going back to the bars but then thought of having to do those awful Tom Jones and Engelbert Humperdinck songs." Hinde supported the group for a little longer, and they were ultimately able to introduce their new act and name – Tundra - at the CNE bandshell in Toronto in the fall of 1970.

When *Band Bandit* took off into the charts, A & M offered Tundra the chance of recording their first album at the Hollywood Studios. "We declined," says Lisa. "We're sick of groups going to the States to record. We wanted to show that perfectly good records can be made in Canada. "

Lisa is an avid supporter of CRTC local content legislation. She's one of the new breed of Canadian musicians - interested in developing a domestic music scene. She says the group passed over several other potential names before deciding on Tundra, the geographical term for the flat and treeless plains of the Arctic regions. There was no symbolism intended, according to Lisa.

Success came quickly for Lisa Garber. "It's so natural that it doesn't feel like anything," she says rather naively. She and Tundra are fortunate; their three months in bars was but a pittance when compared with the fifteen years spent there by a good many of her contemporaries.

6. CONSPIRACY

As sad and disheartening as it may well be, it is difficult to avoid the fact that the media deserves most of the brickbats for the slow, retarded growth of the Canadian music scene.

It has already been made clear herein that the major blame for the mass emigration of Canadian musicians, and the dour bitterness of the musicians who did remain here, can be laid at the doors of the country's radio stations. By not allowing Canadians to take their rightful place on the nation's airwaves, broadcasters effectively crippled any hope of a music industry developing here. If, back in 1965, stations across the country had put a heavy push on a few selected Canadian discs, it is quite conceivable that Canada would still be the home of Neil Young, Joni Mitchell, David Clayton-Thomas and even the Band.

On the other hand, an aggressive press might have been able to force radio into bending. If a few daily newspaper columnists had bothered to write favorably about the local talent scene; if they'd speculated as to why these creative people were not being allowed to utilize the medium of recording, perhaps radio stations would have been embarassed into submission. But all through the fifties and well into the later part of the last decade, there was no word of support in the mass press for the Canadian musicians.

The only publication which drew attention to Canadian rock music was *RPM* magazine, then being run as a losing concern by Walter Grealis. But *RPM* is a trade magazine, and as the newspapers didn't employ anyone familiar in the slightest way with the music trade, the pleas of Mr. Grealis went unheard by the masses.

Don Troiano, lead guitarist of Bush and a veteran of ten years in the Toronto music scene, recalls that prior to 1967, there was absolutely no serious rock coverage. "Our manager, who was familiar with newspaper editor mentality, used to create stunts to get us into print," Troiano says. "We'd have girls ripping off their clothes, mad airport scenes when we were leaving, anything we could think of. And the papers, they'd be out in force covering anything which might look a bit weird to adult readers.

175

"But they never bothered with intelligent discussion of the music we were playing. We were a 'Toronto rock group'; we were never four guys who happened to play music that a lot of Canadians seemed to enjoy.

"There is no doubt in my mind that the narrow-mindedness of radio stations could have been changed by an alert and concerned press. But unfortunately, because we were Canadian, the press automatically assumed, like the radio stations, that we couldn't be any good."

Troiano is right. Although you could hardly expect magazine editors and television executives to know anything about rock music without the information surfacing in the Canadian edition of *Reader's Digest*, young writers employed by local newspapers were guilty of the gravest sins of omission.

Many newspapers employed rock writers on a freelance basis, dropping a vague story or two into the weekend entertainment sections as an ad hoc method of covering all potential age groups, even young people. These writers, with very few exceptions, such as Dave Bist of the *Montreal Gazette*, and Jim Smith of the *Hamilton Spectator* , either didn't appreciate Canadian music or were overwhelmed by U.S. chart domination. If any of these journalists had built up any sort of a readership with Canadian youth and had seen potential in Canadian music, the chances were good that they could have stirred up a lot of interest in local talent.

I will never forget my own introduction to the Canadian music scene. I had been living and working in the English music scene for some eighteen months in a variety of capacities. Opportunities were available but Annie and I had decided that the time had come to move on. We wanted to see North America.

Unable to obtain a U.S. visa because of archaic Australian-U.S. immigration agreements, we settled on Toronto, Canada. We knew no one in Canada, and my only exposure to Canadian music had been a Bobby Curtola record called *Fortune Teller* which I'd written about in Australia, plus a couple of stories I'd read in the English music press about the Guess Who, who had made a promotional trip to London to plug *His Girl*.

We left on a rare sunny morning in London and arrived in the midst of a roaring July thunderstorm in Toronto. A late afternoon stroll down Yonge Street, in the vicinity of Dundas, raised some immediate doubts about the wisdom of leaving the comparative security of the English rock scene.

That premonition haunted us for several weeks. I turned on the radio in the evenings, and after I'd recovered from the initial shock of format Top Forty radio as compared with the BBC and England's pop pirates, I listened to CHUM for several hours.

I was struck by the lack of Canadian records on the CHUM playlist. Then I figured that nights were probably devoted to playing the American *Billboard* Hot One Hundred. I didn't give the lack of Canadian talent another thought until a few days later when 1 went hunting for a job and the local rock scene.

Six weeks later, I was still searching for both. There wasn't a Canadian pop scene, and there weren't any jobs for people lacking Canadian experience. The irony was hard to take.

Finally I found a position writing promotion copy for the CTV network which was a long way removed from the London music world. But I learned a lot about the Canadian music scene from a fellow writer, one Bill Gray, who had once blown sax in a number of rock groups. He wasn't bitter about the non-scene in Toronto; he had been brainwashed like almost everybody else into believing that it was simply not possible for Canada to have a music scene. Such things only happened in the States and in England.

I finally broke into Canadian print on August 31, 1967, when in a moment of desperation I called the editor of the *Toronto Telegram*. Brian Epstein had just died, and I told the editor I had known him and offered my services to write an obituary. The *Telegram* agreed, and a couple of days later I joined the Canadian rock press. Actually, I'd never even met Epstein but it was as good a way as any of busting through the barriers.

From the Epstein obituary, I moved on to various other rock writing endeavors, and eventually became a regular columnist with the *Telegram*. At the time, I wondered why my colleagues devoted little or no space to Canadian talent. There was one writer who did feature local rock groups, but it wasn't long before I discovered that he had some incentive for doing so - he was charging the bands $100 a story for his copy.

Whenever I asked anyone about the local scene, they looked at me as if I were crazy. Sometimes I wrote about the rotten attitudes of broadcasters who were very happy to squeeze millions of dollars out of the Canadian marketplace but were not willing to grant their countrymen equal chance with Americans on the airwaves. It was clear that the greatest single obstacle preventing a growth of Canadian music was the fixed and stubborn attitude of the people who programmed our radio stations.

I had also discovered rather quickly that what little activity did exist was generated by a bunch of back-biters and losers, caught up in petty jealousies and in-fighting.

My reactions were quite similar to those of other non-Canadians who arrived in Toronto around the same time. Terry Brown, one of the finest recording engineers in Canada, bounded into Toronto from a string of successful English hits, including Joe Cocker's *With a Little Help From My Friends*, Manfred Mann's *Pretty Flamingo* and assorted albums by Cream, Jimi Hendrix, Procol Harum and Traffic.

"When I first came over," Brown said recently, "I was amazed by the enthusiasm of the musicians in spite of a stagnant situation. Nothing was being done for them - all they had were jingles and club gigs - but they still believed that one day it would all work out."

The fact that I tended to side with Canadian musicians against the establishment of broadcasters, the Board of Broadcast Governors, and assorted other media wheeler-dealers, soon gave me a bulging list of enemies. How dare an Australian arrive in Canada and start telling well-respected Canadian businessmen that they were doing a disservice to the youth of the country? What would an Australian know about anything?

At that time however, Australia could have taught Canadians a lot about youth culture development. Local rock stars often made the front pages of Australian newspapers; there were national television programs on which artists were not condemned to sing versions of U.S. hits; and magazines devoted lengthy spreads and regular columns to the domestic music business. England was the same. So was every English speaking country in the world, with the exception of Canada. The first fifteen years of the rock era had slipped away, and Canada was still nowhere in the world of music.

Canadian newspapers either ignored or ripped off local artists. Broadcasters simply pretended they didn't exist. Leading magazines refused to believe that any rock act could be good enough to rate a national spread. And television, the ultimate in all mass mediums, either ignored Canadian rock talent or subjected it to the pedantic performance of American hits.

And no one media would criticize another for its apathy on Canadian talent. As Senator Keith Davey pointed out in his recent Report on Mass Media, the corporate entanglements of the media are often so self-conflicting that they leave little room for healthy criticism or competition.

Some people believe that the public gets what is deserves, but this theory can hardly be applied to the music scene. How was the public to know if Canada had good musicians unless somebody gave it the opportunity to judge?

Even after the first effects of the announced CRTC Canadian content legislation became evident, Canadian media continued to ignore local talent. On the day the legislation itself was announced, newspapers accorded banner headlines to the far less significant revelation that the CRTC had decided to bring more Canadian content into television, and generally missed the import of radio content.

My own appearance at the hearings (as a non-industry observer who believed there was more than enough Canadian talent, and that it should be given an opportunity to gain recognition, locally and abroad) was accorded a small mention in the *Toronto Telegram* (which at the time employed me as its rock writer) but was ignored by other papers. It wasn't that I wanted to see my own name in print across the country - I had only hoped that what I was saying to the CRTC would also reach the ears of the Canadian public in columns other than my own.

Towards the latter part of 1970, most of the major dailies in Canada had obtained the services of either a part-time or freelance rock writer. Some of these writers showed an admirable interest in Canadian talent, but others simply carried on their love affair with the U.S. charts. It was still beyond belief that a group from North Bay or Medicine Hat could actually make music equally as good as a Los Angeles band.

The magazines maintained their lack of Canadian music coverage. *Maclean's*, our national kaleidoscope of all things Canadian and long a prime offender, took a leap forward in 1971 with the appointment of a regular music columnist, John MacFarlane, who is at least partly sympathetic to what is happening in contemporary Canadian music. *Maclean's* stepdaughter, *Miss Chatelaine*, continues to defy professional comment. *Chatelaine* could use a lot more inches on Canadian music. *Saturday Night*, for all its fervent nationalism, has yet to discover the booming Canadian rock scene. It is a great pity since the Canadian public is probably still unaware of just what the CRTC has done for the domestic entertainment scene. A step in the right direction was the launching of *Grapevine* magazine in August 1971.

The television industry was equally apathetic. In December of 1970, I presented Jim Guthro, one of the programming decision-makers at the CBC in Toronto, with what I sincerely believed to be a foolproof format for a successful rock TV series. Using the basic approach of the BBC's long-running *Top of the Pops* program in England, I suggested that the CBC could conceivably get Canadian youth to turn on to the crown corporation by presenting the best of the country's rock talent weekly in prime time.

Guthro agreed on the merits of the proposed series, but doubted if I could bring the show in for under $10,000 weekly. After all, he'd spent several fruitless hours trying to persuade the Guess Who to appear in a CBC television special. The last price which had been discussed was $30,000. So I went out and obtained written agreements from almost every top Canadian rock act - the Guess Who included - that they would appear on my proposed program for $2,000 or less per show.

Guthro was astonished to say the least, but nevertheless CBC brass turned the show down. The reasons given were the difficulty in obtaining either a sponsor, a studio and or the money to make the show. My personal opinion is that the CBC couldn't care less about Canadian rock talent.

Even when the mass media does cover anything remotely connected with the Canadian music scene, it inevitably gets its priorities mixed up. Anne Murray made the front page of many newspapers when she was awarded a gold record for million-plus U.S. sales of *Snowbird*. Meanwhile, the same media had virtually ignored the fact that the Guess Who had received not one but five gold records for huge U.S. sales in the same year.

And those people who should know better do not. Late in 1970, some six months after Randy Bachman had left the Guess Who, an established Toronto rock critic called the group's manager, Don Hunter, on the occasion of a concert at O'Keefe Centre and asked if he could interview Randy Bachman.

This is not just an isolated incident. Many of the self-proclaimed authorities on Canadian rock music could not tell the difference between pictures of Joey Gregorash and Rick Neufeld. The natural Canadian inferiority complex towards anything produced domestically is a far-reaching, deeply rooted bias which may never be removed from the Canadian consciousness. It has taken people from other places to recognize and revolutionize the Canadian music industry.

In almost every other nation on earth, local pop stars are household names. If we were to rely on Canadian mass media to keep us informed on what's going down in Canada, we would be lacking in anything approaching a fair and broad picture. We would be led up the proverbial garden path.

7. AN EYE ON THE BALANCE SHEET

Close to two billion dollars worth of records and pre-recorded tapes will be sold in the United States this year. Publishing and other royalties will amount to almost the same figure. Concerts and movies allied to the rock movement will add another billion dollars to the total. Rock is big business - five billion dollars a year in America, and another five billion throughout the rest of the globe.

Canada's contribution to the pie is minute. Last year only about fifty million dollars were spent in the domestic rock scene, and the majority of this was transferred to foreign headquarters. The Canadian music industry, however, is growing, and at a spectacular rate. Informed observers put the annual worth of purely Canadian rock at ten million dollars.

Where does this money come from and where does it go? Canada's acknowledged authority on all things economic in the rock industry is Guess Who producer, Jack Richardson, the president of Nimbus 9 Productions. Jack is one of the new professionals in Canada who knows what sustained success can mean to the cheque book.

We start with a group, any group which has laid out at least $10,000 (in cash or extended time payments, almost always the latter) to purchase the necessary amplifying equipment. Unless the group has recorded previously, it is unlikely that it will receive from its record company anything more than a token advance on royalties, probably $2,000 at the most. Costs of record production have soared in recent years, and most companies prefer to invest all of their working capital in promotion - mailings to radio stations and reviewers, preparation of hype brochures, promotion tours, long distance calls to media VIPS, etc.

As few groups start off with anything resembling a firm financial footing, record companies also find themselves continually shelling out rent and food cheques. The rock musician is a strange breed indeed, and one worthy of scrutiny by a team of sociologists. He spends money as if there was no tomorrow; he is usually married with kids waiting in the wings, he leads a wanderlust life.

The first few months of a group's life are by far the hardest financially. In the pre-CRTC Canadian music scene, such hardship was often prolonged into years. Nowadays there have been notable improvements. Whereas it took the Guess Who a full decade to reach any degree of financial stability, a relatively new national name such as Crowbar reached a similar stage in less than a year.

The key to it all is that less-than-beautiful vinyl device known as a phonograph record. A hit record is a rock group's salvation and very reason for being. With one hit record, a band can become world famous and earn at least $250,000 without ever setting foot in the studios again.

With such an elastic yardstick as mass market taste, it is no surprise that groups can come and go with as much impact as an inch or so of early season snow. Yet despite the many cliches about the fleeting period of success which has been enjoyed by many hundreds of groups with hit records, once they have reached even one-hit status, they never really fade away completely. There is always work in the bars for an entertainer with a well-known hit behind him. The career of Canada's adopted son, Ronnie Hawkins, is ample evidence.

The record is a highly underrated cultural device. Records took The Beatles and a new sub-culture to the far comers of the globe, transcending race, religion and language. Before they had set foot outside London, Liverpool or Hamburg, The Beatles had become a sensation with kids in scores of countries. After the hit records came the press and movies and *The Ed Sullivan Show*. With their particular bent for the non-traditional, the Beatles were media dynamite.

The Beatles' career started and ended with the phonograph record. It comes as no surprise that the record should be the literal centre of the music industry. It is the bullseye that every producer and artist aims for; it is the end of the rainbow for a chosen few; and it is clearly the ultimate in electrical entertainment in the eyes and ears of today's youth. If television ever reaches the penetration levels of the record, it will be a devastating medium.

Fortunes are won and lost every day in the business of record-making. Only two percent of all records (singles and albums) released even recoup their production cost. Still the endless search for a hit group and hit song continues. For many producers, finding a hit has become an obsession. Reality very seldom stands in the way of their efforts.

Making hit records is an art form somewhat akin to producing a priceless painting with the aid of only a piece of canvas and a tube of toothpaste. With the state of the industry in such sad artistic shape at present (due to the moronic tastes of most U.S. radio program directors who want nothing more than the repetition of past hit songs and who shun real originality), it is no easy task to be a successful and happy record producer. Almost every producer has access to ninety percent of the ingredients involved in creating hit records - the problem is that so few producers have the knack of putting these ingredients together in the right proportions at the right moment.

Jack Richardson, as demonstrated elsewhere in this book, is one of the few who knows the formula. He is a sound businessman and a shrewd one, too. Unlike most of his contemporaries, he is also a realist. He attacks the charts with an ear for the right sound and an eye for the budget. "We normally operate on a production cost of between $1,500 and $2,000 per side. It varies a little, depending on the complexity of the group's arrangements." The use of extra session musicians at a cost of about ninety dollars per man for each three-hour session can hike up the costs considerably.

"A single will therefore cost about $3,500, while an album usually runs between $15,000 and $20,000. The most important thing is for the group to be well rehearsed. But invariably something crops up at the last minute. With the recent Alice Cooper album *Love It To Death* we rehearsed exhaustively but still spent sixteen hours of studio time simply tuning guitars."

One of the key reasons for the spiralling costs of production is the blind belief in the latest technical innovation. Whereas most of the big hits of the fifties and early sixties were recorded on four-track tape machines (even *Sgt. Pepper*, the Beatles' lavishly praised, peak period album was cut on eight-track equipment), virtually every hit on the charts today comes from a sixteen-track recorder. Admittedly sound reproduction has improved immensely with the advent of sixteen-track recording, but considering the rapid rise in studio costs, one might expect nothing less than miraculous results.

The average sixteen-track studio costs around a hundred dollars an hour to rent; then there's engineer overtime if it's a night-time session, the cost of raw tape ($90 for a fifteen minute reel), instrument rentals (most studios hire out pianos, organs and other bulky or unusual equipment) and taxes. It usually works out to around $150 an hour, which is $2.50 a minute or almost four cents a second.

It costs no more to record in New York than in Toronto. Indeed, Richardson notes that it is actually cheaper to record in California than in Canada. One of the problems encountered by Canadian studios is crippling import duties on recording equipment manufactured in the U.S., England or Germany. Studio financiers have a valid claim when they point out that the Canadian government is protecting a non-existent industry - tape recorder manufacturing.

If production costs are high, the price of promotion is almost prohibitive. Says Richardson: "Dunhill Records in Los Angeles have figured out that on a first album by a new group, it's necessary to spend twice the production cost on promotion.

"It depends very much on the commitment of a label to a particular act. Many labels throw out product without any promotion just to see if it gets any action. If it creates some excitement, they'll then get behind it with publicity.

"To reach hit status, every record goes through a complicated filtering process," he says. Promotion records are sent to dee jays and music directors who are heavily influenced by what other stations - any other stations - are playing. The actual quality of a new record often has little bearing on whether it receives air time. Top Forty radio is a vast network of imitators and numbers people, the sort of insensitive souls who have maintained the singles rock scene at a dull level of mediocrity. Progressive FM radio was a reaction to the staid, wilted attitudes of Top Forty programmers.

With a new group, it's next to impossible to persuade a music director to listen to a debut single all the way through. There's a saying in the music business that if you're a new act, your record better make it in its first fifteen seconds, or it won't make it at all. Such lore has more than a few grains of truth.

Records don't become hits by accident. It happens because of a friend of a friend, a chance link between a music director and a record company employee, masses of hype spread in every direction, or because of what other stations are playing. In short, making a hit is a long, tedious and often frustrating process.

Few musicians are aware of this fact, and they are quick to criticize their record companies for not turning them into millionaires overnight. The hand of fate notwithstanding, musicians should of necessity think long and hard about recording contracts. It is probably the toughest decision they will ever have to make. The right choice can mean a fortune; a wrong move usually ends up in bitterness and wasted time and effort.

There are many considerations to be taken into account before a group can safely sign on the dotted line. In the past, most groups have found that the best method of selection is to seek out a record company whose product has strongly appealed to them personally, and then to audition for the company's producers. In this manner, many Canadian folk hopefuls have ultimately found their way into the offices of True North Records, which has Bruce Cockburn under contract, or Early Morning Productions, a part of Gordon Lightfoot's operation; blues and hard rock artists turn to Daffodil Records; middle-of-the-road performers usually end up at Capitol. That is not to say that True North could not effectively handle a hard rock group, or that Capitol could not promote a folk artist. But each label does have a particular flare for one of the associated forms of rock music. Your talents are invariably put to better use at a company which already successfully merchandises talents of similar tastes.

The better record companies practise a form of enlightened plant propagation. According to Jack Richardson, labels such as A & M and Dunhill only sign artists in whom they truly believe. "That way they go the whole way. If an artist doesn't make it, you still have the good feeling that everything that could be done has been done. There's nothing worse for a producer than to suspect that his records are not being given understanding and aggressive promotion by the record company. Larger companies tend to lose product; we prefer to deal with the smaller labels which operate in a personalized manner."

Assuming that a group has signed with the right label and receives a royalty rate of about five percent (based on ninety percent of total sales at retail selling price), Richardson says a million-selling hit would yield around $60,000 to the artist in sales royalties.

In addition, a big hit single would yield about $20,000 in mechanical royalties (two cents per single sold if the songs were originals). Performance royalties can vary enormously from song to song. Some tunes are covered by many other artists, thus assuring additional royalty revenue for the composer and publisher.

"A tune like the Guess Who's *These Eyes*," says Richardson, "would yield between $45,000 and $60,000 to the composers, depending on the performance rights society agencies which handle the use of original material with which they are affiliated. We did some calculations recently and found that around $90,000 was lost on four Guess Who hits because of the different royalty calculation methods of performing rights societies."

Thus far, a group with its first million-selling original song has earned about $125,000 in royalties. And that's just the start. Every successful single inevitably spurs at least a moderately successful album, where the royalty payments can be enormous. An album of originals selling 500,000 copies would yield around $200,000 in record royalties, $50,000 in mechanicals, and a further $50,000 in publishing royalties, making a grand total of $425,000 - the hit single exclusive! Then comes concert appearances; any group with a million seller can earn a minimum of $4,000 for each concert. Super groups such as Led Zeppelin and Crosby, Stills, Nash and Young have frequently pulled in $50,000 for an hour's stage work. On at least two occasions, the late Jimi Hendrix received in excess of $100,000 for a single performance.

Pop is the highest-paying act in the history of show business. Little wonder then that the grassroots competition can be lively.

For every group that achieves our simulated success story above, fifty will fall by the wayside. Some will never receive more than a few hundred dollars in royalties. The figures required to just break even on records have risen steeply in recent years.

Jack Richardson points out that almost all recording contracts provide for the company to advance the costs of sessions, with these being deducted from royalties at a later date. Therefore, a group does not receive any royalties on a single record until it has sold about 30,000 copies. The break-even figure for the average album is between 8,000 and 10,000. The record company must bear the brunt of these costs and break-even points. Very few artists will break even on the first few releases.

Richardson is quick to add, however, that the artist is the first to benefit should he overturn the odds and come up with a hit. "On every successful record, the group is the first to realize profit. Certainly the session costs are deducted from royalties, but record companies have many other costs which have to be absorbed after the session costs have been met."

There's a familiar justifying phrase in the music industry that says one hit can make up for twenty misses, and it's true. The risks are great but the rewards are even greater.

Yet it's difficult not to sympathize with the plight of the producer and the record company. "We have got to be very cost-conscious," emphasizes Richardson. "Even with a hit, a producer with no eye on the balance sheet can end up with a successful but bankrupt group, not only financially, but personally as well. The aim at all times is to keep the costs down without sacrificing quality standards. When you go into a studio that's costing $150 an hour, you don't stop for lunch."

8. WHERE TO NOW?

The CRTC regulations have not swept the population off its feet, true enough. A random poll of opinion would as likely reveal an ideological dislike of the ruling, or draw a blank stare, as record support for it. After all, there cannot be many people, even the most destitute musicians, who would not be apprehensive of government intervention in private media.

Yet, at the same time, is it not true that a minority - those involved in what little music business did exist - were being discriminated against? Broadcasters effectively denied local rock musicians access to their audience.

The Canadian Radio-Television Commission decision was that this country had no music industry or pop culture because of the neglect of the media, and they decided that the government should legislate to force radio stations to contribute to the potential growth of this culture. The potential is enormous. The future is absolutely limitless. In its first year, the existence of the CRTC legislation helped more Canadian records reach international success than in any ten years previous.

Yet there is a fly in the ointment.

According to most industry people, the largest single problem now facing the creative music makers of Canada is the entry - of all people - of the radio stations into record production. The hypocrisy of such a move is incredible. The very people who had complained for so long that Canada had no talent suddenly wanted to exploit the likely profit pickings of the CRTC content law.

Only a year before, the broadcasters had been adamantly opposed to the programming of Canadian discs. Then with the passing of a brief twelve months, they did a complete about face and wanted to get in on the making of Canadian records. It gives you some idea of where their heads are at.

Not all broadcasters cared to risk their profits or the possibility of being accused of hypocrisy. A handful showed no concern for either and jumped right on the bandwagon. You'll have little difficulty predicting which station led the herd. Right on, it was Toronto's

CHUM - the station which had probably done the least for Canadian music, though it had been in a position to do the most.

Initially the music industry took scant notice when CHUM announced that it had acquired the Summerlea-Winterlea music publishing companies of Montreal early in 1970 and was forming Much Productions. Some record company executives were actually pleased that CHUM would now suffer first hand the enormous difficulties (financial and otherwise) involved in building an independent Canadian production company. Only a few detected the potential conflict of interest situation which could arise when a radio station was producing its own records for profit, particularly when the station involved was apparently able to sell 10,000 records simply by putting a title on its chart. With that much power, such a production company could hardly fail.

Walt Grealis, the editor and publisher of *RPM* magazine, was one of the earliest and loudest critics of CHUM's entry into record production. "Perhaps they realized that the money they could get from performing rights, publishing and record royalties would make going on the air for Joe's Pizza Parlor look like nothing at all.

"The fact is that any radio station making records has an unfair advantage in the market place. The other record producers don't have a broadcasting license. That's why I am using the power of the printed word to attack the CRTC for not taking action to prevent this by-product of the legislation. If getting your record on CHUM is the only way to have a big national hit, it could conceivably develop into a situation where everyone would go to CHUM and offer them a piece of their record just to have it played. I'm not saying that it would happen, but it could. That's what worries me."

Don Hunter, the manager of the Guess Who, was even more direct in his fears about radio station record production. "At this stage in the development of a Canadian record industry, there must be a distinct separation - record companies must be record companies and radio stations must be radio stations.

"It can do nothing but ill. It should not be allowed; a conflict of interest is inevitable."

Within a few weeks after the legislation era began, it looked like Grealis' fears may have had justification. When the author monitored CHUM over a two-day period, he found that one of CHUM's records (a rather tiresome and mundane thing called *Ordinary Man* by Freedom North) was being played at least as much, and sometimes more, than any other record on the station playlist of some forty discs. Yet this record had received little attention in other markets. At the same time, there were a number of other outstanding non-CHUM produced Canadian records which the station had failed to chart. It was easy to understand the concern of competing producers in the circumstances.

Grealis was confident that the situation would not deteriorate much further without government intervention. "If the CRTC doesn't do something, I'm positive another government department will take action. The U.S. has very strict laws in this area, and I expect Canada will soon have the same."

In an unprecedented statement, the Canadian Independent Record Producers Association came out and attacked CHUM for its entry into record production. Many risked possible financial hardship by standing up for themselves. There are a million reasons a radio station can give for not playing a record. The danger of retaliation is very high.

Record companies and producers depend to a large extent on radio stations for their success. By disagreeing with specific broadcasting policies, a record producer can put himself in a very awkward position. But as Grealis says, the very existence of many members is threatened by CHUM's action. Everything depends on the success of their next record; they must have every opportunity to survive.

"And too, the established foreign-owned record companies aren't going to sink profits into making domestic records if there isn't a fair marketplace for their wares. Several companies have already postponed production budgets pending government action. I believe that most of the large companies are going to stick their necks out and spend a lot of money on Canadian talent. But they'll get their budgets chopped off if the government ignores the situation. There's going to be a swing away from the traditional role of Canadian record companies as simply U.S. branches. They're going to develop an identity of their own and I'd like to believe they're going to stand up for their rights, the way the independent producers have done."

As if the CHUM subsidiary, Much Productions, wasn't enough to contend with, a group of Montreal music people convinced the Canadian Association of Broadcasters that they too should get involved in record production. A company called Astra Records was formed, and the CAB went money-hunting to its membership. Enough capital was raised to launch the company, but there were several stations

190

which refused to get involved. CHUM was one (they, apparently, were involved enough with Much). CKLW Windsor was another. But the loudest radio station critic was Keith James, operations manager of CHED Edmonton. After listening to the Astra prospectus, James commented: "This whole idea is the biggest load of bullshit I've ever seen."

Yet the majority of stations simply did as they were asked - they came up with the bucks to finance Astra Records. Among the first artists to be signed to the label, which Polydor agreed to distribute, were Rick Neufeld (writer of *Moody Manitoba Morning*) and Kurt and Noah. Astra was launched against a background of muttered comments about how the CAB had been attracted by what could only be a futile project.

Twelve months after the CHUM creation of Much, and six months after the arrival of Astra, it was interesting to look back on their respective track records. Despite a disproportionate amount of airplay on some stations, neither CHUM nor Astra had managed to make even a small dent in the Canadian production scene. Neither had achieved an unqualified national hit. And neither had made any impression on the international marketplace.

Grealis feels that the infusion of new blood into the broadcasting scene will bring about even more progress. "Radio jobs change overnight. Young guys like Wayne Bryant, the music director at CHED in Edmonton, are leaders, not followers. They're going to bring about tremendous change."

Bryant himself sees legislation as being a major step towards the creation of a functional domestic record industry in Canada. But he points out the need for other integral areas of the music business to revitalize their approach. "It's fine for the CRTC to tell stations to play thirty percent but someone should tell the record stores to stock one hundred percent of that thirty percent. It's no good giving a record exposure if the kids can't go out and buy it."

Bryant's fresh approach to the business of AM music programming brought other innovators out of their shells. Worthy of mention are Greg Haroldson of CKXL Calgary, Brent Marucci of CJOE London, and Gary Parr of CKLC Kingston.

CHUM's entry into the field of record production is also contributing to some discontent within the Maple Leaf System. Says MLS head Nevin Grant, "A lot of the other stations don't like it, but what can we do? CHUM isn't violating the rules as far as we can see, and we must have the leading station in the country's biggest market to make the system viable. The MLS has tremendous potential, but if it goes down, it will be because of CHUM."

Other problems lay in the booking agency business. In the manner of leeches, Canadian bookers have earned for themselves a terrible reputation within the music industry. Even Tom Wilson, formerly with one of the country's leading booking agents, revealed early in 1971 that "the booking business has degenerated into a sandbox. We're very concerned about it." Terry Filion of Concept 376 was especially bitter about the college booking scene. "Most universities spend three times as much of their government grants on U.S. talent as on Canadian bands," he said.

Despite these problems, the future looks bright. Canada has already produced rock music the equal of almost anything which the U.S. or Britain has come up with. The truly talented Canadians such as Neil Young, David Clayton-Thomas, the Guess Who, Crowbar, Joni Mitchell, the Band, Lighthouse, King Biscuit Boy and others, have not only entered the international rock race but have achieved front line positions tor themselves.

Recent events are most encouraging. As if to prove that the traditional record company branch office-distributorship-for-foreign-records mentality was finally losing its grip, Canadian record companies and artists banded together in August 1971 to begin planning the Maple Music Junket. This was a scheme to fly one hundred leading European journalists, disc jockeys and television interviewers to Canada for a brief look at the booming Canadian music scene. It was hoped that the industry would foot half the estimated $50,000 cost of the junket, with the remainder coming from government subsidies. It was an outstanding idea, and one which would have drowned in a sea of apathy a year before.

Still another venture was *Rock Canada*, a fifteen-hour radio rockumentary detailing the history of Canadian rock music. Produced in Edmonton, this special program was syndicated to many stations in Canada and the United States.

All indications point to one conclusion. Before this decade spins to a close, the world will be looking and listening to Canada for its rock musicians and writers. A healthy industry will pour millions of dollars into the economy; the powerful communication of rock will give Canada a youthful and exciting image with young people the world over.

The potential is very large and very real. In taking the steps it has, Canada has done itself a great service. Now let us all join in.

The Track Record of Canadian Hits

The following compilation of Canadian hits covers the period from the beginning of rock 'n' roll (for purposes of this book, Bill Haley) in 1955 to January 18, 1971, the start of the legislation era.

In assembling this list, the author has included only those discs recorded by resident Canadians at the time of their U.S. chart success. Canadians living in the U.S. or elsewhere have not been taken into consideration. Titles must have reached the *Billboard* or *Cashbox* charts to qualify. Million sellers are marked with an asterisk.

1950s

Johnny Cowell - *Walk Hand in Hand* (Columbia)

Myrna Lorrie - *Are You Mine?* (Quality)

Priscilla Wright - *Man in a Raincoat* (Spartan)

1960

*Beaumarks - *Clap Your Hands* (Quality)

Gordon Lightfoot - *Remember Me* (Chateau)

*Moe Koffman - *Swingin' Shepherd Blues* (Regency)

Ron Metcalfe - *Twistin' at the Woodchoppers'*
Ball (Quality)

1962

Terry Black - *Unless You Care* (Arc)

1963

Johnny Cowell - *Our Winter Love* (Columbia)

Shirley Matthews - *Big Town Boy* (Capitol)

Ian and Sylvia - *Four Strong Winds* (Vanguard)

Lucille Starr - *The French Song* (Quality)

1964

Bobby Curtola - *Aladdin* (Tartan)

Bobby Curtola - *Fortune Teller* (Tartan)

1965

Guess Who - *Shakin' All Over* (Quality)

Little Caesar and the Consuls - *My Girl Sloopy* (Red Leaf)

1966

Count Victors - *Peepin' and Hidin'* (Coral)

1967

Abbey Tavern Singers - *Off to Dublin in the Green* (Arc)

1968

Irish Rovers - *The Unicorn* (Decca)

Irish Rovers - *The Unicom* album (Decca)

Irish Rovers - *Whiskey on a Sunday* (Decca)

Gordon Lightfoot - *Sunday Concert* (United Artists)

Paupers - *Magic People* (Verve/Forecast)

1969

*Guess Who - *Laughing* (Nimbus 9)

Guess Who - *No Time* (Nimbus 9)

*Guess Who - *These Eyes* (Nimbus 9)

Guess Who - *Undun* (Nimbus 9)

Guess Who - *Canned Wheat* (Nimbus 9)

Guess Who – *Wheatfield Soul* (Nimbus 9)

1970

Canada Goose - *Higher and Higher* (Tonsil)

Edward Bear - *You, Me and Mexico* (Capitol)

*Guess Who - *American Woman* (Nimbus 9)

Guess Who - *Hand Me Down World* (Nimbus 9)

Guess Who - *No Sugar Tonight* (Nimbus 9)

*Guess Who - *No Time* (Nimbus 9)

* Guess Who - *Share the Land* (Nimbus 9)

*Guess Who - *American Woman* (Nimbus 9)

*Guess Who - *Share the Land* (Nimbus 9)

Ronnie Hawkins - *Down in the Alley* (Cotillion)

Terry Jacks - *I'm Gonna Capture You* (London)

King Biscuit Boy - *Official Music* (Daffodil)

Gordon Lightfoot - *If You Could Read My Mind* (Reprise)

Gordon Lightfoot - *Sit Down Young Stranger* (Reprise)

The Track Record I

Mashmakhan - *As the Years Go By* (Columbia)

* Anne Murray - *Snowbird* (Capitol)

Anne Murray - *Sing High Sing Low* (Capitol)

Original Caste *One Tin Soldier* (Bell)

*Poppy Family - *Which Way You Goin' Billy?* (London)

Poppy Family - *That's Where I Went Wrong* (London)

Poppy Family - *Poppy Family* (London)

Glossary

acetate - a type of non-permanent record, used for demonstration purposes. **axe** – guitar.

Billboard - the leading music industry publication in the world, produced each week in New York. It carries the weekly listing of best selling records in the United States and elsewhere.

BBG - Board of Broadcast Governors, which until March 1968 was the controlling body of the Canadian broadcasting industry.

Cashbox - the second leading U.S. music trade publication, also issued weekly from New York.

chops - unique, creative drumstick technique.

CIRPA - Canadian Independent Record Producers' Association, whose membership is restricted to domestic producers financing their sessions with Canadian money, as opposed to foreign-owned record companies.

CRTC - Canadian Radio-Television Commission, successor to the Board of Broadcast Governors.

cut - to record or tape.

demo - a demonstration record, usually made upon completion of a recording session. It takes at least a week to cut a lacquer and actually press a record. A demo serves as an interim example of the new record and will only maintain its reproduction quality for twenty or thirty plays. Demo song tapes are also made by artists for examination by record companies.

gig - personal appearance, concert.

hype - to promote or publicize.

keyboards - piano, organ, harpsichord, any instrument with a keyboard.

lease - record companies lease tapes from independent producers for a percentage of sales on the final record.

licks - similar to chops, but used in connection with guitars.

MD - music director, the individual who selects the music to be played on a radio station.

mechanicals - the royalties received by composers for record sales, as opposed to performance rights, which are those royalties given composers for radio and television play of their compositions.

MLS - Maple Leaf System, a network of radio stations across the country which sought to give exposure to Canadian discs.

MOR - middle-of-the-road, adult-oriented, non-rock music.

needle in the red - a technical expression applying to the actual recording of a song using the highest possible volume without distortion. Producers tend to record "in the red" to obtain the best possible range of tones.

PD - program director, above the music director and disc jockey in the executive echelons of radio stations.

picker - guitar player.

playlist - compilation of records which a station is currently playing.

RPM - the Canadian music industry's trade magazine, published weekly in Toronto.

soft cut - similar to an acetate and used for demonstration purposes.

the can - tape is stored in cans or boxes; a tape "in the can" is complete and ready to be transferred to record.

track - Studios use tape recording machines of varying track capacity. Sixteen-track means that sixteen different pieces of music can be separately or simultaneously recorded. The tracks are then mixed, or combined, down to two track (for stereo) or one track (mono). The more tracks available, the more over-dubbing (addition of extra musical effects) can be done.

Publication Information

© Ritchie Yorke 1971

ISBN 978-0-9944400-4-4

Re-published

© Ritchie Yorke 2015

www.ingramcontent.com/pod-product-compliance
Lightning Source LLC
La Vergne TN
LVHW051052080426
835508LV00019B/1834